Critical praise for this book

'Is "young feminist" an oxymoron in a [...] like to call post-feminist? This book challenges "in the box" thinking while addressing a range of issues old and new. Its energy, thoughtfulness and honesty invigorate, even if they discomfort. Highly recommended for feminists, old and young, female and male, of whatever stripe, hue, shape or identity!' *Professor Gita Sen, Indian Institute of Management in Bangalore, India and founding member of DAWN (Development Alternatives with Women for a New Era)*

'Leading the way to the future, this multi-cultural collection of the voices of young feminists illuminates the issues that are or will be in the crucible of feminist struggles to come. It also shows us how the lives of women both have and have not changed in the past few decades. A lively and thought-provoking read. A must for anyone concerned with the future as seen through the wisdom of young women activists today.' *Charlotte Bunch, Founder and Executive Director, Center for Women's Global Leadership*

'This book represents the most powerful, eloquent and thought-provoking collection I have seen in a long time. It brings together a poetic, jarring, often painful chorus of voices. These are not naïve, headstrong young women with blinders on; they are experienced, committed and thoughtful activists whose challenges are complex. Each of the writers in this book brings a rare and sparkling truth to the table – what we do, read, and choose to do with this truth is our choice. These young women have done their job.' *Sisonke Msimang, Open Society Initiative for Southern Africa and AIDS activist*

'This is an exciting book that brings together voices speaking with different accents, but in a common language, about the past, the present and the dreams and struggles to be waged by a new generation of international feminists, standing firmly in the new global order.' *Marysa Navarro, Professor of History, Dartmouth College*

AWID

The Association for Women's Rights in Development (AWID) is an international membership organization, headquartered in Toronto, Canada, with almost 6,000 members in over 100 countries, primarily in the global South. Set up in 1982, AWID has been working to bring about policy, institutional and individual change that will improve the lives of women and girls everywhere. AWID does this by sharing strategic information and creating critical spaces for organizing and strategizing. AWID is one of the few organizations to play the role of facilitator and provocateur amongst gender equality advocates at the global level.

SHAMILLAH WILSON, ANASUYA
SENGUPTA, KRISTY EVANS | editors

Defending our dreams

Global feminist voices for a new
generation

Zed Books
LONDON | NEW YORK

published in association with

The Association for Women's
Rights in Development (AWID)

Defending our dreams: global feminist voices for a new generation was
first published by Zed Books Ltd, 7 Cynthia Street, London N1 9JF, UK
and Room 400, 175 Fifth Avenue, New York, NY 10010, USA in 2005

www.zedbooks.co.uk

Published in association with: The Association for Women's Rights in
Development (AWID), 215 Spadina Avenue, Suite 150, Toronto, Ontario,
Canada M5T 2C7

www.awid.org

Cover designed by Andrew Corbett   ·
Set in Arnhem and Futura Bold by Ewan Smith, London
Printed in Malaysia

Distributed in the USA exclusively by Palgrave Macmillan, a division of
St Martin's Press, LLC, 175 Fifth Avenue, New York, NY 10010.

A catalogue record for this book is available from the British Library.
US CIP data are available from the Library of Congress.

ISBN 1 84277 726 2 hb
ISBN 1 84277 727 0 pb

Contents

Acknowledgements

This book is, in many ways, a tribute to the work and participants of AWID's Young Women and Leadership Programme over the last few years. The voices and experiences of many of our colleagues reinforced the need for an anthology that brings together the visions and analyses of young feminists, from across the world. We would also like to acknowledge our friends and companions in the first Young Women and Leadership International Advisory Group – Anna, Jessica, Nyambura, Shantal, Sheryl and Youmna – who helped to create the programme, and who were a virtual collective space for support and advice, of all kinds. To those who are now part of the Advisory Group – we wish you the same strength and enjoyment.

We wish to extend our gratitude to all the authors who contributed their ideas, their energies, their creativity and their vision to this collection. For us, it is quite remarkable that the entire anthology was put together virtually. The contribution call went out over email, and after selecting the abstracts that would form this anthology, we continued to build relationships with our authors over this medium. What is even more amazing is that we did the editing across continents too (South Africa and India). We thank you for your patience, for your willingness and generosity in working with the challenges that this process might have thrown up, and for helping us to meet (almost!) our 'crazy' deadlines. A special thank you to Gabrielle Hosein and Jasmeen Patneja, whose creative ways of working enhanced and inspired the title and design of this book.

Our heartfelt thanks to our editorial group: Peggy Antrobus, Maria Alejandra Scampini and Alison Symington, who worked with us during the initial stages of this project to develop the process for soliciting chapters, and who then participated in selecting the abstracts that would form the content of this anthology.

This book would not have been possible without the support of Peggy Antrobus, a founder member of DAWN (Development

Alternatives with Women for a New Era, who took an idea from a conversation about the possibility of such a book, and made it a reality; she was responsible for securing the publishing commitment from Zed Books.

We also wish to thank Joanna Kerr, executive director of AWID, who believed enough in this project to give it the institutional backing and support that would see its fruition.

Special thanks to Asha Sara George, Gita Srinivasan and Ashwin Jacob Mathew, for their support and insightful comments through this process. We also wish to thank Laura E. Asturias and Nicole Lisa for translating two of the chapters from Spanish into English.

We would also like to thank Robert Molteno of Zed Books, for his commitment to this book. Anna Hardman has been invaluable as our publishing editor. She has been enthusiastic and supportive, and worked above and beyond the call of duty to support a group of young 'inexperienced' editors. We are excited and grateful that Zed Books has provided a platform for young feminist voices within the international social transformation arena.

Last but certainly not the least, we want to thank the men in our lives – Shingai, Ashwin and Aron – for doing what was necessary to get us through this process. Their love, generosity and patience (particularly the last!) have helped us come through relatively unscathed. It is a tribute to them that our relationships have survived the exigencies of this book.

Unusually, we suppose, we would like to thank each other – it is not an easy collective task (or so we have learnt) to conceive, create and see through the formation of such an anthology. We have had good, bad and ugly moments, and coped with them all, through shared laughter and loving.

This book is for all of those who through their friendships, their inspiration and support have nurtured our growth. Let the struggle continue – A Lutta Continua!

Shamillah, Anasuya and Kristy

Foreword

Often, inevitably, in conversations among older feminist activists about 'movement building', the question is raised of how to attract more young women into The Movement. Sometimes strategies aimed at achieving this objective are proposed and implemented, but frequently they fall short of the goal.

At the same time, young women explain their lack of interest in women's movements with reasons that have to do with the movement's perceived irrelevance to their concerns and with their feelings of alienation from a movement dominated by an older generation that appears to many young women as patronizing, arrogant or misdirected. Sometimes, there is agreement on the need for the young women to 'become involved'. Often the conversations go nowhere.

In 2003 DAWN (Development Alternatives with Women for a New Era) organized its first Training Institute in Feminist Advocacy for young women between the ages of 25 and 35. Given the repute and standing of DAWN, there was no shortage of applicants. The criteria for selection were rigorous: young women who were already engaged, or had a strong interest, in global advocacy work for gender justice, and who wished to sharpen their analytical capabilities and advocacy skills. So it was not surprising that those selected were an outstanding group. Nevertheless, I was in awe of these young women and impressed by the breadth and depth of their knowledge, analysis, confidence and commitment to social justice not just on behalf of women, but starting with women.

The idea of writing this book emerged in my conversations with two of the young women whose involvement in AWID's Young Women and Leadership Programme marked them for leadership in this group. I was just completing my own book on the global women's movement, commissioned by Zed Books as part of their Global Issues Series 'for a new generation of activists'. I mentioned this to them, wanting to know whether the reflections of someone who had come of age as a feminist within the context of the UN Decade for Women (1975–85) and who had been a witness to the evolution of what I wanted to describe as a 'global' movement might be of interest to them. They were enthusiastic; and they shared with me their own ideas about a book that would present the voices, perspectives and analysis of young women, the new generation of activists!

The editor of Zed Books, Robert Molteno, thought it was a great idea and the young women moved it forward with a confidence that contrasted with my own hesitations about taking up Zed's invitation to write a book. I thought it was a measure of the generation gap, and of how much more advanced and confident, in every sense, these young women were from my generation at that age.

Today young women represent a significant constituency within the larger movements for global justice around the World Social Forum (WSF) as well as the Ministerial meetings of the WTO, the joint annual IMF–World Bank meetings, and those of the leaders of the major industrialized countries (the G-8). They are engaged there as advocates, organizers, protesters and strategists. Not all are feminist (or would describe themselves in this way). The word is alienating to some (as it was to many in my generation, myself included, until I understood the relevance and importance of feminist analysis and politics to the larger struggle for social justice). Within these spaces, young women are already helping define social movements around the globe.

Reading *Defending Our Dreams* reinforced my early impressions of the confidence, knowledge and commitment of the women of this generation. More than this, I was struck by the breadth and originality of the analysis. The chapters in this volume answer the questions: what do young women mean when they say that their issues are different from those of their mothers, and grandmothers? How is young women's organizing different from that of earlier generations? What do young women bring to strengthen and re-energize women's movements? And why is it important to the future of women's movements that the link between older feminists and young women's organizations be strengthened?

This book highlights a range of issues of concern to young women today. Some of these are not unfamiliar to the veterans of past struggles but even 'old' issues are experienced and approached differently, reflecting the altered contexts and perceptions of the new generation. Some new issues covered in this book are:

- new technologies, from reproductive technologies and genetically modified organisms (GMOs) to ICTs;
- HIV/AIDS and sexuality;
- faith and families – issues not often explored by earlier generations;
- 'feminist' men – a point of controversy for my generation;
- the international criminal court (ICC) in relation to violence against women and legal reforms that could improve women's human rights; and
- 'intersectionality' – a concept my generation barely understood and never used until it emerged in the context of the UN Conference Against Racism, Xenophobia and Other Forms of Exclusion in 2001.

Some long-established issues experienced and approached differently include:

- trafficking in women, showing how the 'apparatus of development' has been hijacked by women's and feminist movements, to make it into a 'project';
- poverty, a refreshing, futuristic approach to this pernicious issue;
- sexuality, discussed without self-consciousness, and seen as central to understanding the political forces and institutions that challenge women's agency;
- migration and cross-border adoption, presented from the perspective of those who have lived the reality;
- difference, diversity and identity in their organizing emerged with greater clarity and realism than they had for many of us; and
- identity politics as a source of deep divides but also as a positive force for organizing.

Very striking is the way in which the authors combine personal introspection with an analysis of global issues. The link between 'consciousness-raising' and *conscientization* (relating personal experience to a structural analysis) takes feminist consciousness-raising to a new level, transforming the personal into action that reaches beyond personal concerns: for many of these young women, their experience of their own multiple identities is the basis of their organizing. While they speak from their own experience they link this to an analysis of the larger issues facing us today in a way that the earlier experiences of consciousness-raising often failed to do. For some earlier generations of feminists there was a choice, a trade-off, between self-reflective, analytical work, and engagement in struggle. This anthology makes it clear that this combination is no longer unusual.

Some authors are comfortable working with men, individually and in the larger movement for global justice (for example, the World Social Forum) and challenge our assumptions about the very nature and objectives of women's movements. Some seek dialogue with women's movements, while others underscore the difficulty of this engagement with women who continue to treat them as 'children'.

While for this generation the use of ICTs is commonplace, many of the authors nevertheless emphasize the personal contacts, the friendships that clearly transform their lives and their work, combining cyberspace with intensely personal relationships.

As I read the chapters in this book, I understood why it is crucial for this intergenerational dialogue to continue, and indeed, why more young women should take leadership in women's movements. It is not a matter of acknowledging and detailing old and new issues, but of distinguishing the methodologies with which these writers analyse and approach the issues. The work is securely grounded in contemporary conditions and experience. It highlights what is at stake for feminist ideology, theory and practice, and for intergenerational organizing precisely because it presents the issues and analysis of the generation that is central to the changes taking place. Their interpretation of what is happening is central to how the issues might be approached. These young feminists have not only reaped the benefits of the organizing that has gone before, they are grappling with issues that their seniors cannot fully understand, let alone address effectively. In these chapters women of an older generation will recognize the same energy, passion and creativity they brought to women's organizing in their time, taking new forms, re-energizing and strengthening movements for social change.

As the authors say, beyond the 'myriad forces' at play in our world today, their lives are 'also shaped by the energy of youth, hopes for a better future, friendship, love, creativity, vision and a passionate advocacy for equality and justice' (proposal for the publication). The experiences, perspectives and visions of young women and girls are therefore unique and invaluable both in understanding the current world order and in shaping a better future.

For this reason more attention needs to be given by the women's movement and young women's groups to the ways of opening up intergenerational dialogues that can move beyond mutual suspicion, perceived threats and insensitivity to finding the complementarities that would allow both to work on common agendas. Attention must also be given to ways of facilitating the transition from young women's involvement in their own movements to the organizations and networks of older women.

In the context of the celebration of 30 years since the launch of the UN Decade for Women, which produced enough Programmes and Platforms of Action to last many lifetimes, it is clear that we have to go beyond the quick-fix number of the '12 critical areas' of the Beijing Platform and the '8 Millennium Development Goals' to deeper levels of transformation of the power relations that foreclose the realization of our dreams for gender equity and global justice. This book gives us hope that this new generation of feminist activists will advance the struggle in ways that are more deeply grounded ('making politics, personal' is a recurring theme – both implicit and explicit – in many of the chapters) while taking advantage of the incredible advances in ICTs.

In this book, the authors do not merely clarify what young activists are thinking or doing. More importantly, they speak from the position of their experience of intersectionality, their passions, struggles, their dreams. The result is something fresh and creative and powerful.

The regeneration of feminist politics depends on the generation represented in this volume. This is an exciting book! It illustrates both the legacy of the best efforts of earlier feminist activism as well as the energy, creativity and clarity of this generation. Finally, beyond the contribution this book will make to young women's organizing, it will inspire young women to live their lives differently, as much as it will leave the older pioneers in awe of the richness of our legacy.

Peggy Antrobus
Barbados, April 2005

Introduction: our dreams, our nightmares, our voices ...

SHAMILLAH WILSON AND ANASUYA SENGUPTA

We came to 'being young' rather late in life. No, this is not an existential puzzle to be resolved while sitting in a Parisian café; we came to be called 'young feminists' much past the age for being 'young', or so we thought. Both of us – like many others of our generation(s) – had joined struggles for justice wherever we were located, in geography and in historical context. We had been out on the streets against apartheid, against the caste system, against fundamentalism, against communalism, and both of us, across the globe from each other, against war and violence. We had challenged and angered, listened and learned from older activists, many of them women, and we had found ourselves part of, almost unconsciously, almost imperceptibly, 'the women's movement', 'the development discourse', 'the social sector' ... More consciously, and sometimes more perceptibly, we grew to understand and to accept a certain set of values upon which we tried to base our lives and our living.

We rarely called ourselves anything. We were Shamillah and Anasuya, 20-something, big on dreams, touched by nightmares, living our lives in honest confusion and mundane struggle. And then suddenly, one day, our lives changed. We went from being small-town local girls to women reaching out across countries, across continents. In our work and in our experience, we went international. We were suddenly called many things. 'Young', 'feminist', 'activist', 'practitioner', 'academic' ... and the identities that we traversed at home, on the street, in the village, in the city, became labels. Gender, sexuality, race, class, caste, region, religion, language – these were all issues we were self-consciously analysing for ourselves, and with others. Along the way, we were being called 'third-wave' 'next-generation': terms we could not understand or appreciate; the histories and contexts of women's struggles back home were very different from the apparently easy classifications we were encountering. We were also discovering, in uncomfortable and uncertain ways, our new positions of privilege. Yes, we were black, brown, South African, South Asian, but we seemed to have moved from speaking for ourselves to representing others. When did that happen? Was it okay? Was it true? Were we okay? And ... were we true?

We have still not answered all of these questions. And we are still uncomfortable with labels. But we have learned one thing – we speak for ourselves, and when others listen, if they hear echoes of other lives, other energies, other confusions ... then that is what we do. Labels are useful because they help create communities; we can try and transcend those labels without leaving behind the communities, but that is part of the struggle.

Why this book?

This book comes out of our friendship. Unsurprisingly, as it so happened, we met at an AWID–AGI conference on Organizational Change, somewhere in Cape Town, in 1998.[1] So this book symbolizes the ways in which we have kept in touch with each other since then – over years, and across continents, helped along by new technology and old touch. It also symbolizes our understanding of friendship in general – 'friendship cannot be true unless it is open, inclusive, convivial – unless a third is fully welcome'.[2]

Over the past few years, while trying to negotiate our international identities, we have begun to realize the magnitude of the world stage on to which we were being gently led. The impact of those forces that currently shape our lives, such as globalization, war, conflict, poverty, violence, HIV/AIDS ... it is hardly surprising that nightmares jostle with our dreams, that our personal processes of 'growing up' and 'growing adult' are accompanied by politically charged moments and events. Sharing these experiences and moments with others, we realize that as 'young' women (young in age, and possibly, experience), we are experiencing these forces differently, and that this diverse analysis is not only useful, but necessary. Young women – young feminists – today are experiencing both old and new challenges, personally and politically, and we need to address them in creative ways.

A friend of ours once said:

As a young Arab woman living in the United States, my identity is multiple. Constrained by the limiting US-based notions of identity, I have moved through various categories, but have always had to name myself in reaction to assumptions. In the gaze of the mainstream, as an Arab woman I am oppressed, as an Arab I am inherently violent, and as an immigrant I am suspicious. Most recently, if I am young and Arab, I am dangerous. I feel that until notions of identity are no longer built from ashes of global colonial, military and economic agendas, young people will consistently lose their languages and I will keep on giving geography and history lessons every time I say my name.[3]

We are straddling many complex identities and locations; we are both insider and outsider, rooted in our origins and yet diasporic in our natures. Very often the only way we survive is by using spaces in between: spaces where we create our own families and communities. Feminist communities have been one such space, where we have flourished and grown. We are a generation of feminists who dream and imagine – like those before us and, no doubt, like those after us – many other worlds. We defend those dreams in our engagement as advocates, organizers, spokespersons, protesters, researchers and strategists in social movements across the globe. We believe that our energies, friendship, love, creativity and passionate advocacy for equality and justice can spark holistic visions, fresh analyses and new strategies for change. We hope that we will embody our own visions of leadership – of being both follower and leader, of being inspired, and becoming inspiration.

What is this book?

This book is an attempt to bring together a set of voices from across the world who straddle multiplicity themselves; within the book too, there is a breathtaking range of identities, experiences and issues that are thereby represented. Yet we make no claim to be all-inclusive or all-representative. We are not attempting any geography lessons. We believe these voices will speak for themselves, and possibly others, with clarity and precision, in analysis and in reflection. As far as we are aware, this is the first anthology of its kind – an international collection by young feminists from over eleven countries, representing all populated continents, and including a piece on male advocates for gender equality by a male feminist (they exist!).

As editors, we have been overwhelmed by the sense of responsibility we have felt while putting this anthology together. From the initial support of Peggy Antrobus (who is the spirit of all that we believe is feminist leadership), to the enthusiasm of the publishers, to the extraordinary abstracts we received for our contribution call ... We have been amazed, astounded, humbled and (in our lesser moments) quietly triumphant. The fruition of this book feels like the endorsement of our belief in our friends, our fellow travellers in these strange and complex journeys of feminist engagement. They have redeemed our belief in full measure; each chapter is a testimony to their personal activism and analysis.

In Chapter 1, Suzan Pritchett sets the tone for the rest of the book by interrogating how the New Global Order fosters dualisms, instead of cooperation, between women and feminist movements.

In Chapter 2, Aziza Ahmed takes on discourses around sexuality, HIV/

3

AIDS and reproductive health and how they shape the understanding of individual experiences of sexuality among young women.

In Chapter 3, Alison Symington looks at why young women act, react and engage distinctly from older generations, not only with respect to economic justice issues but also in terms of the broader and more complete picture of their lives.

In Chapter 4, Ann Elisabeth Samson looks at new technologies and their potential impact on our bodies, our environments, our work and our safety.

In Chapter 5, Haidee Swanby (with Shamillah Wilson) explores the politics inherent in the proposal that genetically engineered crops will address food insecurity.

In Chapter 6, Sushma Joshi interrogates the anti-trafficking movement in Nepal and its methods that are geared towards maintaining purity and national sovereignty rather than labour and migration rights, which limits its own effectiveness.

Indigo Williams Willing explores the politics underlying transnational adoption, in Chapter 7. Her account moves beyond the usual focus on adoptive parents and highlights the less publicized issues of displacement and discrimination, through deeply personal and analytical reflections.

In Chapter 8, Anasuya Sengupta presents an imagined reality where poverty is no longer the major dilemma constraining social justice. By taking us into another realm, she addresses many of the questions we are currently engaging with, and uses this method of exploration to pull us out of normative 'in the box' thinking around poverty eradication.

In Chapter 9, María Alejandra Scampini reflects on the potential of the World Social Forum as an alternative space for engagement for young social advocates in search of new ways of addressing the challenges we face in this global order.

Jennifer Plyler illustrates, in Chapter 10, instances of young women in Canada building radical movements of action and solidarity. She shows that these young women, who epitomize 'think global, act local', are leading new and militant struggles against the forces of imperialism, colonialism, racism, sexism and poverty.

In Chapter 11, Zakia Afrin and Amy Schwartz look at the establishment of the International Criminal Court (ICC) as a possible means to ensure justice for women in the context of sexual violence and gender-based persecution. They explore the enforceability of the ICC, its possible influence on domestic legal systems and the implications for international and national legal reform that could significantly improve women's rights.

In Chapter 12, Kristy Evans takes us on a virtual journey to explore some of the existing internet and communication technologies and their potential uses in feminist activism (communication, building solidarity, advocacy and research).

In Chapter 13, Gabriela Malaguera González creatively explores sexuality and desire, using the female archetypes of Scheherezade and Freud's Dora to pose provocative questions with regard to the impact that feminism has on younger women, especially in the realm of their relations to men.

As though in response to Gabriela's questions, Dean Peacock has a conversation in Chapter 14 with other male feminists who share their processes of becoming involved in issues of gender equality, the impact their work has had on their personal lives and their understanding of the role of men in the broader struggle for women's rights and gender equality.

In Chapter 15, Paromita Vohra provides a personal exploration of her own involvement in media advocacy, and critiques the ways in which the intuitive and open-ended richness of art and feminism has been abandoned in the attempt to 'mainstream' issues.

Salma Maoulidi, in Chapter 16, through a personal reflection on faith, family and relationships, shows that it is not only the external that grounds our choice and realization of advocacy and activism, but the internal and personal trajectories of our lives.

In Chapter 17, Shamillah Wilson addresses the 'internal' and 'external' challenges for the feminist movement, and its potential to 'be' the leadership and change that it wants to see.

Every chapter in this anthology explores, in different ways, some of the myriad questions that crowd our present global order, and analyses its disorders. Globalization, fundamentalisms, sexualities, financial institutions, new technologies, trafficking, transnational adoption, poverty ... The chapters also offer new ways of strategizing around these issues, new spaces for change – the World Social Forum, radical activist groups and networks, media advocacy, the International Criminal Court, and internet activism. Finally, we end with a call for an old slogan with renewed implications – making the personal political is also about making the political, personal. What is our own integrity and accountability, as advocates for feminist justice, for social change, in the ways we theorize and practise? In our strategies and our imaginings? How do we resolve our nightmares? Do we need to defend our dreams? Where do we go from here?

Are we really gonna 'make a difference'?

When AWID set up the Young Women and Leadership Programme, it was an opportunity to understand the issues that were particular for young women, as well as their relationship with the feminist movement.

5

Young women today do face different realities from those faced by previous generations, while at the same time benefiting from the gains of earlier feminist struggles. In this new global order, feminism provides a critical framework, a political lens, through which to analyse and develop visions and strategies for a just world. Feminist and women's movements then provide a particular vehicle with which to make real those visions. As an ideology and a movement, feminism offers solidarity, commitment rights, understanding of power as personal and systemic, and a willingness to challenge an inequitable status quo. However, for many young women the gap between discourse and practice fuels scepticism about the relevance of feminist movements – have we become part of a well-oiled institutionalized development apparatus? Are we part of the problem? Are we really gonna make a difference?

Sisters, friends, fellow travellers – we'll make a difference if we're able to learn and appreciate history and memory and wisdom, and yet have the courage to take our own risks in new contexts with new issues. Along with some of the old ones just the way they were, or bottled in new ways. We'll make a difference if we are able to work with participation and cooperation and shared learnings, in honest, transparent, intimate ways, without letting self-reflexivity and angst become personal diarrhoea. We'll make a difference if we are able to straddle the many levels of ideology, theory, discourse and practice, in our personal lives and out there. And if we are able to bring out there back home when needed, and the personal out to the streets when needed, but not to the extent that whom we are sleeping with or not is our only understanding of feminism. Our passions, our relationships, our friendships, our energies should be manifest in the ways we are up close and political. We'll make a difference when the many levels we straddle – in geography and in action – are as fused in our heads as they should be in our bodies; when we are as honest and as responsive to the issues at the local as we are to the global. But equally honest that the language, the metaphors, the negotiation at these levels are differently done – and that we must learn the skills and the strategies with which to juggle the multiplicity. We'll make a difference when we move from self-consciousness to consciousness – when we accept that women (or men!) who do brave and courageous acts, who move out of confined and imposed spaces for themselves and others, are feminist whether they call themselves that or not. And that we don't need to call them feminist either. Feminist is, as feminist does.

Notes

1 The Association for Women's Rights in Development (AWID) and the African Gender Institute (AGI), with their partners, held an international conference called 'Transformation for Gender Justice and Organizational Change' in 1998.

2 M. Rahnema with V. Bawtree (1997), 'Twenty-six years later: Ivan Illich in conversation with Majid Rahnema', in *The Post-development Reader* (Halifax: Zed Books, Fernwood Publishing).

3 Youmna Chlala (2003), *Young Women and Leadership Diary* (Ontario: AWID).

1 | Will dualism tear us apart? The challenges of fragmentation in identity politics for young feminists in the New Global Order

SUZAN PRITCHETT

The politics of irreconcilable differences

Jane[1] and I were best friends until the age of 16. Our friendship was the kind based on similar background, shared ideas and a mutual curiosity that extended beyond the boundaries of our small Midwestern community. Both growing up on farms amid the rolling hills of north-western Iowa, Jane and I spent many an afternoon planning our futures and mapping our destinies. While we debated the directions our future lives would take us, one thing was never questioned: the sanctity and longevity of our friendship.

As our high school years drew to a close, Jane and I made radically different choices in the colleges we were to attend. She chose an evangelical Christian university with a fundamentalist mission, while I chose a small college founded on liberal ideologies and a commitment to diversity. Little did we know at that point in our lives, in addition to choosing higher educational institutions, we were also choosing identities that would irreconcilably divide us.

The winter break of that now infamous first year of college will be one that I never forget. Jane and I came back to our hometown changed women, whose beliefs, politics and identities had diverged so much that they were impossible to reconcile. Jane refused to speak or engage with me based on my 'new-found' highly suspect liberalism. Feeling hurt and slightly bewildered, I chose to do the same to her, finding her conservative fundamentalism too alien and hostile to address.

Looking back on it now, I laugh at how close, yet so very far away, we were to each other. We grew up on neighbouring farms in the heartland of the United States. We both had chosen to study religion: Jane focusing on the evangelical possibilities of spreading the Christian message globally, I on a feminist exploration of religious pluralism. We have both gone on to attain master's degrees and travel and explore the world, albeit from different vantage points. We could/should have had so much to share. Yet, however much our lives resemble each other's, Jane and I are sharply divided by the identity politics of our lived realities.

I cannot, I admit, bring myself to understand her chosen path in life, and I think she too would agree that she finds my curiosity and acceptance of the multivariate ways of living and doing, as a woman, anathema to her personal and religious philosophy. Yet no matter how long it has been since I have spoken with Jane, no matter how enraged I am by her politics and/or her judgements of me, I also lament the lost possibilities: especially the possibility that our friendship, as young women, could have been a site for productive dialogue that might have included and celebrated our different political perspectives. I know there is much that I could have learned from Jane, and I would hope that she could have learned from me. Our continued friendship and bonding could have been an enormous source of strength. It is our chosen polarized identities, however, that have torn us apart; and so, I fear, we will for ever be.

I am sure my personal story is not unique. As young women, life is about change, growing up, learning, experiencing and pursuing those things we deem important. We choose different paths, different geographies and different politics. Our lives grow apart. But it is not this type of growing apart to which I address this chapter. Instead, it is the divisive 'apart' that proved to be the demise of my friendship with Jane: the 'apart' of political polarization and dualistic fragmentation, which largely characterizes the politics of identity for young women in the New Global Order.

When I speak of the New Global Order, I am referring to a world illustrated by the powerful forces of war and militarization, religious fundamentalisms and the spread of globalization and free-market democracy. I speak of my personal national landscape coping with the traumatic upheaval of the events surrounding 11 September 2001 and the subsequent re-masculinization of foreign and domestic policy. I am reflecting on an international climate characterized by increasing disparities between nations and between people, and continuing inequality between men and women. At every turn in this tumultuous climate, young women are being faced with dualistic politics and polarized identity politics that continue to threaten the solidarity of the feminist movement.

As young feminists with a vested interest in the future of our movement, it is important to analyse the impact of the powerful binaries embedded in the forces of the New Global Order. We must inquire into how the current global political climate is fostering dualism instead of cooperation between women. Has the transnational feminist movement been made stronger by the possibilities of the New Global Order? Or has it been weakened by the proliferation of competing, diverse identities that have proven stronger, providing more to women in the turbulent changing climate of rampant militarization, globalization and neo-liberal economic restructuring? How can we, as young feminists, best use our positioning and our voices to challenge dualism and bring women closer together instead of further apart? Through this brief chapter I begin to explore and open up debate surrounding some of these questions.

Why identity, why now?

Identity politics is not a new phenomenon within the feminist movement and has long been the centre of debates separating philosophical strands and chronological waves of feminist thought. It should also be noted that identity politics surrounding feminism and feminist solidarity is not limited to a particular geographical location, despite the Western media obsession with the 'Backlash' and specific references to a new 'Third Wave' in which women return to a reassertion of their femininity and partake in a bargain with patriarchy.[2] Instead, identity politics is a factor shaping women's realities across the world from the post-communist states of Eastern Europe to the provinces of Pakistan to, as it has been seen, the heartland of the United States.

Valentine Moghadam, a prominent scholar of identity politics, notes that identities, in a post-structural cultural analysis, are products of historical and discursive practices, primarily influenced by culture, the state, mass media, religious bodies and educational institutions.[3] She asserts that identities are neither fixed nor primordial, but instead fluid intersectionalities that are shaped by social and cultural surroundings and 'reflect the symbiosis of the economic, the cultural, and the political' in both the national and international context.[4] Therefore, any analysis that undertakes a study of identities and intersectionalities must also be concurrently analysing the surrounding climate and addressing the various powerful forces that vie for attention and reflection in women's chosen identities. Thus we are able to see that far from being outside the sphere of influence, women's identities are but a part of the complex web of characteristics that define the New Global Order.

So why identity and why now? Because now is a momentous time in our history as a movement and our role as young feminists within this movement is paramount. The traumatic events of 11 September 2001, the upheaval caused by global restructuring and the continuing threat of future military actions and terrorist strikes have resulted in a reassertion of identity from all sides of the political spectrum. Within the discourse of our highly charged atmosphere, the politics of dualism has been used to garner power and as Moghadam asserts, 'hold together what is [perceived to be threatened]'.[5]

The New Global Order, and the identity politics that is being played out within it, are largely about a struggle for power. Neo-liberal economic theories of development and structural adjustment are empowered through support from the major economic players. Alternative visions of development are quietly sidelined. Moderate and pluralistic religious voices are not loud enough to grab the media's attention. War is presented as the only solution to an already astonishing amount of suffering, sacrifice and loss of human life. Within these powerful discourses, the battle for identity and women's allegiance rages on.

In this search for a place in the New Global Order, women, as it will be seen, have been torn apart as they seek to find meaning, security and sense in what feels like, if not actually is, 'a world gone mad'.[6] It is our role, as young feminists, to recognize that feminism, our analysis and vision, must provide meaning in this New Global Order, be it mad or completely sane. We must recognize that the current discourse of our global political and economic environment has worked to undermine the value of the feminist identity. We must use our voices to find ways to overcome the simplicity of binary oppositions that continue to tear us apart: personally and politically.

The fragmenting impact of war and militarization

Increasing militarization in the New Global Order has had devastating impacts on women's solidarity. From the 'clash of civilizations' theory to the rise in armed conflicts, including the wars in Afghanistan and Iraq, violent forces have divided women across the political and geographical spectrum.[7] In his now infamous speech trying to convince the world of the validity of war, George W. Bush declared 'you are either with us, or with the terrorists'.[8] Such a dualistic mentality has fostered the fragmentation of women by offering only two viable identity alternatives: 'us' or 'terrorists', both of which from a feminist perspective are gendered and divisive. In her analysis, Susan Hawthorne aptly points out:

> The homogenizing of 'us' is a useful tool for the focus of dominant culture.
> It turns a diverse ... political culture into a monoculture. And in times of
> war and conflict, the monoculture gets much more airtime than the forces
> of resistance.[9]

Feminism as an identity has been undermined by the promotion of the 'monoculture' of binary opposition as the 'resistance' characteristics that we as feminists value: complexity, diversity, deconstruction and critical analysis becoming highly suspect. It is a dangerous world for those with identities that do not fit neatly into the boxes: 'us' or 'terrorists', and consequently, feminism as a chosen identity has suffered and women have been divided by unnecessary political compartmentalization.

11

Governments have contributed to this increasing fragmentation by encouraging neighbours to question each other, to be wary of 'otherness' and those who do not look like 'us'. Joseph and Sharma, in their carefully documented analysis of the effects of global terrorism on gender, cite the US Patriot Act and the Terrorism and Information and Prevention System as leading to polarization and anti-solidarity.[10] The mentality of questioning and suspicion, rather than celebrating the 'other', splits bonded groups of women apart and slowly wears away at the progress of the transnational feminist movement. One is left to ask: for whose benefit are these binary oppositions, fuelled by the fires of war and militarization, being constructed? It is probably sufficient to say, not for the benefit of women.

The upheaval caused by war, terrorism and increasing militarization has also led to a resurgence in nationalism and a reinforcement of traditional gender ideologies. The group Transnational Feminists have made it clear that militarization and nationalism are not gender-neutral, but are instead 'highly sentimentalized narratives that ... reinscribe compulsory heterosexuality'.[11] The media's portrayal of 'the masculine citizen-soldier, the patriotic wife and mother, the bread-winning father who is head of household, and the properly reproductive family' has further assaulted feminist solidarity and identity.[12] Women choosing not to adhere to traditional gender roles are thrust into the 'other' suspect category and further alienated from possible solidarity with their sisters.

Such an analysis of the fragmenting impacts of war and militarization cannot be complete without noting the tangible costs that women have faced. As military spending has increased, social sector spending has decreased: a burden, which women are largely left to bear.[13] Internationally agreed human rights standards have waned in the face of state security as 'right and wrong, legal and illegal have come to be defined by each state, separately'.[14] This all comes with a tacit [un]recognition of the lives that have been lost: both women's and men's. Women have been torn apart by the costs of war and militarization across the world and young feminists are challenged to make feminism a viable, stalwart, desirable identity, as women are forced to choose their place in this rapidly changing and challenging world.

Fundamentalism's divisiveness

Fundamentalism, from a plurality of religious traditions, has been an equal threat to feminist identity and women's solidarity in the New Global Order. As major social upheaval has been caused by war and global restructuring, religious fundamentalism has flourished in reaction to the changing social and political climate.[15] Valentine Moghadam has noted that 'a central manifestation of fundamentalism – be it Islamic, Christian, Jewish, or Hindu – is an attempt to circumscribe women's freedom and identity', and increases in fundamentalist practices have resulted in further divisions between women of conservative and liberal political and social values.[16]

The New Global Order has seen a teaming up of politics and religious fundamentalism at the centre of the world stage, notably through the neo-conservative politics of George W. Bush. On his first day in office, he enacted the Global Gag Rule, cutting off all aid to international family planning organizations that provide abortion services.[17] This decision was no doubt based on his very own fundamentalist politics, which seeks to subordinate women's bodily freedom and integrity. The impact of his decision has been felt by women across the world and has provided a further barrier between the freedoms enjoyed by women in the North and their sisters in the South. This same fundamentalist politics also continues to divide women domestically along rigid liberal/conservative political lines. In many countries, women are equally divided around issues of reproductive choice and the role of religion in the state; this is especially evident in the recent US presidential election results.

It is important to note that while religious fundamentalism often works as a cohort to the power of political will, it also plays an important role in circumscribing women's role inside of communities. Fatou Sow notes that fundamentalist forces assume that women are the bearers of culture, morality and national identity.[18] Fundamentalism asserts that 'women cannot assume a modernity that might threaten the fragile moral and cultural balance of societies … Women's rights are perceived as anti-cultural and anti-religious.'[19] Inside the New Global Order, with the pace of change continuing to threaten the cohesiveness of communities and identities, it is important to understand that fundamentalist discourse and the discourse of feminism and women's rights are most often at odds. With the power of political will firmly behind fundamentalist forces, it is the struggle for women's rights that is most often lost.

Young feminists must continue to analyse the impacts of fundamentalist politics on our movement. We must prepare ourselves to be further challenged by fundamentalist mentalities that threaten our complex and complicated discourse. We must not forget that it is not only men who play the fundamentalist role, but that 'women are also fundamentalist policy-leading characters, acting as spokespersons in the defence of family, morality, and decency'.[20] Fundamentalisms are on the rise across the globe and the past has taught us that feminism and fundamentalism occupy competing space in the context of women's identities. This will no doubt provide a challenging future for our movement. As long as fundamentalist politics drives governments and societies, women will continue to be both subordinated and divided.

The challenge of globalization and neo-liberal economic restructuring

In addition to increasing militarization and hostile ideological and religious fundamentalisms, the promotion of globalization and neo-liberal economic restructuring has contributed to the weakening of feminist identity. In a definition cited by Marchand and Runyan, we find that the two characteristics most relevant to the fragmentation of identity politics for women are the spatial reorganization of production and the massive transfers of population from South to North and from East to West.[21]

The spatial reorganization of production has had devastating impacts on women's solidarity and empowerment. From the policies of the World Bank to the privatization of public goods and services, women have been asked to accommodate rapidly changing market, state and international systems with their unpaid labour and care-giving. While attempting to reconcile the gulf between provision and need, poor women have suffered disproportionately compared to their 'better-off' sisters and the rift between North and South, rich and poor has widened, making solidarity across borders a formidable challenge.

Simultaneously, globalization has resulted in what Marchand and Runyan describe as 'a redefining of boundaries and identities'.[22] While women have been asked to assume a larger role, participating actively in the public sphere of the market, they have simultaneously been pressed to strongly adhere to gendered identities within the private sphere, providing continuity and identity for households, communities and states in the rapidly changing climate of globalization. The reassertion of traditional gender roles, as a coping mechanism in globalizing contexts, works to further divide women on all sides of the economic and geo-political spectrum, leaving the feminist identity and women's solidarity deprived of power in the face of neo-liberal economics.

Mass population transfers also typify our New Global Order and a major consequence of population shifts has been threatened ethnicities and communities, and the reactionary forces of nationalism. Through gaining momentum in order to protect, as previously discussed, that which is deemed to be threatened, nationalist forces have circumscribed women's identity and have pitted women from diverse ethnicities, geographies and communities against each other. Nickie Charles also notes that nationalist

14

forces in a globalized context are often highly suspicious of feminism as an identity because it is seen to be either a colonial, Western import or a divisive identity that weakens the national struggle against the adversary faction.[23] Thus, globalization and neo-liberal economic restructuring have added to the divisiveness of our global political landscape and have provided a further challenge to women's solidarity.

Divided and conquered?

The above analysis has revealed ways in which the powerful forces of the New Global Order have fostered a dualistic discourse that threatens to undermine the power of the feminist movement and women's solidarity. Far from being gender-neutral, normative moral orders, the forces of the New Global Order have united in posing a threatening challenge to women, who are lost in the sea of identity politics. How can we be loyal to a feminist cause when we are forced to choose a side in this ideological battle of militarization, fundamentalisms and globalization? How can we advocate for gender equality and holism when we are continually confronted by dualism and a wearing away of the foundations of our transnational solidarity movement?

What must be recognized is that dualism and binary opposition are political tactics fostered by those in power in order to maintain hegemonic control and support. Diane Bell provides a helpful conceptualization in warning: 'Beware of binaries ... The juxtapositions are not a matter of simple opposites but rather mask the power of one side of the binary to control the other.'[24] It comes as no surprise, then, that in the construction of simplistic, dualistic politics that states 'you are either with us or against us', feminist voices, with their celebration and embrace of plurality and multi-perspectivalism, are often left powerless in the face of rigid dichotomies.

Valentine Moghadam has explained the difficulties of feminist multi-perspectivalism in saying:

> Women have been exposed to contradictory, dissonant messages and practices, filled with false expectations and aspirations. This has rendered them vulnerable and receptive to an ideology that simplifies reality and promises escape from role conflict and ambiguity.[25]

Thus, women in the New Global Order have fallen into the trap of fragmentation and have had their potentially powerful solidarity torn apart. The neutral middle ground where ideas and politics could once be contested has turned into an ideological battlefield where the consequences of militarization, fundamentalism and globalization are most acutely felt.

Women and young feminist leaders have unduly suffered in this ever-increasing rift, as they are pitted not only against their ideological foes, but also against their feminist sisters. As the opening to this chapter reveals, Jane and I have been divided by the politics of our chosen identities and are currently occupying space in the peripheral 'no-woman's land' where constructive dialogue with the 'other' remains elusive. bell hooks suggests that it is the downfall of our movement: not have to transformed these hostile landscapes into sites of strength and solidarity. 'So far, feminist movement has not transformed woman-to-woman relationships, especially between women who are strangers to one another or from different backgrounds.'[26] I believe it is now the foremost challenge for young feminist voices to overcome this fragmentation and devise a way forward.

The role of young feminist voices in overcoming fragmentation

The question, although not a novel one, now rests with us. How best can we achieve a sustainable movement that is not only able to withstand the powerful antithetical forces of the New Global Order but that continues to value diversity, complexity and multiple perspectives? How do we attempt to overcome the fragmentation between women and among feminists?

The New Global Order brings with its many challenges increased opportunities for analysis and activism and for extending beyond the boundaries of our dualisms and polarization. Technological advancement has made communication across borders, be they geographic or ideological, possible where they once were not. Increasing amounts of travel across national borders continues to open the eyes of the world to 'other's' realities: a first step in overcoming fear and distrust of the 'other'. International development has finally made it to the front page as world leaders begin to respond to our global activism and unrelenting demand for justice.

Despite the opportunities, however, feminist engagement with the forces of the New Global Order has brought us only so far. We have been able to give the beasts of fundamentalism, militarization and globalization a name, analyse their effects on women and on the feminist movement, and theoretically unite against them. However, what we have failed to do is dialogue with, and impact upon, the forces themselves; no doubt a weighty task considering that feminist identity is the very modernist force that New Global Order demonizes.

Clearly, if the feminist movement is to continue as a dissonant voice and an alternative identity for women who choose to reconsider mainstream or fundamental gendered ideologies, young feminists must continue to respond to the forces of the New Global Order with equally powerful, contextualized and viable responses. This involves a thorough understanding of the locations and reasoning of our adversaries. We must stop shying away from those things we believe to be 'outside' our feminist framework and venture into lands unknown. We must admit to harbouring our own fundamentalisms and own up to our propensity to be closed and unrequiting. It is important to remember that 'at any moment that we're dealing with people different from ourselves, the likelihood is that they carry a similar list of hopes and fears in their back pocket'.[27]

In her work on activism and reaching beyond the boundaries of the feminist, liberal movement, Anasuya Sengupta provides tangible ways of overcoming divisions in identity politics. She describes the work of an organization, Culture Move, that takes political and social discussions into unexplored activist spaces in her national context: pubs. She notes:

> While we need the sense of solidarity and community we feel protesting together on street corners and at rallies, we do not, at all, reach out to those with power and influence, and we certainly do not change the way most young people in schools and colleges think ... if we have to do whatever it takes to reach out, we should be prepared to make music videos, we should be prepared to go on pub crawls![28]

If we are at any point able to open up dialogue with religious and political leaders, who gain power from these fragmenting politics, with our sisters, who find no strength from our analysis, from the women whose realities have been ignored by our movement, we must start by moving beyond the boundaries of our activism and begin to communicate and listen to the so-called 'other'. We must make every effort to re-establish dialogue and communication with those from whom we have been torn apart. We must be the ones to begin transgressing the binaries of the New Global Order and make the first step towards co-operation and solidarity.

It has been a long five years since Jane and I have made the opportunity to engage with each other. I truly miss her, and I can only hope that *some day* my politics of identity as a young woman committed to diversity, multiplicity, peace and equality will overcome our polarization and resonate with her too. Perhaps *today* is the day. I think it is time for me to pick up the telephone and make a very important call.

Notes

1 Name has been changed.

2 Anonymous (1997), 'Wimmin are from Mars, women are from Venus', *The Economist*, 343 (8022): 87–9.

3 V. Moghadam (1994), 'Women and identity politics in theoretical and comparative perspective', in V. Moghadam (ed.), *Identity Politics and Women:*

17

Cultural Reassertions and Feminisms in International Perspective (Oxford: Westview Press), p. 3.

4 Ibid., p. 9.

5 Ibid., p. 9.

6 Ibid., p. 19.

7 S. P. Huntington (1998), *The Clash of Civilizations and Remaking of World Order* (London: Simon & Schuster).

8 G. W. Bush (2001) 'Address to a joint session of Congress and the American people', see <www.whitehouse.gov/news/releases/2001/09/20010920-8.html>.

9 S. Hawthorne (2002), 'Fundamentalism, violence and discrimination', in S. Hawthorne and B. Winter (eds), *September 11, 2001: Feminist Perspectives* (Melbourne: Spinifex), p. 342.

10 A. Joseph and K. Sharma (eds) (2003), *Terror Counter Terror: Women Speak Out* (London: Zed Books), p. xxii.

11 Transnational Feminists (2003), 'Transnational feminist practices against war' in Joseph and Sharma, *Terror Counter Terror*, p. 266.

12 Ibid.

13 R. Saigol (2003), 'Ter-reign of terror' in Joseph and Sharma, *Terror Counter Terror*, p. 48.

14 Ibid., p. 46.

15 M. Marchand and A. S. Runyan (2000), 'Feminist sightings of global restructuring: conceptualizations and reconceptualizations', in M. Marchand and A. S. Runyan (eds), *Gender and Global Restructuring: Sightings, Sites and Resistances* (London: Routledge), p. 18.

16 Moghadam, 'Women and identity politics in theoretical and comparative perspective', p. 17.

17 K. Viner (2002), 'Feminism as imperialism', *Guardian*, 21 September 2002.

18 F. Sow (2004), 'Fundamentalisms: positions and debates', in *DAWN Special Supplement for the World Social Forum, Mumbai, 16–21 January 2004*, p. 4.

19 Ibid., p. 4.

20 S. Corrêa (2004), 'Religious fundamentalism and secular politics: different sides of a single thought', in *DAWN Special Supplement for the World Social Forum, Mumbai, 16–21 January 2004*, p. 2.

21 'The manifestations of globalization ... include the spatial reorganization of production, the interpenetration of industries across borders, the spread of financial markets, the diffusion of identical consumer goods to distant countries, massive transfers of population within the South as well as from the South and the East to the West, resultant conflicts between immigrant and established communities in formerly tight-knit neighborhoods, and emerging worldwide preference for democracy.' In Marchand and Runyan, *Gender and Global Restructuring*, p. 10.

22 Marchand and Runyan (2000), 'Feminist sightings of global restructuring', p. 18.

23 N. Charles (1996), 'Feminist practices: identity, difference, power', in N. Charles and F. Hughes-Freeland (eds), *Practising Feminism: Identity, Difference, Power* (London: Routledge), p. 20.

24 D. Bell (2002), 'Good and evil: at home and abroad', in Hawthorne and Winter, *September 11, 2001*, p. 433.

25 Moghadam, 'Women and identity politics in theoretical and comparative perspective', p. 19.

26 b. hooks (1997), 'Sisterhood: political solidarity between women', in D. Tietjens Meyers (ed.), *Feminist Social Thought: A Reader* (London: Routledge), p. 489.

27 M. DuPraw and M. Axner (1997), 'Working on common cross-cultural communication challenges', accessed 2 February 2005, see <http://www.wwcd.org./action/ampu/corsscult.html>.

28 A. Sengupta (2004), 'Fundamentalisms of the progressive?' DAWN panel on 'The Many Faces of Fundamentalism', 18 January 2004, World Social Forum, Mumbai, India.

Will dualism tear us apart?

2 | Channelling discourse, effecting change: young women and sexual rights

AZIZA AHMED

An 11-year-old raised his hand and asked: 'If my friends want condoms, where can they get them?' He was among 50 young people participating in a youth forum on HIV/AIDS. His peers nodded in his direction, affirming the value of his question. In Barbados, where sex is illegal under the age of 16, there is no place for young people to access condoms legally. The member of government representing children's services quickly replied: 'You are not to be having sex; it's illegal. Next question.'

Despite the assertions of the government representative, the 1998 Caribbean Adolescent Health Survey indicated that in a cross-section of Caribbean adolescents, of those reported being sexually active, over 40 per cent experienced their first sexual intercourse before the age of 10; a further 20 per cent of youth experienced their first sexual intercourse before the age of 12. Over half of these adolescents reported that they did not use any form of contraception during their last sexual encounter.[1]

A young woman at the session raised her hand: 'What about the taxi-drivers who have sex with young girls?' The children began to discuss this newly presented issue among themselves and the adults nodded in recognition of this challenge. In agreement with several members of government in the room, one young woman suggested that, in fact, young women should stop enticing older men. Another young woman proposed a solution to the audience: 'Well, why not just arrest the girls?'

These attitudes and experiences are not specific to the Caribbean. As a second-generation South Asian Muslim in America, the idea of the woman as temptress to the apparently uncontrollable sexual drive of men becomes integral to how one begins to internalize sexuality: as something to be controlled, limited, hidden and kept a secret.

And yet of course, even in America, the self-proclaimed anti-venom to all things potentially touched by Islam and now the 'saviour' of women in the Islamic world, one often hears discussions on rape and sexual violence quickly turned to blame the woman and her role in bringing it about. Accompanying a friend to church on Sunday, I listened to the minister tell a story of two women wandering through a dark street, one of whom was raped. The minister explained that the woman who had not been raped had been saved because she had accepted Christ and was protected by guardian angels that appeared in the form of two men walking next to her.

I wondered at that moment how women who might have been sexually assaulted and who attended church every Sunday internalized this statement. Had they not accepted Christ enough? Were they not truly Christian? Were they to blame for the wrongs committed against them?

How do we identify and cultivate the power within ourselves to define our own sexuality, amidst different discourses and realms of experience spanning from shame to celebration, occurring across continents and cultures, and marked by centuries of constructing and resisting social norms?

The control of sexuality is regulated by the privileging of heteronormativity,[2] whiteness, maleness and idealized body images. These external forces are absorbed internally to influence our experiences of sexuality, which are inherently personal and intimate.

Writing about something so universal to humanity, yet so unique to every individual, poses a challenge for me based on the problematic assumption that my experiences of being young, being a woman, being of colour are experiences that speak not only for myself, but for many others.[3] The definitions of the terms I use to describe myself differ through time and space and by person. Being young, for example, may be a state of mind and not just a numerical age. Being young for some also means being married with its concomitant sanctioning of certain sexualities. The ways in which we identify ourselves are based on a negotiated process of who we are, who we choose to be, how we identify ourselves and how others label and control us.

This chapter seeks to explore how the current discourses around sexuality, HIV/AIDS and reproductive health shape the understanding of individual experiences of sexuality among young women. The analysis will allow us to place ourselves better in this dialogue, and create conversations where there is currently a void, in order to leverage our own power in shaping global and local actions that impact on our sexualities.

Changing paradigms and global contexts

The sexual rights movement has a long history, and the struggles have led to countless sacrifices from women around the world. Sonia Corrêa documents the movement in her article 'From reproductive health to sexual rights: achievements and future challenges'. She notes the efforts to legitimize the term 'reproductive health' from the mid-1980s to the 1990s and the parallel term 'reproductive rights', utilized mainly by women's groups who struggled for acceptance within mainstream development efforts. Corrêa also describes the process by which women's groups came together to create a strategy by which to review the neo-Malthusian principles that dominated the field of population.[4,5] After decades of activism and collaboration with various partners within the broader international health community, it was the Beijing Platform of Action in 1995 that embodied the core principles behind sexual rights:

> The human rights of women include their right to have control over and decide freely and responsibly on matters related to their sexuality, including sexual and reproductive health, free of coercion, discrimination and violence. Equal relationships between women and men in matters of sexual relations and reproduction, including full respect for the integrity of the person, require mutual respect, consent and shared responsibility for sexual behaviour and its consequences.[6]

This history foregrounds the current involvement of young women in the discourse on sexual rights. With each generation comes a new and unique struggle around sexuality and sexual rights, entrenched in the socio-cultural and political economic norms of the past. Today young women find that our conversations around sexuality are confronted by contexts fuelled by a growing global conservatism, driven by global development agendas and emerging health paradigms.

This conservatism is marked by the pivotal events of 11 September 2001 and the United States' continued hegemonic relationship to the global community. The administration of the US government utilized the events to rouse support for their biggest allies, the Christian right, with reference to the 'War on Terror' and a parallel war on women's rights.[7] The hypocrisy of the US government was perhaps best demonstrated to the world in the violations of people's rights at the Abu Ghraib prison. US soldiers carried out acts of hatred and homophobia, while the government coopted the language of human rights to justify their presence in Iraq. While the world's citizens struggle against such demonstrations of power, other conservative forces and nations, including the Vatican and Islamic countries, are able to merge their own agendas with that of the US government's; ironically, they are all allies in the war against women.

The rise of conservatism, bolstered by this cooptation of human rights language, has led to a more specific assault on sexual and reproductive health and rights, beyond the actions in Iraq.[8] Such conservatism is seen in the active stance against lesbian, gay, bisexual and transgender (LGBT) rights both internationally and domestically, and the increased funding to abstinence and faith-based programmes.[9] Additionally, the current climate in the US ceases to permit a free flow of criticism of the government, as individuals fear being called 'unpatriotic', thus squelching much-needed discourse and dialogue domestically on the actions of the administration.

The global conservative agenda continues to ignore the rights of adolescents to access appropriate sexual and reproductive health care while perpetuating notions of a 'traditional nuclear family' that undermine the rights of sexually diverse communities. In doing so, more people are shut out of appropriate sexual health and rights programmes, information and services, only increasing vulnerability to HIV/AIDS and other STIs. It appears, then, that in their questionable efforts to save people from hell, many faith-based organizations are making staying alive a challenge.

Alongside this agenda of conservative forces, we have the emerging dominance of restrictive development agendas. The Millennium Development Goals (MDGs) came out of the United Nations Millennium Summit in 2000. The MDGs outline time-specific goals that governments are using as a yardstick by which to measure development and improvement in people's lives.[10] Peggy Antrobus includes in her critique of the MDGs the fact that the indicators fail to represent the reality of women, who continue to suffer socio-economic marginalization throughout their lives.[11] Other feminist critiques articulate how sexual and reproductive health and rights have been left out of the goals and indicators, resulting in the absence of these issues from mainstream development discourse.[12] This omission leaves women in a void with programmes that do not address their needs and with indicators that do not begin to 'measure' their realities in any concrete way. The omission further reinforces the marginalization of sexually diverse groups and young people.

What do we know about young women's sexuality on a global scale? Very little, as the few indicators we currently have tell us about 'behavioural norms', which may provide insights into women's sexual behaviour, but they say nothing about the socio-political realities impacting on women's abilities to demand and exercise sexual rights, to gain access to sexual health information and to condoms, to negotiate with sexual partners or how pleasure and desire factor into women's sexual decision making.

Globally, there are two major discourses on the realization of sexual rights – one regarding the HIV/AIDS epidemic and the other regarding reproductive health and rights – that intersect but often operate as separate paradigms. These initiatives have been largely separated due to funding structures that often dictate that HIV/AIDS programmes be developed and implemented outside reproductive health programmes. Both separately and together, however, HIV/AIDS and reproductive health programmes tend to marginalize sexual rights.

Reproductive health programmes, both historically and today, focus overwhelmingly on maternal and child health, and women as reproductive agents.[13] This has led to the exclusion of broader sexual health issues outside those of reproduction. This focus also leads to programmes targeting only women of reproductive age and/or who are mothers, often leaving little or no services for very young or older women who fall outside reproductive years, or women who cannot or choose not to have children. Historically, reproductive health programmes have had a purely hetero-centrist view of reproduction and have neglected to create appropriate and accessible services for sexually diverse people.

HIV/AIDS programmes, an intersecting paradigm to that of reproductive health, have attempted to utilize the existing reproductive health approaches to respond to the epidemic. Such programmes have therefore reinforced the same vacancies created by the narrow maternal and child health framework. Hence the responses to these programmes also lack an integrated sexual rights perspective, and ignore the real drivers for engagement in sexual behaviours that often determine individual vulnerability to HIV/AIDS.

In some countries, where funding has created entirely new structures to deal with prevention of mother-to-child transmission (PMTCT) initiatives, maternal and child health programmes have little interaction with HIV/AIDS responses. Additionally, PMTCT programmes have tended to focus on mothers for the benefit of the children. Responses to the HIV/AIDS programmes have often served further to marginalize individuals of sexually diverse communities, and programmes that have not effectively responded to this stigmatization increase the vulnerability of already highly vulnerable populations (sex workers, men having sex with men, and so on) with little information or access to services. Finally, global discourse and programming on HIV/AIDS has been affected by the global conservatism mentioned earlier, which consequently impedes the development of appropriate programmes.

This persistent hetero-normativity, fuelled by fear and ignorance, is illustrated in the mental and physical violence inflicted on LGBT communities globally, in reaction to the notion that HIV/AIDS has been brought to those practising 'normal' sexual behaviour. The extreme responses to 'aberrant' behaviours of sexually diverse communities are exemplified by recent discussion around the decriminalization of homosexuality in the Caribbean.

The *Jamaica Gleaner*'s editor quotes the Jamaica Labour Party spokesperson, Anthony Johnson, revealing the bias and discrimination faced by the LGBT community:

Studies have shown that it's about three per cent of persons in societies worldwide who suffer from a psychological problem in which they feel they are attracted to people from the same sex, the rest of those who are engaged in the practice do so for other reasons, including material gains. Judging from this, I would not say it's prevalent in the schools, it may be there, yes, but no I don't think it's widespread.[14]

In addition, a recent dialogue in Barbados on the decriminalization of homosexuality and sex work inspired outrage amongst members of the general population:

Has anyone followed through the further ramifications of decriminalizing homosexuality and prostitution? Do we wish to *see* homosexual couples holding hands, kissing, and making out on our beaches? Do we wish to *see* the children at school openly practising this behaviour? Do we wish to *see* a gay Kadooment Band 'wukking up'? Do we wish Barbados to be known as the gay capital of the Caribbean, attracting gay cruises and tours? Do we wish to *see* ads on TV, or in the press, advertising gay bars and restaurants? Or even 'legitimate' brothels? Do we wish to *see* classified ads offering sexual services? Do we wish to *see* prostitution offered as a career option to our schoolchildren?

Come on Barbados! Are we going to allow our country to slide even deeper into sexual immorality?[15]

In the midst of continued negative discourse in the Caribbean, and many other parts of the world, further attention is being paid to the problems of stigmatization and discrimination. These conversations tend to argue against isolating individuals with HIV/AIDS, however, failing to recognize the stigmatization and discrimination faced by members of marginalized sexual groups.[16] In addition to the vulnerability of contracting HIV, when members of marginalized groups become HIV positive, they often face 'double' the discrimination. By neglecting to focus on the integral issues of diverse sexualities, HIV prevention and education programmes lack effectiveness.

Sexual rights contest certain approaches to development and exist outside the confines of the context of 'reproductive health'. Sexuality affects the way we interact with the world, from shaping our interactions with other people to the way we create an identity for ourselves. Therefore, it is necessary to carve out a discussion on sexuality and sexual rights within existing structures, where sexual rights are either intentionally or unintentionally invisible from dialogue, negotiations, treaties and the frameworks (for instance, the Millennium Development Goals) designed to improve people's existences.

Situating young women: sexuality redefined in changing circumstances

HIV/AIDS and new technologies are also factors that have had a particular impact on the way young women define and internalize their sexuality today. The use of the internet and related information and communication technologies are disintegrating cultural boundaries while creating new demarcations of borders. While some of the world's people have access to an unprecedented amount of information, others are further marginalized by lack of access to technology: women continue to die in childbirth and lack the basic information and resources they need around reproduction. That being said, for many, new reproductive technologies and innovations have altered the face of reproduction. Women are capable of conceiving at a later age, advances in medical science have addressed issues of infertility and advances in abortion technology and science have given women easier and safer access to abortion.

Other technological developments are affecting the way in which we access information and knowledge of the sexual realms. For example, many children (normally boys) are playing video games such as the infamous *Grand Theft Auto*, which is popular in the US. It is globally marketed on internet forums in reference to violence and 'prostitution': these references are meant to make the game 'exciting' and therefore worth playing. The struggle for the rights of sex workers seems to fall at the wayside in these virtual realms where rights don't matter as much as scoring points. We have yet to understand the real impact that these games will have on future generations, especially in terms of increasing desensitization of violence that the international media and ICTs bring with them.

Alongside video games, access to new realms of sexuality through the internet is unlimited. While gazing at sexual imagery is far from new, the interaction that young people are able to have is particular to our generation. For instance, interaction globally through chat rooms and instant messaging has altered our notions of boundaries and distance. While chat rooms and instant messaging have facilitated communication around relationships and sex, particularly for young people in clandestine relationships, these media have also been abused by individuals seeking to gain illegitimate access to young people through virtually unregulated spaces. The open access to sexuality offered through the internet is unregulated with regard both to the material that can be accessed and the environment – young people are often alone in the virtual world, left to their own direction with few limitations.

This lack of regulation can have benefits, however, as young people who would not otherwise have access to sexual education material can access it through this medium. For example, young women who would like to seek information about abortion services and sexual health can do so without needing permission or being constrained by money barriers in the 'real' world. While experiencing such unregulated access to information and new frameworks within which to understand our sexuality, we are also left to dissect what we see and hear given the politicization and commercialization of our images, including in information campaigns and education systems.

The use of the internet as a conduit to young people (and between young people) points to a new era of policing and policy, which is developing, and will continue to develop, around social interactions, access to information, and behaviours on the internet. The formation of this policy is a critical place for young women to bring their perspectives in order to create a safe environment while protecting the right to access information.

A second factor that is necessary to highlight, in terms of its impact on the way young women define and internalize their sexuality, is HIV/AIDS. Statistically, young women now make up 60 per cent of the 15–24-year-olds living with HIV/AIDS, and are 1.6 times more likely to be living with HIV/AIDS than young men.[17] Feminists have persistently called for an increased focus on young women and girls because of increased vulnerability to sexual violence and an inability to negotiate condom use. Additionally, gender norms in many countries prevent young women from accessing much-needed services and education regarding HIV/AIDS. Feminists have identified one of the gaps in HIV/AIDS programmes as being the lack of acknowledgement of sexuality among children and youth.[18]

As young women today, we are a generation that must negotiate sexuality through the lens of HIV/AIDS, as many of us were born and experienced our first sexual interactions in this new era. For us, there was never a time when sex and death were not potentially synonymous.[19] Unlike previous generations, who might have negotiated sex with uncertainty, I often hear my peers discuss sexuality and engage in sexual decision making in the context of fear – that of contracting HIV and STIs. We live in a new generation where walking into a nightclub bathroom, we can look above the sink while washing our hands, and be reminded of HIV; we look at a condom and the warning about HIV is largely emblazoned on the side. We walk into the doctor's office and while being firmly recommended to take a pregnancy test, despite informing the doctor we are not pregnant, we are also encouraged to be tested for HIV. This experience might be different even for those 'youth' born five to ten years before I was, which speaks of the drastic changes that can occur within one generation. These changes have not only affected the environment in which we exercise our sexuality but also speak to the changes occurring in interpersonal sexual relationships. Desire has changed and spontaneity has been removed in a new generation, and we are now advised to stop and ask our partner how often and when they have been tested for HIV and other STIs.

The experience of disease affects the socio-cultural norms around sexual interaction. Additionally, power dynamics are magnified between genders, as those who are charged with the responsibility of condom use have been given, unwittingly, a new realm in which to control another individual's sexuality. Many of the public service announcements in the US, for example, speak to men advising them to 'protect their partners'. Geared towards the heterosexual relationship, such programmatic responses relegate more responsibility, but also power, to men in the face of disease. The shifting sexual dynamics that young people face need to be better understood and integrated into the programmatic and policy responses designed on the global level, through the integration of the perspectives of young people.

Finally, in keeping with feminist approaches to sexuality, we must look beyond women and girls as merely victims, and instead argue that programmes must incorporate specific perspectives of young women's agency, their sexuality (in its diversity) and sexual realities. Only then can prevention, education, and care and treatment programmes become effective.

Young women reshaping discourse

Young people, and young women in particular, must deal with the reality of new geo-political norms, technological revolutions, virtual realities and HIV/AIDS in order to start the process of reshaping discourses around sexuality. While young women may not have entered into sexual activism with the knowledge of the battles over discourse at Cairo or Beijing, they clearly need to address both discourse and practice in their activism today.[20] What are some concrete strategies by which to initiate this process?

Demanding dialogue and inspiring a paradigm shift Young women must harness the challenges that create barriers by becoming the bridge that connects non-traditional allies and groups who may not have joined hands previously in order to build a stronger movement. We must bring to the fore the various experiences specific to our generation that need to be better heard and understood. Within this, we need to articulate language and action around sexual and reproductive health rights that have been coopted by global forces and reinforced by the current geo-political environment of fear and increasing conservatism.

With specific regard to sexual and reproductive health rights, we must acknowledge the continued gap in reproductive health programmes that lie between the frameworks of maternal and child health programmes and HIV/AIDS. To explore the gap between reproductive health and the arena of HIV/AIDS, we must be willing to bring realities and contexts to the table, to take risks, and to move discourse a step further. HIV/AIDS, perhaps, offers us opportunities to discuss sexuality in environments previously unwilling to consider the issues. However, we need to be creative with how we use such opportunities. We need to create spaces to discuss our sexual realities, sexual decision making and sexual behaviours. This process must be driven by young people and be inclusive of the range of gender and sexual diversities that comprise our global populations. We also have to engage in emerging discourses around erotic justice, from our different locations, to ensure that our perspectives are integrated into this discourse.[21]

A great challenge for us is the process of bringing the micro-realities of individual lives to the global stage, with honesty and integrity. An accompanying challenge is also in being able to confront the different levels of macro-structures that govern women's lives. Religion, for instance, serves as an example of the interaction of the personal and societal understandings of sexuality, as we recognize that organized religion often trumps an individual's desire to change the norms that define the structures of these religions. Riffat Hassan quotes Fatima Mernissi, in describing this phenomenon in the context of Muslim women's lives:

> One of the distinctive characteristics of Muslim sexuality is its territoriality which reflects a specific division of labor and specific conception of society and power. The territoriality of Muslim sexuality sets ranks, tasks, and authority patterns.[22]

Hassan further elaborates that it is often socio-cultural interpretation, and not Islam intrinsically, that may drive the differences in the treatment of men and women in the context of religion. But it is under the guise of a religious framework that many of us experience a problematic allocation of power based on gender norms. Religion is only one of the many macro-structures that govern women's lives. Others may be community-specific or perhaps more entrenched with regard to race, class, caste or ethnicity.

We need to fight for the right to respect sexuality on each front at which a challenge arises; support for this may come from different backgrounds and locations. For instance, the Convention on the Rights of the Child (CRC) includes protection against sexual exploitation, and the right to comprehensive sexuality education.[23] More recently, the Brazilian Resolution in the United Nations attempted to include discrimination on the basis of sexual orientation as a violation of human rights.[24] Our allies may include sensitive video game programmers and sympathetic religious leaders.

Finding new ways of understanding 'progress' In the midst of misplaced indicators and problematic cultural norms, how does one find a realistic understanding of how women, men and others along the gender continuum experience life? In attempting adequately to design indicators and measures of women's progress in the arena of sexual and reproductive health and rights, one might argue that we need to identify and dissect these structures to find out how they retranslate into tools by which individuals set their personal sexual norms. In doing so, we must recognize how factors (or alternative frameworks) outside the scope of these macro-structures, such as pleasure, pain, love and infatuation, affect how people interact as sexual beings, and particularly how women interact as human beings. For example, we seem to be quite content to use fear of abuse as a constant justification of why women do not encourage the use of condoms during sex. Is this really the only reason we are willing to acknowledge? Why must all control of sexual interaction be framed in terms of male pleasure and/or physical and mental control in relationships? Could it perhaps be that the lack of success of condom-based prevention programmes in some parts of the world may in fact be due to women's physical desire to engage in sexual activity without a condom? Are we permitted to discuss pleasure explicitly? One group of women, of the Pleasure Project, feel that the best way to educate around safer sex is by addressing the primary motivators for having sex: desire and pleasure.[25]

All women calling for the recognition of pleasure and desire within the context of HIV/AIDS, and other discourses around sexuality, face the challenge of not having their voices heard in a global discourse that has intentionally or unintentionally omitted these issues. The silence is particularly deafening when it relates to pre-adolescents and adolescents; little wonder that programmatic responses are at times ineffective at changing high-risk behaviours.

Exercising inclusivity In the context of a discussion on sexual rights, young women must question what it means to be 'young women', what biological and cultural norms define our status as young and define our position as women. Where people are able to be open about their sexuality or their status as intersex, transgender, transsexual (the list continues), the scope of what it means to be a young woman may broaden, not only to whom society deems a young woman, but to who self-identifies in this way. Fighting for this greater sense of inclusion within a broader discourse on sexual rights requires an explicit call for the participation of members of sexually diverse communities, and the voice and direct involvement of young people. This inclusion must be empowered with the right to question and transform existing forms of privilege and power that serve to sustain discriminatory social norms.

Conclusion

We, as young women, must embrace our own sexuality, demand that it be recognized, and demand that a space be created within both feminist discourse and a global activism that addresses the nuanced nature of a sexuality shaped by the realities of our times. We must continue to recognize the common experiences of ourselves, as young women, across the globe, who transcend lines of culture, border, class and time, facilitated by technology. In turn, we must recognize that only *some* young women are able to access this revolution, and that the borders of only some of our existences may not be based on country or nationality, but rather may exist in a virtual realm demarcated by power lines and wires. In addition to all else, we must build on the culture of the women's movement, in identifying our commonalities and continuing to support one another across the lines of religion, age, class, race, gender, sexuality and other social demarcations that divide us. As we move into new realms that dictate new realities, young women must continue to be inclusive and without boundaries in our demanded space of discourse. For it is in this space that we will continue to effect change in a continuing revolution.

Notes

1 Pan American Health Organization (1998), 'Caribbean Adolescent Health Survey'.

2 Hetero-normativity is defined as: 'Those punitive rules (social, familial, and legal) that force us to conform to hegemonic, heterosexual standards for identity. The term is a short version of "normative heterosexuality"' in D. Felluga (2003), 'Introducton to theories of gender and sex', see <http://www.sla.purdue.edu/academic/engl/theory/genderandsex/terms/index.html>.

3 In the United States, being 'of colour' means you are non-white and therefore a minority.

4 Neo-Malthusian principles reinforce the Malthusian doctrine that argues that the betterment of a standard of living is not possible without a decrease in competitiveness brought about by the control of reproduction. Found in B. Hartman (1995), 'The Malthusian orthodoxy', see <http://www.hsph.harvard.edu/rt21/globalism/HARTMANNc2.html>.

5 S. Corrêa (1996), 'From reproductive health to sexual rights: achievements and future challenges', see <http://www.hsph.harvard.edu/Organizations/healthnet/reprorights/docs/correa.html>.

6 Ibid.

7 J. Lobe, 'Conservative Christians biggest backers of Iraq war', Common Dreams News Centre, <http://www.commondreams.org/headlines02/1010-

02.htm>, accessed 10 March 2005; Max Blumenthal, 'The Christian Right's humble servant', alternet. <http://www.alternet.org/election04/20499/>, accessed 10 March 2005.

8 F. Girard (June 2004), 'Global Implications of U.S. Domestic and International Policies on Sexuality', IWGSSP Working Papers, No. 1.

9 While terms around sexuality are often loosely defined and culturally specific, the following definitions provide an introduction to understanding terms. The definitions are quoted from various LGBT and sexuality organization sites.

Intersex: 'Technically, intersex is defined as "congenital anomaly of the reproductive and sexual system." Intersex people are born with external genitalia, internal reproductive organs, and/or endocrine systems that are different from most other people. There is no single "intersex body"; it encompasses a wide variety of conditions that do not have anything in common except that they are deemed "abnormal" by the society. What makes intersex people similar is their experiences of medicalization, not biology. Intersex is not an identity. While some intersex people do reclaim it as part of their identity, it is not a freely chosen category of gender – it can only be reclaimed. Most intersex people identify as men or women, just like everybody else' (Intersex Initiative, <http://www.intersexinitiative.org/articles/intersex-faq.html>).

Transgender: 'an umbrella term used to describe all forms of thinking or behaving over gender lines' (Sexuality.org, <http://www.sexuality.org/l/incoming/trbasic.html>).

Transsexual: 'A person assigned by the anatomical structure of the body to one sex, but who feels and wishes to function as a member of the opposite sex. Some transsexuals choose to undergo sex reassignment surgery to change their bodies to match the sex that they feel they really are' (Positive Space, <http://www.positivespace.utoronto.ca/Definitions.htm>).

10 UN (2005), 'Millennium development goals', see <http://www.un.org/millenniumgoals/>.

11 P. Antrobus (2003), 'Presentation to working group on the MDG's and gender equality', UNDP Caribbean Regional Millennium Development Goals Conference, Barbados.

12 Ibid.

13 S. Corrêa and G. Carega (2004), 'Is sexuality a non-negotiable component of the Cairo Agenda?', see <www.dawn.org.fj>.

14 Editor's Forum, *Jamaica Gleaner*, 12 October 2003, <www.jamaica-gleaner.com>.

15 Barbados Nation Opinion (27 November 2003).

16 A. Ahmed (2004), 'Gender Review and Assessment of HIV/AIDS Programs', presentation of research for UNIFEM.

17 UNFPA (2005), 'Women and AIDS', see <http://womenandaids.unaids.org/themes/theme_1.html>.

18 A. Germaine (2004), 'Reproductive rights: a vital strategy to fight HIV/AIDS', see <http://www.iwhc.org/docUploads/AdrienneGermain102704.doc>.

19 This may have been historically true for women through the ages, but HIV/AIDS has had a specific global impact and influence on young minds, both in the present discourse around it and the scale of information about it.

20 The International Conference of Population and Development, at Cairo (1994), and the Fourth International Conference of Women, at Beijing (1995).

21 R. Petchesky (2004), Presentation at DAWN Anniversary Celebration on 'Erotic Justice'.

22 R. Hassan (2004), 'Religious conservatism: feminist theology as a means of combating injustice toward women in Muslim communities/ culture', see <www.ncwdi.igc.org/html/hassan.htm>.

23 Much as could be expected, the United States is the only country in the world, besides Somalia, which has not ratified the CRC. See <http://www.un.org/News/briefings/docs/2002/childcaucaspc.doc.htm>.

24 The Resolution on Sexual Orientation and Human Rights was proposed in the UN by Brazil in 2003, postponed twice, and is now to be discussed in 2005. For more information see <http://www.ilga.org/news_results.asp?LanguageID=1&FileCategory=44&ZoneID=7&FileID=58>.

25 The Pleasure Project: <www.the-pleasure-project.org/more.html>.

3 | From tragedy and injustice to rights and empowerment: accountability in the economic realm

ALISON SYMINGTON

There is no common perspective or view of young women today. Our ideas, interests and goals are as diverse as our appearances and our homes.[1] Yet it is fair to say that we have some common experiences, which shape both who we are and who we will become. For example, as young people we have universally experienced a lack of power, whether because of our age and our dependence on others to meet our needs and fulfil our rights, or because of poverty, discrimination, lack of opportunity or limits placed upon our freedoms. Moreover, we all live in consumerist cultures; no matter where we live in the world, McDonald's, Levi's and Coca-Cola and the values of profit, consumption and accumulation have crept into our societies (although their manifestations and impacts can be quite distinct). And for the vast majority of young women in the world, a sense of unfairness and/or injustice at the institutions and ideologies that structure our lives and our world is also a common experience. How we, as diverse young women, respond to this unfairness is the focus of this chapter.

In focusing on questions of how young women today are responding to and shaping our world, a key area to consider is necessarily that of economic rights, macro-economic institutions and the predominant international economic ideologies. If we look at the structures and actors that have the power to influence policies and behaviours around the world, rich country governments and finance ministers the world over, chief executive officers of transnational corporations, international and regional financial institutions and wealthy individuals figure at the top of the list. Comparing these contemporary powerhouses to those that dominated 20, 50, and even 100 years ago, we see both new actors and new ways of exerting power. We also see more global uniformity in the exertion of this power and the global reach of the powerful, which have become greatly amplified with the advent of new communication and transportation technologies that enable constant communication and exchange without geographic or time limitations. This is a whole new world.

Some of the most powerful economic forces in the world today are relatively new to their positions of power and have been structuring the rules by which they will play the game as they go along. Their influence and what it means to engage with them will only really be known by those who are in the younger generations today, and in particular by those who continue to be excluded from their bounty, including women, indigenous peoples, the disabled, racialized peoples, the poor, migrants, and others who are marginalized by patriarchal and colonial structures and ideologies. The intention of this chapter is modest: to sketch out a preliminary picture of this economics-dominated world and its implications for young women today, and to consider some of the diverse responses and modes of engagement that are beginning to take hold and will continue to unfold and develop in the coming years. It is hoped that this contribution will add to an understanding of why and how young women act, react and engage distinctly from older generations and in diverse ways from each other, not only with respect to economic justice issues but also in terms of the broader and more complete picture of their lives.

Money makes the world go round

It is difficult for folks of my generation to imagine an existence without cash. Even in remote areas and predominantly subsistence-level economies, goods and services are today bought, sold and traded for money in one form or another. Earning an income is not only a desire but also a necessity for most young people today, and social services and staple goods are provided in accordance with available resources to pay for their provision. Products produced far from where we live and made by people with whom we will never have any personal contact are widely available. Currency exchange rates, foreign investment and development assistance have direct impacts on our daily existence (even if we are not always aware of how). This is common sense and barely merits notice by most young people today, yet not that long ago the situation was markedly different.

If we step back a couple of generations, in most parts of the world formal education would not have been widely available to young girls. As young women began to gain access to educational opportunities, quite a predictable equation emerged of education leading to employment, and thus leading to security. Most essential products were produced locally or at least in the nearby vicinity, and labour was divided according to age and gender within families and communities, with each person (particularly those who happened to be female) expected to make a contribution to the collective good. Moreover, in many parts of the world welfare and social-ist state systems emerged, with a clear idea that the government owed a duty of care to its citizens (even in colonial models, the idea of a duty of care owed by the colonizer to the colonized was common, if completely misplaced within the broader ideology and violence of colonial encounters). The specifics of what this economic model looked liked in different locations varied widely, but we can each cast our mind back to stories told to us by our older relatives, and histories taught to us in school or elsewhere, to find a sense of the cohesiveness, localness and opportunities that characterized these earlier times.

I do not wish to suggest that earlier times were easy, or that they were not characterized by great injustices, including widespread violence and discrimination, for that is simply not the case. What I do want to highlight is the different role of money, and of economics and economic institutions, in the way our worlds were organized. The challenges faced by young women today are new and distinct from those experienced previously, and the manifestations of discrimination and inequality are likewise distinct and pervasive.

So if we want to understand this new world of challenges faced by young women today, we need first to understand the cast of characters.

First and foremost, there is the World Trade Organization (WTO). While it has been described as the 'institutional face of globalization' and is perhaps the most powerful and wide-reaching of all international players today, the institution is in fact only ten years old. Based in Geneva, it was formed to oversee the series of trade agreements that had emerged from the 'Uruguay Round' of negotiations on an international trade agreement called the General Agreement on Tariffs and Trade (GATT) and to implement a dispute settlement process with respect to members' rights and obligations under these agreements.[2] As of February 2005, 148 states are members of the WTO.[3] Officially, the WTO is a member-driven 'one-country, one-vote' organization. In practice, however, there is a long-standing custom of decision-making 'by consensus', and the richer countries exert disproportionate influence within the organization. While some of the world's least-developed countries have minimal capacity to participate in negotiating sessions, the richer countries have large staffs of trade specialists, lawyers and expert negotiating teams. In addition to this global trading body, numerous regional trading bodies (such as MERCOSUR, CAFRA and NAFTA) serve similar roles at the regional level.[4]

The World Bank (the International Bank for Reconstruction and Development, in full) plays a close supporting role to the WTO.[5] Originally established in 1944, the Bank is the world's largest supplier of development capital and advice. It is headquartered in Washington, DC, and has 100 country offices. The Bank is primarily engaged in three activities: lending, development research and economic analysis, and technical assistance. It provides funding from public sources for development programmes in areas such as health, education and environmental protection, focusing on national legal, political and economic structures. It promotes reforms that it believes will create long-term growth and stability, while lending to governments and using the profits generated from the loans to finance its operations.

Over the years, the activities and policies of the World Bank have shifted significantly, from its original role in rebuilding Europe after the war, to its central role in development finance today. Over the past ten years, significant shifts can be seen in the terminology used by the Bank to describe its work, including, in more recent times, venturing into the realms of gender equality and rights. What remains steadfast through these shifts, however, is the underlying policy framework, which is based on an unwavering belief in neo-liberalism (see description below) as the only way. In terms of the evolution of these players, it is critical to understand that many of the policies that are being cemented today in international law through the WTO were initially put into place through World Bank structural adjustment policies and development programmes. Working with the World Bank, which has a global scope, are the regional development banks (such as the Asian Development Bank), which have similar operations and missions.[6]

The third in this trio of international financial institutions is the International Monetary Fund (IMF).[7] The IMF was also established in 1944. Its focus is short-term balance-of-payments crises. Its three main areas of activity are surveillance of exchange rate policies, financial assistance to members with balance-of-payments problems, and technical assistance with respect to policies, institutions and statistics. In a nutshell, the IMF formulates economic policy based on the mantra 'tighten your belt' and it has created a body of international monetary law.

Together, these three institutions have set in place the set of economic policies and prescriptions that pervade our world today and are the driving force behind globalization. Commonly referred to as neo-liberalism, this policy framework primarily arose as a response to the economic downturn and international debt crises of the 1970s. It is based on an unwavering belief in 'free markets', promoting competitive market capitalism, private ownership, 'free trade', export-led growth, strict controls on balance of payments and deficits, and drastic reductions in government social spending. More than a theoretical model or set of economic tools, neo-liberalism has become *the only way*. In the 1980s, the international financial institutions began to impose these economic prescriptions on countries that accepted loans or aid through them as 'conditionality', a central feature of structural adjustment policies, which were intended to pull poor countries into conformity with this model and hence propel them into 'development'. In most areas of the world, marginalized peoples have not benefited from neo-liberal policies and it is common for women to suffer disproportionately from disruptions to their local economies, from the continual undervaluing of their work, and from the increased insecurity brought about by the increasing prevalence of casual and flexible jobs alongside the privatization of essential services.[8]

The other key actors that have gained awesome power in recent years are corporations. The statistics on the magnitude of corporate power are now well known: of the world's 100 largest economies, 51 are corporations, not countries; the world's top 200 corporations account for over a quarter of the economic activity on the global level, while employing less than 1 per cent of the global workforce; and the average CEO in the United States made 531 times what the average worker was paid in 2000.[9] Most transnational corporations are headquartered in developed countries but may have operations, supply chains and distribution networks that stretch across many borders. Corporations have been granted extensive rights as investors and have wielded increasing power to influence policy at the international level and within countries.

Where do people fit within this system? Well, primarily they are con-sumers. People buy things, they consume products and services. If the good is valued, then people will pay for it. The limited purchasing power of poor people means that they are quite invisible in the system. To the extent that they are explicitly considered, they are most seen as anomalies, as recipients of charity and as drains on an otherwise efficient system.

The point of this sketch is in terms of understanding the structures, influences and realities of young women today. These economic institutions and the ideologies that they promote and enforce are essential components of the fabric of our lives. If we pour ourselves a glass of water to drink, take our mother to see a doctor, go to a dance club with our friends or participate in an employment training programme, these institutions and ideologies have influenced the availability and accessibility of the services and products available to us, and they impose restrictions on the types of regulations governments can impose on products and service-providers. Whether we live in peace or conflict, in health or illness, if we are restricted by religious and cultural tradition or free to explore and experiment, these institutions and ideologies put parameters around the choices our govern-ments can make, and the options and opportunities available to us. And not only do they structure what is and is not possible within the given context, but those who are young today do not really know any other system. We may have read about other economic models, or experienced elements of

Symington | 3

38

them in our childhoods or in certain aspects of our lives. We may have dreamed of alternative markets, solidarity economies and non-monetized systems and rights-based social policies, but money has always been a factor in making our world go round, to an extent that was unimagined and indeed impossible prior to the advent of globalized, modern information and communication technologies.[10] If young people question this reality, it is not because they have considerable experience with an alternative that they prefer, nor is it because they want to choose between various systems that are available to them. For young women today, the money has always been there and economic institutions have always structured their world, to a greater or lesser extent.

So when a young woman today looks for a job, it is not necessarily the job that she desires in order to achieve her dream; it may be the only job that is available to her and will provide her with some needed income. When a young woman obtains condoms in an attempt to protect herself from HIV/AIDS, she may be able to do so only if she has money with which to pay for them and if the corporations that manufacture them find it economically profitable to make them available in the area where she lives. When she prepares dinner for her siblings, she may need to consider the relative costs of grains, vegetables and meats to determine what she can serve, even if nutritional deficiencies result or traditional foods are omitted. This is the reality of most young women today. Whether or not they know the theory of neo-liberalism or the history of international economic institutions, they know the reality of their impacts intimately.

I believe it is important to start with the recognition of the place of money and economic institutions in the lives of young women today. I do not want to oversimplify the complexity of the rich experiences of young women or to under-emphasize the importance of the pursuit of wealth in the colonial project and throughout history, but this everyday lived reality is the necessary starting point for most young women as they engage with issues of social justice, with gender roles and discrimination, and with technology and with cross-cultural interactions, among other issues. Of course it does not determine who a young woman is and what her dreams are, but it does structure her existence in a multitude of ways. Moreover, young women necessarily come to issues of social justice, development and equality differently from older generations simply because of this different starting point. This is a reality that I believe is often overlooked in discussions of 'intergenerational dialogue' and 'movement-building' within feminist circles, yet is essential in moving forward meaningfully.

Alternatives in the works

While the neo-liberal economic system has a firm grasp today and dominates almost everywhere, that of course does not mean that it is universally accepted, welcomed or left to function without contestation. Young women are active among those struggling against the tragedies and injustices brought about by this system and all it entails. For example, in Seattle in 1999 and Cancun in 2003, many young women took to the streets to protest about the World Trade Organization and have been involved in the numerous 'anti-globalization' rallies ever since. Many young women are active members of local anarchist groups and radical anti-poverty organizations such as the Ontario Coalition Against Poverty in Canada, and anti-corporate protests such as those against Chevron in Nigeria.[11] And many young women are embarking on careers in the public service, in NGOs, as lawyers, economists and policy analysts and as educators and organizers to challenge the system.

By now, it is well established in extensive academic and popular literature that the international trade, aid and investment regimes do not work for women, young or old. They do not contribute to the eradication of poverty, nor do they advance women's rights and gender equality. It is probably safe to say that few young women today could imagine a world without international trade, foreign investors or overseas development assistance, but can they imagine a system in which these forces contribute to equality, peace and justice? Many young women just try to get the best deal they can for themselves within the existing system, paying little attention to notions of social and economic justice. But on the other hand, many are extremely active and committed to the causes, taking part in diverse forms of action, activism and studies towards a more fair and just world.

One of the interesting phenomena with respect to globalization and neo-liberalism is that they are often discussed as if they are inevitable and as if they exist in a complete vacuum. Somehow, policy-makers and 'experts' have become adept at debating development as if it does not involve people, trade as if it is an end in itself, and international investment and production supply chains as if they are the only option. Most financial institutions and international economic actors talk of human rights as if they are unnecessary, purely political, confrontational, and really just a distraction from the important matters at hand. In fact, discussions often go on as if human rights do not exist, alternative models and values are absent and irrelevant, and by and large, humans and the environment are similarly irrelevant. But surely for most of humanity, the values of human rights, of equality, justice, dignity and happiness, are much more in line with what we truly value. Surely the stark disjunctures between these competing value systems and discourses are the intersection points at which people really live, struggle and survive. To my mind, it is at these points of disjuncture and collision that alternatives are concocted, gestated and experienced.

Young women using human rights

International human rights law is one of the tools that we have at our disposal in the quest for a fairer global economic system, and a tool that seems to appeal to many young women. I can only speculate as to why, but I believe it is at least in part because human rights present a principled, alternative and comprehensive vision of how our world can be organized. Using human rights tools makes one *for* something concrete, opposing the complex, multi-faceted and seemingly seamless world of global capitalism with an equally complex, multi-faceted and rigorous set of principles and prescriptions. Increasing numbers of young women are attending law school or studying human rights in graduate school, and many are volunteering or working for civil society organizations that work from a human rights framework. They are increasingly using law and human rights to challenge injustices and undemocratic, unaccountable structures in the economic realm. Exploring the potentials for using human rights frameworks to demand justice and accountability, then, is a good example for understanding young women's engagement with economics into the future, and for understanding the shift from seeing poverty and inequality as tragedies to seeing them as injustices to be challenged and rectified.

Impassioned debates about the relationship between trade and human rights have raged in recent years. Trade purists, at one extreme, have argued that trade liberalization is the best way to maximize wealth, which leads to increased employment and improved living standards. They argue that these automatically lead to improved human rights protections. At the other extreme, human rights purists have insisted that human rights standards should be a precondition to participation in an international trading regime, arguing for measures such as 'social clauses' in international trade regimes and trade sanctions against human rights violators. For young women seeking gender and economic justice, however, there are numerous options between these extremes and 'outside of the box' possibilities. Young women are coming into the human rights movement at a time when standards and norms have been articulated and ratified by states in 50 years' worth of negotiations and treaty ratifications, but also at the nascent stage of the struggle to really implement, actualize and operationalize these norms. A new set of skills is needed to take human rights to the next stage (including, for example, skills in developing targets and indicators as well as working with policy-makers to develop rights-based policy frameworks), with emerging new understandings of the intersections between the economic realm and the social, cultural, civil and political realms. It is a unique and pivotal moment in social justice and economic history, a moment in which young women are playing a decisive role.

As young human rights advocates know, non-discrimination is one of the most fundamental principles of human rights, and poverty is increasingly understood as a total lack of economic, social and cultural rights. By using the analytical frameworks, the legal principles, the moral imperatives and the mobilizing power of human rights, we could effectively work towards an international economic system that is supportive of poverty eradication, sustainable development and the full attainment of human rights for everyone. This is a truly exciting and inspirational prospect! The challenge for young women who are stepping into this area is to figure out how to apply and fully implement human rights in our globalized world. A central part of this challenge is to determine how to apply human rights principles practically, to ensure that the rules of international trade contribute to the type of world, characterized by justice and equality, which many young women want.

Incoherence in international law

The international rules of trade and human rights are both enshrined in highly developed bodies of law. These two areas of international law have developed simultaneously, yet in isolation from one another, resulting in competing and sometimes incompatible obligations on states. While there is no essential conflict between the objectives of trade law and those of human rights, the potential for conflicts does exist, and they are amplified by the different values, assumptions and power players underlying each regime. For example, trade rules with respect to agricultural products, patent protections on pharmaceuticals and the provision of essential services often have negative impacts on people's enjoyment of their human rights to food, to health and to education. Furthermore, because those who most often benefit from trade liberalization are those who already have access to markets, infrastructure, credit and land, trade liberalization may exacerbate existing inequalities and have particularly egregious impacts on the rights of women, indigenous peoples and other marginalized peoples. Rather than supporting each other in the struggle towards development and equality around the world, trade law and human rights law have produced a set of incompatible and incoherent rules, institutions and values.

International law doctrines dictate a hierarchy of legal norms and provide guidance with respect to conflicts between different bodies of law. According to this doctrine, in the event of actual conflict, human rights law would often prevail over trade rules (because of its status as customary international law), but wherever possible provisions should be interpreted and applied in a manner that avoids conflicts. Irrespective of legal theory or doctrine, however, international trade rules have effectively become dominant because the trade system is better resourced, has effective enforcement mechanisms and is tied to the dominant ideology and power structures in the world today. This is not to say that human rights are unhelpful in terms of advancing women's rights and development within the international economic system. We must, however, use human rights mechanisms strategically, with our eyes open to the actual political and economic realities with which we are faced today. We must rise to the challenge of exposing the incoherence and hypocrisy of states and develop the doctrines and mechanisms necessary to make it work.

Many young women are discovering how the language of human rights can be an effective tool for mobilizing and motivating people to demand accountability and justice. In designing effective campaign messages, for example, it is extremely useful to reveal the hands of power at work in a particular situation. It is easy for the average person to understand as tragic the fact that approximately 40 million people are living with HIV/AIDS today, a growing percentage of whom are women,[12] or to feel distressed that there were 700,000 new HIV infections in children in 2003, most of which resulted from mother-to-child transmission because most women do not have access to treatments aimed at preventing transmission to their children.[13] Similarly, hunger, drought and food insecurity in poor countries and the extreme malnutrition suffered by so many throughout the world can readily be understood as a terrible thing by most. But until the powerful actors and institutions that created and/or are maintaining this situation are revealed, people may only recognize this deprivation as a misfortune.

But the HIV/AIDS pandemic, hunger and food insecurity are *injustices*, with national and international institutions and actors significantly responsible. In other words, they are largely preventable and solvable problems, if human will is there to resolve them. Injustices require corrective action and redress. The human rights framework is a valuable tool for revealing some of the injustices behind ill health, malnutrition, homelessness, the lack of access to essential services, unsafe working conditions and gender inequality. By naming a specific human rights violation, identifying the persons or institutions responsible for that violation, and claiming redress, the injustice is laid bare and can be used to mobilize a constituency to advocate for change. While misfortune elicits sympathy, injustice evokes outrage, passion and motivation to make a concerted effort to bring about change. Young women are using human rights frameworks to mobilize action against injustice in this way.

Human rights can also be used to lobby governments, demanding that they fulfil their international obligations (this is a more 'traditional' form of feminist activism). But what is more novel, and also promising, is using international mechanisms such as investor–state dispute resolution panels, domestic tort claims provisions, the World Bank Inspection Panel and other economic mechanisms within economic institutions and other areas to challenge injustices by asserting principles of equality, accountability, transparency and human rights.[14] Truly innovative work is being done to stop environmentally damaging mining practices, to protect indigenous rights, to guarantee access to essential services such as safe drinking water, and to empower workers to claim their rights in factories all over the world. And finally, tools and principles are being developed that use human rights as the basis for policy development, so that governments implement policies that are based on their rights obligations rather than their perceptions of 'need' or 'charity', or, as is so often the case, purely in response to political expedience and interest group demands.[15] These developments are taking human rights into their next stage of development, moving into empowerment and accountability for women and excluded peoples.

Certain human rights principles are quite helpful from a policy perspective, if one is focused on advancing economic rights and equality. For example, human rights norms render some policy choices impermissible, especially those with a disproportionate impact on the poor or that exacerbate inequalities because even short-term violations can not be justified in terms of 'the greater good' or as necessary in the pursuit of a longer-term goal. These parameters can have a huge impact on the efficacy of policy. We also know that human rights have a particular preoccupation with vulnerable individuals and groups: because they face the greatest obstacles in maximizing their capabilities and exercising their full and equal rights, they are prioritized in terms of policy interventions. Human rights principles also force decision-makers to consider trade-offs explicitly, as opposed to hiding behind the idea of unintended externalities or the notion that some 'adjustment' or safety nets will be needed in order to achieve greater economic efficiency. In theory, this implies that policy-makers need to address the consequences, for example, if the reduction of duties on textiles is going to leave women workers unemployed, the loss of revenue from tariff reductions is going to cause budget shortfalls leading to reductions in social spending, or the liberalization of trade in certain agricultural products is going to transfer production from small-holding, female farmers to large-scale mechanized farms.

From a gender equality perspective, the provisions of the WTO agreements, as well as most regional trade agreements, are quite interesting in that they aim to create a rule-based, predictable, transparent system where each member is equal (often referred to as creating 'a level playing field'). But years of feminist theory and gender equality activism have made it clear that treating unequal parties equally does *not* produce equality. Treating all poor countries and all rich countries alike does not result in equality any more than does treating all men and all women equally, or applying the same rules to persons of different ethnicities, different sexual orientations, different levels of ability, or any number of other attributes. 'Level playing fields' puts the stronger in a position to do better. Substantive equality, the standard used in human rights, produces equal outcomes.

What would the international trade regime look like if it operated under the principles of substantive equality and attempted to put all countries, large or small, rich or poor, into a position where they could obtain the same substantive results in consideration of their actual means? What would trade policy look like if it considered the differing capabilities of individuals and groups all over the world, and attempted to put in place policies and programmes that would allow them to achieve substantively equal outcomes? There is a tremendous amount of diversity in terms of levels of wealth, industrialization and trade capacity in trading blocs, and in terms of genders, classes, races and levels of capabilities within our societies. Only approaches grounded in ideas of substantive equality can bring about equality and justice. Herein lies the challenge. Young women can start fresh from their experiences and perspectives to help develop these doctrines. As we go forward, we do not have to be tied to given meanings and past experiences that privilege elite interests and profit-maximization values.

The international legal elements of trade are one piece of the puzzle for us to understand. And international law, especially international human rights law, is one tool for us to use strategically. The argument is not that the WTO should take over responsibility for human rights or gender equality, nor should all young gender justice advocates devote their energies to trade issues or international law. Trade, however, can and does have negative impacts on women of all ages and the tools of human rights, used creatively and strategically, can help restructure our economic systems so as to promote accountability and justice for all. Boiled down to the most basic arguments, governments have voluntarily undertaken to protect human rights as well as respect trade rules. These commitments seem to call for a type of policy coherence, a concept that is currently considered quite 'sexy' by international institutions. But the policy coherence being promoted is within a market fundamentalist growth imperative paradigm. Intellectually and politically, many young women are working to tie all of these pieces together into a functional and just global vision.

An economically just future?

Trade is only one component of the macro-economic system. Investment, currency exchange and aid are also important elements, and all of these are tied to the provision of basic services, employment and educational opportunities, and to equality and empowerment within our communities. We do not need complex statistics or deep theoretical analysis to understand how dire the situation is in the world right now – extreme poverty thrives, millions lack access to basic shelter, water and food necessary for survival, and the natural environment is being decimated at the same time as wealth accumulates and luxury overflows for a select few. Within the so-called 'global feminist movement', basic issues of poverty are not always front and centre, with 'sexier' issues such as erotic justice, spatial theory and reproductive technologies garnering more attention. But to my mind, poverty and economic rights are the most fundamental issues there are. Our humanity rests on our ability to solve this disaster, which is not natural or inevitable but is located in institutions and structures created by humans (mostly men, of course).

We must work from foundational principles such as justice, equality and accountability. Discussions of aid, development and concessions will not get us anywhere without people and humanity being centred and the values we are working towards being clearly articulated. Civil society must generate the will for change to happen and average people must choose to live their lives differently. There is no magical formula or perfect disciplinary approach to social justice and gender equality.

Many young women are facing up to this challenge, mastering a critical analysis of economics and developing skills in advocacy, policy-formulation, public protest and mobilization. It is up to us to decide how to address the neo-liberal global economic system – whether to challenge it, work within it, attempt to reform it or disengage from it. But if we want to really change it, to divert the present course towards one of justice and equality, we must resist the current tendency to shy away from 'smarts'. Intellectual leadership is as important as charismatic leadership in implementing rights and articulating alternatives. These systems and ideologies are complex: life is not simple, and the problems of poverty and injustice are monstrous. We need a dose of humility alongside our confidence, some silence in addition to the noise we can generate, and a critical analysis with solid evidence and proposals to back up our dreams and visions.

Much of this work is done by young women outside the 'global feminist movement', including research done in universities and research institutions, activism through non-feminist organizations and initiatives, service provision by various institutions, and policy work by women who do not define themselves as activists or their work as internationally oriented. A mosaic of approaches, experiences and perspectives, from all over the world, come together to create alternatives based on rights, empowerment and accountability. There is a new world of challenges from and for young women, but also a new world of possibilities.

Notes

1 It should be stated off-the-top that I am a young, middle-class white woman who lives in Toronto, Canada. I am a researcher for an international organization, educated in the fields of international development and international law. My comments necessarily emanate from my position, location and experiences, representing only my own personal and ever-evolving perspectives and realities.

2 See the WTO website for an explanation on the WTO: <http://www.wto.org/english/thewto_e/thewto_e.htm>. See also M. Trebilcock and R. Howse (1999), *The Regulation of International Trade*, 2nd edn (London and New York: Routledge); L. Wallach and P. Woodall (2003), *Whose Trade Organization? A Field Guide to the World Trade Organization* (New York: New Press); or M. Matsushita, P. C. Mavroidis, P. Mavroidis, T. Schoenbaum and T. J. Schoenbaum (2003), *World Trade Organization: Law, Practice and Policy* (Oxford: Oxford University Press).

3 WTO (2005), 'Members and observers', see <http://www.wto.org/english/thewto_e/whatis_e/tif_e/org6_e.htm>.

4 For more information see: NAFTA Secretariat at: <http://www.nafta-secalena.org/DefaultSite/index_e.aspx>; the Regional Trade Agreements section of the WTO website is: <http://www.wto.org/english/tratop_e/region_e/region_e.htm>.

5 See World Bank website: <http://www.worldbank.org>, <www.imf.org> or A. Symington (2002), 'AWID Facts and Issues No. 5: The World Bank and Women's Rights in Development'.

6 See Asian Development Bank website: <http://www.adb.org>.

7 See IMF website: <http://www.imf.org>.

8 See for example D. Elson and N. Cagatay (2000), 'The social content of macroeconomic policy', *World Development*, 28(7); D. Elson and H. Keklik (2002), *Progress of the World's Women 2002: Gender Equality and the Millennium Development Goals*; UNIFEM (2003), *Progress of the World's Women 2000* (New York: UNIFEM).

9 The Corporate Accountability Project (2004), 'How the system works (or doesn't work) and what to do about it', see <http://www.corporations.org/system>.

10 Globalization is not a new phenomenon, nor are international trade,

investment and capital flows. The globalization lived by young women today is distinct in several ways, however, from previous international interactions. This globalization dates back to the early 1970s and has been driven by firms, transnational corporations, states and financial institutions. It has resulted in increasing interconnectedness, and an intensification and speeding up of global interactions and processes. What we see as a result is a stretching of social, political and economic activities across frontiers such that events, decisions and activities that take place in one region can have significance for people in another region. D. Held and A. McGrew (2000), 'Rethinking globalization' in *The Global Transformations Reader: An Introduction to the Globalization Debate* (Cambridge: Polity Press). Important elements of this globalization which define the experience of it are the facts that is it based on neo-liberal capitalist ideals and that it is reliant on modern information, communication and transportation technologies.

11 CorpWatch (2002), 'Youth protesters take over Chevron oil rig, leave peacefully', see <http://www.corpwatch.org/article.php?id=2428>, or Corp-Watch (2002), 'Women protesters say deal with Chevron off', see <http://www.corpwatch.org/article.php?id=3088>.

12 Centers for Disease Control and Prevention (2004), 'Division of HIV/AIDS prevention: basic statistics', see <http://www.cdc.gov/hiv/stats.htm#international>.

13 WHO (2004), 'International women's day: women and HIV/AIDS 8 March 2004', see <http://www.who.int/fch/depts/gwh/en/IWDtwo-pagers0403.pdf>.

14 For example, claims under the North American Agreement on Labor Cooperation (NAALC), a side agreement of the North American Free Trade Agreement (NAFTA), with respect to labour rights violations in *maquilladoras* in Mexico; use of the Alien Tort Claims Act in the United States to sue corporations for their actions overseas; and use of the World Bank Inspection Panel to challenge government decisions with respect to access to health services.

15 See the reports of the UN Special Rapporteur on the Right to Health, Paul Hunt, for a discussion of rights-based approaches to policy-making, including Report to the General Assembly, 10 October 2003, A/58/427, *Report to the Commission on Human Rights: Addendum on Mission to the World Trade Organization*, 1 March 2004, E/CN.4/2004/49/Add.1, and others.

4 | Seeking techno-justice[1]

ANN ELISABETH S. SAMSON

Genetic modification has become a reality in our world today, due to advances in biology and our understanding of the human genome. Genetic modification, or altering human genes to 'fix' a problem or disease, will soon further commodify and industrialize the process of childbearing.[2] In fact, some scientists claim that human cloning is an easy next step.[3] At the same time, agribusiness companies want to sell genetically modified (GM) seeds with 'terminator technology' to farmers around the world.[4] These 'one-time use' seeds do not produce crops appropriate for sustainable livelihoods. The seeds can blow into, for example, a rural women's food plot, whether she knows it or not, and may permanently affect her community's natural ecosystem.

Increasingly competent information and communication technologies (ICTs) are making the world smaller: email, internet and cell phones make life and social justice organizing easier, but issues of unequal access and misuse still dog technological advancement in this area.

Since 11 September 2001, we have witnessed huge financial investments by governments in the North and South in military and surveillance technologies. While weapons used 'against others' or technologies promoted to 'protect us' are proliferating, major questions of human rights and civil rights protections are surfacing.

At present, the most money in private scientific research and development is being spent on nanotechnology, which promises the 'manufacture and replication of machinery and end products ... from the atom up'.[5] Like genetic technologies, some see 'nanotech' as an answer to the world's toughest problems – pollution, disease, ageing and hunger. Others recognize that the infinite possibilities of these technologies might also have infinite dangers.

New technologies directly affect our bodies, our environments, our work and our safety and these developments are happening and fast. While there is uncritical public support for much of this 'modern progress', human rights activists, social justice advocates, and religious leaders are all critically analysing the real (and imminent) potential of fundamental changes in our lives: both good and bad.

In this chapter, I will address the politics of new technologies and contextualize it in our current global order. I will also explore some of the new technologies and the gender issues inherent in them and look at how we, as feminists, can seek gender justice in a techno-science world.

The politics of new technology

Most technological developments happen in research laboratories outside government regulation and outside the knowledge of civil society.[6] The expansion of new technologies is becoming increasingly corporatized through forces of globalization. Simply stated, technology is being developed for profit, not justice. Take, for example, the area of health technology and drug development.[7] The biotech pharmaceutical industry is now about US$30 billion annually and is growing by about 10 per cent each year.[8] The emphasis on research and development of the drug Viagra and its competitors (for erectile dysfunction) dwarfs any effort to focus research resources on better malaria treatments, when, according to the WHO and UNICEF, malaria kills 3,000 children a day.[9, 10]

New technologies are ubiquitous and have effects that extend beyond the local area in which they are produced.[11] What makes now and the not-so-distant technological future different from the past is that the promises are bigger, the possibilities are real, and thanks to their incredible potential and the forces of globalization, they are spreading rapidly.[12]

Technological development brings benefits to large numbers of people and is often appropriately understood as a testament to human prowess. However, in an era of increasing privatization, new technologies are brought to the market with few or no regulatory mechanisms in place. This is particularly worrying when some new technologies have the potential to change our environment and our lives drastically. The convergence of these trends brings us to a crucial historical moment.

Rhetoric about 'amazing' new technologies that will solve long-standing social problems such as hunger, disease and poverty pervade both debates and agendas of development and human rights, and even women's rights. It is true that new technologies have potential benefits; they also carry with them certain risks. While certain new technologies can be helpful and seem promising, the idea that they might be a 'magic bullet' for social problems is almost laughable. And in some cases it is possible, and in fact probable, that certain technologies might be a hindrance to human rights and development.[13] Of course this hasn't stopped the efforts to identify, develop and use new technologies to promote development.

It is important to note how technology develops and is used in different parts of the world. New technologies are pervasive and invasive, particularly in developing countries where they tend to 'leapfrog' over more traditional technologies. For instance, the fastest growth rate for wireless telephone users is in Africa and in China; five million new mobile phone users subscribe every month, largely because the infrastructure required for landlines is far more expensive and difficult to build than the newer, more adaptable cell phone.[14] In this case, the newer technology is more appropriate than the older one. 'Leapfrogging' means technologies offer particular promises for the South as a tool for development.

Civil society must develop a framework for analysing and questioning technology – particularly about the links between science, technology and business – as there is significant pressure from people who stand to make a lot of money from the creation and subsequent use of these technologies, and who will break down every barrier to do so.

What exactly are the 'new technologies'?

The technological areas focused on in this chapter have been chosen because of their urgency, novelty and irrevocableness, as well as their relevance not only to development, but also to women's rights. While it is difficult to imagine a technology that might have the same kind of effect on a woman in urban Canada as on a woman in rural Kenya, for instance, the technologies are related, and the effects will be related through processes of globalization, as well as the use of technology for development initiatives.[15] And because many of these technologies will drastically change our environments, bodies, work and safety, they are issues for women everywhere. The kinds of technologies being developed and distributed now are different: they are attached to ever-bigger promises to do anything and to solve any problem. Increasingly, resources for development are being focused on them.

New genetic technologies

Genetic technologies have been applied to humans in the form of reproductive technologies, genetic testing and drug development, and they are becoming more and more invasive. Soon, it will be possible (and accepted?) to change humans at a genetic level – and these will be the kinds of changes that will be passed on to future generations. Critics of the unrestrained development of new human genetic technologies claim that these technologies have the potential to technologize (further) new eugenic or racist ideologies as well as exacerbate the differences between rich and poor.[16] Women's rights are particularly threatened by new genetic technologies because of their reproductive and care-giving role as well as the fact that the development requires extensive testing on women and their genetic material.

'Reproductive technology', typically thought of as the technology most related to gender issues and women's rights, traditionally refers to a range of devices and procedures for assisting, preventing and/or manipulating contraception, fertility and reproductive practices. What makes 'new' reproductive technologies (NRTs) different is not only their increasing effectiveness and invasiveness, but the globalized system of profit-seeking and control in which they are being advanced. Not only are these technologies being used to manipulate contraception, fertility and reproductive practices, but they are creating new ways to have and influence characteristics of potential children. Never before have reproductive technologies been manufactured and marketed with such intensity. Yet the dialogue as to the ethics, potential dangers to and consequences for women's bodies remains largely uncritical and unbalanced, often neglecting to examine the different experiences of NRTs depending on location, class, race and gender.[17]

There is serious concern over the commodification of human life and the marketing of women's bodies. Policies in some countries make the selling of one's eggs and surrogacy services (as products) illegal.[18] These policies are based on a principle of non-commodification where it has been recognized that the harvesting and selling of life forms is problematic. Yet, even as these practices are banned in some countries, there remain opportunities and reasons for women in other countries to engage in them. Judy Norsigian (co-founder of the Boston Women's Health Collective) worries that financial incentives may encourage low-income women to take unnecessary risks to donate eggs for experimentation by taking potentially dangerous drugs or undergoing risky surgeries.[19]

Genetic research on health problems are those that by and large affect Northern, more affluent groups. For instance, many geneticists are looking at Alzheimer's disease and Parkinson's disease in the North. In developing countries, infectious diseases are more prominent and so the causes of death and illness are very different between the two. As infectious diseases and HIV/AIDS increase in developing countries, life expectancies are decreasing, or at least not increasing at the same rate as their Northern counterparts. Because people are dying younger, research into diseases such as Alzheimer's in these contexts, for instance, becomes less pertinent. In addition, the kinds of answers that are available to us are often skewed and favour a pill or marketable treatment rather than diet, behaviours, social support or feeling valued. If the vast majority of people in the world have the genes to be healthy if they have good life circumstances, it would be more effective to focus on the whole range of social circumstances that allow people to live better lives, rather than use scarce societal resources for testing variant genes.

Robotics, surveillance and military technologies

Historically, governments, for weapons or other military needs, funded the majority of technology development. The present 'war on terror' has led to many more companies investing in the development of biometric devices and surveillance techniques to identify people at a distance, in the name of 'safety'. In March 2005, a group of US scientists organized a letter of protest against the US government's science spending priorities, charging that 'biodefence research since 2002 has diverted researchers away from potential breakthroughs in basic research' by pouring money into researching potential bio-weapons such as anthrax, plague, smallpox and the Ebola virus rather than research focused on significant diseases.[20] Funding for the US National Institute of Allergy and Infectious Disease (NIAID), the part of the National Institutes of Health that deals with pathogens, went from US$53 million in 2001 to US$1.4 billion in 2004.

GM crops, with the dependency on GM seeds and the ability to alter the production of a certain crop, as well as the development of diseases that could infect crops, create real possibilities of using food as a weapon.[21] However, there are many intersections of altruistic technologies with military or security needs. Currently, a Danish biotech company is developing a genetically modified flower that could help detect landmines, which could really benefit communities recovering from war and violence.[22]

Surveillance technologies are proliferating, particularly after 11 September 2001, as a result of better ICTs. Consider consumer technologies such as the RFID (radio frequency identification), which is an inexpensive, industry-standard product-tagging system.[23] The RFID is an electronic tag embedded in a product you might buy in a store. The tag allows the item to 'tell' a nearby computer what and where it is. For some, this has the potential to be a frightening technology. 'In a world where every product is embedded with identifying technology, the possibility would exist for companies to know what you're doing, in real time, in almost every aspect of life.'[24] As with many new technologies, the potential uses and promises for this technology are vast, as is the potential for harm. Unfortunately, the harm done is disproportionately experienced by women.

Information and communication technologies

Globalization and ICTs[25] have connected people around the world and made learning, educating and social justice organizing easier. ICTs have the potential to bring information and education to women and men in many parts of the world, increasing their individual and organizational capacities, and enhancing networking, participation and advocacy. ICTs can also provide ways to extend and support participatory democracy by increasing participation and transparency of information. At the same time, these tools are used profitably for exploitation: pornography, human trafficking, gambling, extortion and fraud.

Despite the expansion of new ICTs in the South, access and connectivity is still concentrated in large cities, which means that for rural areas in particular, and in much of the world, the radio rather than the internet remains the primary source of information. For example,

> In Africa, each computer with an internet or email connection usually supports a range of three to five users. This puts current estimates of the total number of African Internet users at around 5–8 million. This is about one user for every 250–400 people, compared to a world average of about one user for every 15 people, and a North American and European average of about one in every two people.[26]

ICT policy is only beginning to reflect gender concerns, but there remains much more work to be done to ensure gender equality as policies further develop.

Nanotechnology[27]

Nanotechnology represents the convergence of robotics, molecular biology, chemistry, physics and information and communication technology – every kind of modern science. It is focused on bottom-up construction, in which molecular machines assemble molecular building blocks to form products, including new molecular machines. It is based on the biological principle that molecular machine systems and their products can be made cheaply and in vast quantities.[28]

The promise of developing pollution-free industry, and other countless uses, makes nanotechnology a promising commercial endeavour.

> Perhaps the most exciting goal is the molecular repair of the human body. Medical nanorobots are envisioned that could destroy viruses and cancer cells, repair damaged structures, remove accumulated wastes from the brain and bring the body back to a state of youthful health.[29]

Other important uses for nanotechnology are focused on manufacturing and production processes.

The increase in nanotechnology-based weapons could destabilize the world's power structures because the manufacturing of these weapons will be much less expensive and faster, and the weapons themselves will be much smaller than anything available today. For example, 'smart bullets', created by adding sensory and computer technology to bullets, would allow them to navigate with greater precision. Materials are also in development to make soldiers' uniforms capable of providing exterior support when a soldier is injured or tired, as well as using tiny sensors to constantly monitor the soldier's health.[30]

At present, nanotechnology is focused primarily on developing new materials for consumer products and manufacturing; with the amount of resources currently dedicated to exploring this area, progress will be made soon on some of these other applications. Before nanoscale technology invades our lives, gender equality advocates should engage in debates and critiques of nanotechnology using past experiences with other new technologies to guide the path.

What does gender have to do with it?

Women's rights are particularly threatened by new genetic technologies because their development requires extensive testing on women and their genetic materials. Now, as debates rage on about cloning and other reproductive and genetic technologies, the issue of experimentation and testing is often overlooked. Beyond safety, there are a number of other specific women's rights issues that need to be addressed: access and equity, reproductive choice, commodification of life and, specifically, women's bodies.

In terms of GM foods and other agricultural technology-related issues, a gender analysis is crucial. Women are the (subsistence) farmers of the world; however, in most patriarchal systems they have very little access to resources and very little power. In other words, they are doing the work to feed their families and communities but really have no platform whatsoever to get their needs met. And women have typically been the holders of indigenous knowledge and wisdom, including seed-saving and food and medicine preparation. So, many of the new technologies discussed here are eroding this role completely. Technologies can and do transform gender relations and roles, and, therefore, gender impacts of technologies must be more fully understood.

The widespread availability of ultrasound technology in India and China (and elsewhere) has increased sex-selective abortion. While sex selection is banned in both countries, prenatal testing continues to be used for social sex selection purposes. In both places, there is a clear cultural preference for male children. But when accurate technologies are added to this, the technologies are used to strengthen patriarchal attitudes and institutions. In this case, the technology is used to reinforce social inequalities and rendering women an 'endangered species',[31] ensuring the continued propagation of gender inequalities. Ultrasound and abortion medical technologies are both determinants and causes of discrimination. 'New' technologies such as pre-implantation genetic diagnosis and sperm-sorting only make sex selection easier by allowing intervention before conception.[32] These pre-conception selection techniques are already being used and marketed in some wealthier parts of the world. The existence and use of these technologies force gender equality advocates to ask new questions and develop new analyses on reproductive rights.

Much of biotechnology is being sold as improving health. Thus far, the effects of modern medical technologies have extended lifespan dramatically without extending the quality of life. Here again, medical technology has an unanticipated impact on gender roles. The care of the elderly and the increased amount of work to care for them generally falls on women because it is usually a woman's responsibility to keep her family healthy and care for them if they fall ill. Gender relations are also transformed as reproduction, thanks to assisted reproductive technologies, moves into the laboratory and the domain of (male) scientists. What is the impact of this move on gender roles and more specifically on women's conceptions of their bodies? While some things are immediately related to women and their specific social or biological roles, this does not mean that women should not be involved in debating other technologies such as biological weapons. Women are marginalized in most avenues of life and science.

With nanotechnology, and the promising future that combines all these different technologies, there seems to be very powerful pressure to develop technologies because the capability exists. This puts all the decisions currently made about science and technology in the hands of scientists, engineers, universities and private industry – very male-dominated realms. And in nanotechnology research and development, the field appears to be the same. Women don't often see these issues as a priority. Yet, historically, new technologies have made very real impacts not only on women's lives individually but on gender relations as a whole. With nanotechnology, some of the most promising uses will be applied to manufacturing and other areas where communities in the South, and women in particular, will be drastically affected by the changes.

The way science has been constructed, both historically and literally, includes cultural biases, social constructions and inequalities – and for this reason, women's movements cannot afford to ignore it. However, it is important not to solely focus on these blatantly obvious facts and traditional gender issues, even though with genetic technologies, for instance, women are certainly going to be taken more advantage of than in most other fields. Despite the existence of the specific gender implications of new technologies, it is important to understand the human implications as well. As Bill McKibben has pointed out, many new technologies are not only about the assertion of male power over women but also about a whole new idea of power over human beings in general.[33] The way in which these technologies would have to work, germline genetic engineering in particular, is through intervention of the foetus – get an embryo, remove it, manipulate its DNA, re-implant it or raise it outside the womb. In many practical ways, this kind of invasive technology will have all kinds of repercussions for women, but in the philosophical realm, it is the goal and identity of human beings that is threatened.

Feminist engagement with science and technology

Feminists, especially the younger generation of feminists, are not strangers to technology. At the beginning of the twentieth century, when many European and North American feminists were fighting for the vote, they were often part of larger social movements that included, on occasion, prohibition and health issues, such as public health and hygiene. During this period, responsibility for the health and well-being of society was largely placed on women as the mothers and care-givers. In addition, Malthusian movements during this period often involved women activists who worked for the rights of poor women to have access to birth control as a way to prevent poverty and all the problems associated with it.[34]

Feminism, and the related field of women's studies, inherently question patriarchal models (such as science). And since scientific research and new technological development are not intrinsically value-free, they need to be analysed and explored, and in many cases, debunked in a political and deliberate way. In the 1970s and 1980s, as feminism and women's studies moved into academia as well as into activism, feminists began to critique traditional 'science' and 'technology'.

Feminists also started the women's health movements in the 1970s and 1980s, and have long been working on environmental issues related to new technologies, protesting nuclear weapons and energy and toxic dumping. At the same time, a number of feminists and environmentalists called for a new kind of eco-feminism or 'feminist theory and activism informed by ecology ... concerned with the domination of women and the domination of nature'.[35] Maria Mies and Vandana Shiva describe the evolution of eco-feminism:

As activists in the ecology movements, it became clear to us that science

57

and technology were not gender neutral; and in common with many other women, we began to see that the relationship of exploitative dominance between man and nature (shaped by reductionist modern science since the 16th century), and the exploitative and oppressive relationship between men and women that prevails in most patriarchal societies, even modern industrial ones, were closely connected.[36]

Science and technology have often been seen as male worlds, based on models of rationality. A gender critique of this model might challenge the definition of rationality as disembodied and instead focus on a fuller, more relational concept of what science is. This can be done by looking at all aspects of the 'stream' of technological development, from research and development and decision making about what questions to ask to the dissemination of technology for consumer use. Who has access to the process and to the decisions about how the technology is applied? How do new technologies inform gender stereotypes or gender relations?

Making sense of technology and social justice

Technological developments must be contextualized in a bigger picture. The technologies themselves are interrelated, the governments seeking to regulate are linked by trade and aid relationships, and the companies looking to develop and sell them use the processes of globalization to reach bigger and bigger markets and to locate more resources and raw materials for that development. In this sense, new technologies are not unlike many of the other issues faced today by civil society. However, we are at a crucial historical moment, because of the rapid development and distribution/dissemination of science and technology with little to no regulation; the rhetoric and 'inevitability' of human technological prowess; and with the potential of these technologies for development. Once many of these technologies, such as inheritable genetic modification and GM foods, are adopted, there will be no turning back. And the majority of civil society has been silent.

There are many technologies that will affect women in differing contexts differently. Ultrasound, for instance, has the potential to make birth and pregnancy much safer. However, let us look at the use of ultrasound in India, where there is a great disparity in women's access to ultrasound technology due to income and position within society. For those who *can* access ultrasound technology, it has become possible for women of different backgrounds, despite the fact that it is now illegal, to abort a female foetus because of a preference for male children. This availability and use of ultrasound technology is one of the reasons girl-to-boy ratios in India for children under 6 years of age have declined over the last ten years.[37] In this case, the use of the technology indicates that politics, power relations and the social value placed on having boys determines whether the technology itself is harmful or exploitative for women.

Then there are issues such as human cloning, which affects us as a species. If any countries permit it, because science and technology are global, it will happen. It then becomes a global issue, because it will move wherever it can. We (humans) are all living in this world together and it becomes a species issue whether we're going to move towards cloning humans or not. Now, as debates rage on about cloning and other reproductive and genetic technologies, the issue of experimentation and testing is often overlooked. Much of the stem cell research and cloning mentioned in these debates will require huge amounts of eggs, which must be donated by women. Egg donation is invasive and potentially dangerous. Debating the merits of cloning and this kind of human experimentation is premature without considering the health and safety of the women who would be required to pursue the research. In this case the need is for international instruments and policy dialogue.

Where is the innovation of these technologies located? They are mostly in the North, though more recently also in the South, mostly in the private sector, in male-dominated spaces and associated with trends where commercial applications are coming out of universities. Both scientists and institutions now seek ownership of their knowledge, in order to protect it and reap potential profits.

When taken together, the examples listed above begin to show the bigger picture of how the introduction of new technologies might affect different women (and men) in different parts of the world or in different economic situations. Also, these examples show that it is not possible to examine one specific technology without recognizing the influence of others. How do we take these intersections into account?

Ensuring gender justice in a techno-scientific world

At this point, it is evident that definitions of social justice must necessarily include technological justice. The conception, development, dissemination and application of new technologies should be held accountable to the same democratic standards that other global processes must. Decisions should be openly debated and subject to public scrutiny. These crucial questions cannot be left to the decisions of businesses and individual scientists.

To ensure social and gender justice, there needs to be an understanding of the intersectionality of identities and discriminations, which pays attention to systematic oppression in terms of new technologies. Gender analysis plays a particular role in some obvious technologies related to reproduction, various genetic interventions and advances in 'moulding' children. However, gender considerations go well beyond a woman's reproductive capacity. Women have a distinct set of interests and gender roles in different parts of the world and in different realities.

What we really need to do is to slow down and ask more questions about how, and what, technology is developed and for what reasons. We need to figure out how to integrate gender issues in the development of technology and for what reasons – not just react to specific technologies. For example, if women were able to direct contraceptive technology, what would it look like? Would we have different options? Would they be focused on population control? This applies to all technology: is there an ulterior motive or at the least a non-participation of women in the process? Whom will this benefit and how? And what are the policy implications of this? Technologies do not just *happen*.

It will be vital to find a balanced approach to technologies that takes into account these differences as well as feminist concerns, with the ultimate goal being to find and encourage technologies that promote and improve quality of life and help secure human rights for all. This will depend largely on who controls them, what access people have and what space there is for regulation and control. Using a social justice perspective means these issues must be addressed both vertically (within a particular reality) and horizontally (across regions and technologies) as we modify the environment and the very nature of human beings and try to monitor the impact of these technologies.

The roles of young women specifically must be considered. Just as 'younger' economies adopt new technologies and leapfrog over older ones, young women tend to be early adopters of new technologies while their older counterparts are more reluctant. As a result, the relationship of young women (and men) to these technologies, including how they adopt them and adapt them for their own purposes, must be carefully considered. In addition, younger generations are the targets of advertising campaigns seeking to market the latest technologies – they are the target group for ICTs such as cell phones and other communications devices, as well as the newest reproductive technologies. In the free market world of technologies, young people have incredible (buying) power and they are crucial for the success of new technologies.

A specific problem of women's entry into debates about science and technology is the level of expertise and specialization required to be involved, in addition to a certain 'technophobia'. So far, women's participation in developing technologies is certainly less than our representation in the population at large. Where are women in the production of these technologies? Women, in terms of technology, tend to be presented as the labour or the receivers of the technology, rather than as the creators. New technologies are also often tested on women. What is missing is the acknowledgement and valuation of women as innovators in essentially every field (not only token famous female scientists): in areas such as farming and agriculture, smaller animal breeding and innovative ecosystem management, to name but a few areas.[38]

Ultimately, gender equality advocates everywhere will need not only to be more familiar with the language and the technology itself, but also equipped with a 'big picture' vision of what the implications of such technologies are, for their communities, their environments, their bodies, food, work, safety – their lives.

Notes

1 The research for this chapter was done as part of the author's work for AWID's Gender Equality and New Technologies Programme.

2 Richard Hayes (2002), 'Beyond cloning', *World Watch*, July/August.

3 'Cloning' refers to the creation of an exact copy of existing genetic material. Hypothetically, this can be done for research purposes or for reproductive purposes, creating an embryo or child with only one genetic parent. Cows, sheep and even a household cat have already been cloned. And, on 7 August 2003, a group at the Laboratory of Reproductive Technology in Cremona, Italy, announced the birth of the world's first horse clone, named Prometea. Fergus Walsh (2003), 'First cloned horse unveiled in Italy', *BBC News UK Edition*, see <http://news.bbc.co.uk/1/hi/sci/tech/3129441.stm>.

4 Seeds (crops) are bioengineered to last one or two generations, not allowing farmers to 'save seed'.

5 Pat Mooney (2001), 'ETC century', Dag Hammerskjold Foundation, p. 44, see <www.etcgroup.org/article.asp?newsid=159>.

6 Most laws regulating scientific and technological development are too antiquated to be adequately applied to the newest technologies.

7 Health advocates have identified this as the '10/90 Gap', where 10 per cent of resources are put towards affecting 90 per cent of the population and vice versa. Largely affluent markets in developed countries determine the global research agenda. There are huge disparities in spending on health research conditions that affect different socio-economic classes – within as well as between countries.

8 Alison Langley (2003), 'Engineered drugs open new issue of regulation as patents expire', *New York Times*, 9 August 2003, Section C, p. 1, col. 5.

9 Pfizer, the pharmaceutical giant that makes Viagra, spent US$4.8 billion on the research and development of new drugs, and US$11.3 billion on marketing, advertising and administration in 2001. These data suggest the focus

of marketability of a drug as a driving factor for research and development. From Families USA (2002), 'Profiting from pain: where prescription drug dollars go', <http://familiesusa.org>.

10 WHO and UNICEF (2003), *The Africa Malaria Report*, see <http://www.rbm.who.int/amd2003/amr2003/amr_toc.htm>.

11 For our purposes, we will use 'technology' – both the word and the concept – to describe the practical application of scientific knowledge. In other words, technology is the usable, tangible result of scientific research and development. In this sense, we can talk about medical technologies being pharmaceuticals, diagnostics and treatments, and we can also refer to information and communication technologies and mean both hardware and software. Technology will also be machines or tools that help us work. While it is a flexible (and huge) term, it is, at the same time, specific – it is the marriage of science with consumer goods, commercial and military interests.

12 Debates about the wisdom of introducing GM foods are everywhere – in North America, where farmers in Canada are suing multinational seed companies because their crops are contaminated with GM crops from neighbouring fields, to India, where farmers are fighting back by saving their seeds and refusing to buy GM. Technology is a truly global concern.

13 In fact, many activists contend, on the very issue of GM crop introduction, that they 1) do not actually increase yield, and 2) enhance inequalities (particularly of gender) because subsistence farming suffers and the majority of subsistence farming in the world is done by women. This is, of course, a greatly simplified explanation of a complex issue.

14 UNDP (2003), 'Pragmatic plans for a wired planet', *UNDP Choices: The Human Development Magazine*, see <http://www.undp.org/dpa/choices/2003/december/index.html>.

15 Some examples of international institutions looking to technology as a tool for development include the UNDP (*Human Development Report, 2001: Making New Technologies Work for Human Development*, see <http://hrd.undp.org/reports/global/2001>) and the WHO (Genomics and World Health: *Report of the Advisory Committee on Health Research, 2002*, see <http://whqlibdoc.who.int/hq/2002/a74580.pdf>).

16 R. Rapp and F. Ginsburg (2002), 'Standing at the crossroads of genetic testing: new eugenics, disability consciousness, and women's work', *GeneWatch*, 15(1), see <http://www.gene-watch.org/genewatch/articles/15-1crossroads.html>.

17 K. Evans and A. E. S. Samson (2004), 'Facing the challenges of new reproductive technologies, AWID Facts and Issues, No. 8', see <http://www.awid.org/publications/primers/factsissues8.pdf>.

18 Laws regulating the buying and selling of eggs and sperm are on the books in France, Germany, Italy, Switzerland, Australia, Brazil, Peru, Austria, China, South Korea and Canada.

19 A. Stevens (2002), 'Cloning debate splits women's health movement', see <http://www.womensenews.com/article.cfm/dyn/aid/935/context/archive>.

20 D. MacKenzie (2005), 'Top US biologists oppose biodefence boom',

see <http://www.newscientist.com/article.ns?id=dn7074&feedId=online-news_rss091>.

21 In 1999, *Scientific American* published a report by researchers at the University of Bradford (UK) that chronicled crop and livestock bio-warfare research in South Africa, the UK, the US, Russia and Iraq dating back to the Second World War. The Iraqi work took place in the 1990s and included bioengineering of wheat pathogens that could have devastated food security in the Middle East. P. Rogers, S. M. Whitby, and M. Dando (1999), 'Biological warfare against crops', *Scientific American*, 280(6): 70–5.

22 D. Bailey (2004), 'GM cress could seek out landmines', *BBC News Online*, see <http://news.bbc.co.uk/2/hi/europe/3437019.stm>.

23 F. Manjoo (2004) 'Everything is watching you', see <http://www.salon.com>.

24 Ibid.

25 Information and communication technologies (ICTs) refers to the internet, email, telephony, mass media and communications, as well as the related hardware and software to support them.

26 APC (2002), *The African Internet: A Status Report*, see <http://www3.sn.apc.org/africa/afstat.htm>.

27 One nanometer is one-billionth of a metre. Nanotechnology is the manipulation of matter at this incredibly small 'nanoscale', on the level of single atoms and molecules.

28 G. Stix (1996), 'Waiting for breakthroughs', *Scientific American*, 274(4): 94–9.

29 Ibid.

30 B. J. Feder (2003), 'Defense Department expands nanotechnology research', *New York Times*, 8 April 2003, Section C, p. 2, col. 1. Much of this research is being conducted at MIT's Institute for Soldier Nanotechnologies, whose motto is 'Enhancing Soldier Survivability'.

31 Ibid., p. 190.

32 High-tech sex selection procedures are becoming more available around the world. Many advertisers on the internet, such as the Fertility Institutes (located in the United States and Mexico) claim accurate pre-conception sex selection services, 'SEX SELECTION WITH 99.9% GUARANTEE OF CHOSEN GENDER', for US$18,480. Another company has advertised in the *New York Times* Sunday Style section, asking, 'Do you want to choose the gender of your next baby?'

33 Telephone interview with Bill McKibben, 31 July 2003.

34 This is not unlike some arguments for fertility control, particularly in the South, where hunger and poverty and other social problems are linked with huge poor populations. In this kind of argument, women are given the responsibility for solving societal ills by controlling their own fertility. One doctor, Stephen Mumford, a self-proclaimed neo-Malthusian, promotes the quinacrine sterilization method as a way to control immigration to the United States by having fewer Southern poor people wanting to immigrate.

35 N. R. Howell (1997), 'Ecofeminism: what one needs to know', *Zygon* 32(2): 231.

36 M. Mies and V. Shiva (1993), *Ecofeminism* (Halifax: Zed Books), p. 3.

37 India Census (2001), see <www.censusindia.net>.

38 Interview with Pat Mooney, 25 July 2003.

5 | Smoke screen or solution? Genetic engineering and food insecurity

HAIDEE SWANBY WITH SHAMILLAH WILSON

Despite the existence of international legislative instruments such as the Universal Declaration of Human Rights (1948), which states that every human being has the 'right to adequate standard of living', including food; the International Covenant on Economic, Social and Cultural Rights (1966), which ensures 'an equitable distribution of world food supplies in relation to need'; and the Universal Declaration on the Eradication of Hunger and Malnutrition (1974), which declares that 'every man, woman, and child has an inalienable right to be free from hunger and malnutrition', we are still faced with the reality that 842 million people suffer from chronic hunger and a child dies from malnourishment every five seconds.[1, 2]

In the 1979 World Food Programme Report, food security was conceptualized as an 'assurance of supplies and a balanced supply–demand situation of staple foods in the international market'.[3] The report also emphasized that increasing food production in developing countries would be the basis on which to build their food security. Against this backdrop, genetically engineered crops have been marketed as the solution to food insecurity throughout the world. The proponents of these crops argue that they will tackle food insecurity by increasing yields on less land, by developing crops that are more nutritious, and by simply producing more food. It sounds logical enough, but a deeper look at the real reasons for hunger in the world makes it apparent that this is simply an effective tag-line in a very expensive advertising campaign. As Apuh Shah explains:

> Economics and politics at all levels (international, national and local) have often prevented food from reaching hungry people, not a lack of production. These same causes have also created, or contributed to, a lot of poverty, which prevents people from being able to afford food in the first place.[4]

Global food availability does not ensure food security to any particular country and what is available in the world market (or surplus in the US or Canada) cannot necessarily be accessed by famine-affected people who are in need of food. The economies of the countries in which famine-affected people live cannot usually generate the foreign currency needed to purchase food from the world market.[5] The issue of world hunger and food security is not only about producing enough food but also about the ability to access food that is available. In addition, while many politicians, farmers and consumers may have accepted genetically engineered crops as a universal panacea, the stark reality is that the main responsibility for the world's food security falls on the shoulders of small-scale women farmers responsible for feeding their families and communities. Their needs go beyond technology and agriculture-related concerns to include health care, depleting natural resources, land tenure rights and access to credit and other vital resources such as appropriate extension services and education.

In this chapter, we explore the complex issue of food security: its relationship to women, the notion of genetic engineering as the solution and the issues associated with this, as well how different movements, including the feminist movements, have engaged with these issues. Finally, we will propose some ways in which we can start addressing these issues as feminist advocates.

Genetic engineering (GE): the answer to food insecurity?

Biotechnology and GE are terms that are often mistakenly used interchangeably; however, they are not the same. Biotechnology and civilization have evolved together. Biotechnology, then, is the use of living organisms to create a product, service or process useful to humans. Some forms of biotechnology with which we are all familiar include the domestication of plants and animals through selective breeding, as well as using yeast – a living organism – to make bread rise or to ferment beer. Newer forms of biotechnology are more laboratory-based, such as using tissue cultures to develop disease-free plant material, or marker-assisted breeding to assist us in efficiently breeding crops and animals with particular characteristics, such as resistance to drought or disease. These forms of biotechnology are not generally controversial, as most agree that they are beneficial and relatively risk-free.

GE is a very modern form of biotechnology:

> a set of techniques for isolating, modifying, multiplying and recombining genes of different organisms. It enables geneticists to transfer genes between species belonging to different kingdoms that would have no probability of interbreeding in nature.[6]

Theoretically, the benefit of such a procedure is to produce plants and animals with desirable traits in an efficient and precise manner. In contrast, classical breeding is a rather lengthy and random affair, and breeders are limited to traits found within the species being bred.

Genetically modified organisms (GMOs) are living, breeding, mutating organisms with lives of their own, interacting in complex ways throughout ecosystems.[7] If we realize, years from now, that we have made a mistake, there is no way to recall them. Agribusiness insists that GE is nothing new because we have been breeding plants and animals for millennia, but the reality is that this newest phase of biotechnology stands apart from other forms of 'biotech' because it has unique risks. In recognition of the novel and unknown risks that GE poses, world leaders have negotiated an international treaty dealing solely with this technology called the Cartagena Protocol on Biosafety under the auspices of the United Nations.[8] The Biosafety Protocol acknowledges that 'scientific knowledge about GMOs is incomplete, and allows countries to take measures to prevent harm to the environment and human health, in the absence of scientific certainty about that harm'.[9]

From the green to the gene revolution: can GE really stamp out hunger?

Hunger has precious little to do with the amount of food produced in the world; yield is an arbitrary indicator of food security. In 2001, Argentina harvested enough wheat to meet the needs of both China and India, yet Argentina's people went hungry. Argentina's status as the world's second largest producer of GM crops, largely for export, could do nothing to solve its very real hunger problems at home.[10]

The promotion of GE technology as an answer to food insecurity is an illustration of insufficient understanding of who is producing the world's food and their actual realities, as well as the real causes of food insecurity in the world. GE crops are developed to work within a model of industrial agriculture advanced by the 'Green Revolution' since the 1950s and 1960s that is inappropriate for resource-poor farmers.

The Green Revolution advocated moving away from the planting of diverse crops and the use of natural available resources to intensive crop production systems, growing only one crop at a time with the help of external inputs such as chemical fertilizers, pesticides, herbicides, irrigation and mechanization. It promised an end to world hunger. The idea was not to grow diverse and balanced food for the family, but rather to grow high volumes of cash crops to sell. This approach bypassed the problems of women farmers, who have little capital input for this methodology and often little capacity for the financial skills needed to make a success of it.[11]

This methodology remains inappropriate for the majority of small-scale farmers around the world and yet the newest development of the Green Revolution, the 'Gene Revolution' (based on genetic engineering

67

techniques), is being aggressively marketed as the new solution to world hunger. The gene revolution still works in a mono-crop, high-input framework. However, the inputs have become more expensive and there are more restrictions and obligations on farmers growing them.

Thus, as we engage with GE technologies as potential quick fixes to the effects of poverty, such as hunger, we have to be critical about whether this solution will really address the root causes. If not, then what else are we doing towards addressing the real reasons of poverty and hunger? Is this solution a respite from hunger, or is it a ruse to increase dependencies on developed nations and at the same time increase disparities between rich and poor?

The costs of the new technology

First, if GE is meant to address issues of poverty, the fact that it is such an expensive technology creates access issues for small-scale farmers from the beginning. GE seeds are often double the cost of conventional seeds, with a technology fee on top, plus contractual obligations to buy the corresponding chemicals, as well as bans on seed-saving or seed-sharing. Farmers must apply for loans to obtain the capital to buy the technology and, in turn, must sell their crops to pay back the loan (which has now grown considerably with interest). If the crop fails, if there is a problem getting it to the market, or getting a decent price for it – all very likely scenarios – farmers are left with no food, no money and a debt that could cost them their home, land and livelihoods. In addition, the risks that genetic engineering present are the destruction of the very basis for future production. By degrading the soil and generating pest and weed problems, it makes it increasingly difficult and costly to sustain yields. Farming in industrialized countries versus developing countries is, for the most part, fundamentally different. Industrial agriculture is large-scale, capital-intensive, highly mechanized and market-driven. For people in developing countries, agriculture is often much more than a commercial or subsistence activity; it is imbued with significant cultural and social connotations.

The promotion of GE and the industrial agricultural framework in which it works is misguided, at best, and highly calculated to create dependence, at worst. The promotion of industrial agriculture to replace the highly diverse, cheap and often environmentally sound practices of indigenous peoples could be disastrous. The FAO estimates that we have already lost over 70 per cent of our agricultural diversity in the last century and the continued promotion of industrial agriculture threatens to erode that diversity even more, along with the rich knowledge and skills associated with those resources.[12]

According to Dr Tewolde, general manager of Ethiopia's Environmental Protection Agency and chief negotiator for the 'Like Minded Group', in the Cartagena Protocol:

> GE threatens to make the problem (of food insecurity) worse, creating dependence on corporate-owned agricultural inputs such as seed, decreasing the need for labour, decreasing agricultural diversity, promoting agribusiness over family farms ... the causes of the shortage are many, complex and primarily not technological but structural. What is needed is good national governance and a fair North–South trading and financial relationship.[13]

In a declaration of over 300 small-scale farmer leaders from all over Africa at the World Summit on Sustainable Development (WSSD) in 2002, farmers said 'NO to GMOs', saying that their indigenous seed and rich practices, not GMOs, were the solution to hunger. They called for assistance with water, land tenure, infrastructure and appropriate technology.

Second, the 'human cost' has a huge impact on food security. Other than consumers of food, humans are also food producers, especially women. The proponents of GE crops make all sorts of assumptions, with very little knowledge of what women need and value in their lives. The FAO estimates that rural women are responsible for half of the world's food production, producing up to 80 per cent of the food in most developing countries. Despite this, women remain invisible to policy-makers and service deliverers who persist in perceiving farmers as predominantly male.[14]

While promoting new technologies such as genetically engineered crops, policy-makers ignore the fact that the needs of women food producers go beyond (new) technology, farming techniques and agriculture-related concerns. Women also have to deal with time constraints associated with factors such as depleting natural resources. This means that women must spend more time foraging for wood for fuel, or walking further to fetch water; consequently, their time for working in the fields and caring for their children and home becomes increasingly stretched. The impact of HIV/AIDS on communities of food producers means that caring for sick and dying family members results in less time for working in the fields and for livelihood-related work.[15]

For women, there are also issues of rights to land tenure, access to credit and other vital resources such as appropriate extension services and education. During a GE workshop in Kenya in early 2005, in informal conversations with fellow participants, we talked about the fact that the vast majority of African women may not own land or handle the finances of the home. Excluded on the grounds of customary law and religious grounds, often only men have rights to property, income and legal livelihoods.[16] As one man said, 'if my mother goes to the market with a goat, no one will buy it. Everyone knows that the goat does not belong to her so how can she sell it?' In a meeting with the Landless People's Movement in South Africa towards the end of 2004, women spoke out about the fact that they could cultivate a piece of land for 20 years, only to be thrown off the land when their husband died. Although women are at the centre of subsistence food production, UN statistics tell us that women do not even own 1 per cent of the world's land.[17]

Thus, once again, if we are to address issues of (food and other forms of) security, our challenge is to ensure that the rights of women as producers are protected to enable them to become efficient producers of diverse, quality food that fits in with their lifestyles and livelihoods. Throughout the process, we need to make sure that women are empowered with rights, information and access to resources that enable them to make choices about their roles in society.

The third cost of GE is that of uncertainty. Thus far, much of the criticism thrown at GE is the lack of proper testing of the effects of GMOs. One possible effect is that the increase of the use of pesticides has long-term implications for the health of subsistence farmers (considering that most of them are women).[18] If women's health is endangered, once again their ability to produce food, and hence ensure food security, is at risk.

Finally, the cost to the environment and the diversity of the crops is an effect that cannot be underestimated. If the diversity of crops is reduced, the benefits that the diversity gives – resistance to disease, better ability to cope with environmental extremes, and increased yields – are also reduced.

Economic and political agendas

Genetically engineered crops were created not because they're productive but because they are patentable.[19]

Hunger is both an issue of economics and politics (rather than simply an issue of agriculture and technology). Any sustainable solution would have to address political, economic and social factors that play a part in maintaining this status quo. This includes domestic and international policy, unfair trade and intellectual property rights regimes, as well as the insurmountable burden of unfair debt that has been placed on developing countries. All of these factors either enable or disable food security. Conflicts, wars and natural disasters are also factors that need to be taken into account in relation to food insecurity.

While biotech companies claim that GE food is the answer to world hunger, the act of patenting knowledge may be the real 'threat to food security'.[20] The introduction of GE food has the potential to decrease food diversity, and bring about environmental conditions that will affect our ability to produce food in future. Patenting laws go against the interest of poor people around the world and allow biotech companies to benefit from patenting indigenous knowledge, often without consent. Vandana Shiva explains:

> Biopiracy and patenting of indigenous knowledge is a double theft because first it allows theft of creativity and innovation, and secondly, the exclusive rights established by patents on stolen knowledge steal economic options of everyday survival on the basis of our indigenous biodiversity and indigenous knowledge. Over time, the patents can be used to create monopolies and make everyday products highly priced.[21]

Corporations are using the plight of the developing world as a marketing strategy to gain acceptance of GE food as well as creating dependency via intellectual property rights. The Trade Related Aspects of Intellectual Property Rights (TRIPs) Agreement of the WTO has been a bone of contention between the North and the South, as it not only allows, but obliges, members to apply patents to living organisms. According to Arnold Apoteker,

> [life] has become another invention that is patented just like any other mechanical process. Biotechnology companies are rushing into patenting living beings, micro organisms, plants, animals, even human cell lines, despite national laws which exclude patenting of living beings. The WTO and the US support these multinationals and are trying to impose patenting on the rest of the world, which will finally give a handful of companies almost full monopoly of genetic resources by limiting the access of farmers, who have in fact been their guardians for thousands of years.[22]

Many developing governments, and Africa in particular, have been vocal about the impact that TRIPs could have on the survival and social practices of their people. It is an ethical issue, but a very practical one too. Over 80 per cent of farmers in Africa rely on farm-saved seed.[23] Patenting seed, which prohibits this practice, spells starvation for those who cannot afford to buy seed annually.

GMOs have been called the first living pollution, spreading where they will and contaminating farmers' varieties, which have been carefully bred from generation to generation. The system of exchanging seed is informed by a 'moral code of reciprocity of giving and taking between the earth, communities, neighbouring villages and poorer villages and is essential to the preservation and continued development of the genetic diversity'.[24] However, this will come to an end if patented genes begin to contaminate crops. At stake are 10,000 years of intellectual efforts in favour of corporate claims to ownership on crops and the integrity of the gene pools that provide us with materials for breeding crops resistant to new diseases and climatic conditions. Although GE crops are the sole property of the corporations that develop them, a liability and redress regime that makes corporations responsible for damage is yet to be developed, anywhere in the world. Instead, farmers must pay the polluters for patent infringements! It is one of the greatest ironies that corporations lay claim to these seeds when there is profit involved but do not take responsibility for the damage they cause.

In addition, the use of pesticides presents an economic opportunity for corporations who manufacture and sell them. Over 70 per cent of the GE crops on the market today are engineered to resist Monsanto's herbicide called 'Roundup'. These crops are engineered to work only with that chemical, and the seed and the chemical are the patented property of the corporations that develop them.[25] In Brazil, which has some of the richest biodiversity in the world, large multinational corporations have already patented more than half the known plant species.[28] In all of this, corporations are cashing in on 'public knowledge'; the need to make a profit overriding 'indigenous knowledge and the rights of indigenous people, sustainability of local ecosystems, and even the ability of nations to provide food security and protection of the global environment'.[27]

The politics of GE are 'often played out through the politics of international trade'.[28] For developing countries, this is not good news, since they are the weaker parties in the equation. The US has made it clear that rejecting GE crops constitutes unfair trade practices as defined by the WTO. They have sued the EU at the WTO for their slow adoption of America's GE exports. In so doing, the US has sent a strong message to weaker trading partners that they will implement strong laws to regulate GMOs at the peril of sanctions.[29] Despite not having signed the Cartagena Protocol, which sets out safety measures for the trans-boundary movement of GMOs, the US is leading the way in assisting developing countries with the development of their domestic laws on bio-safety. Analysis of the kinds of bio-safety frameworks that they are assisting to develop shows that they are designed as permitting systems for the influx of GMOs, rather than to be regulations to ensure the safety of environment, health and socio-economic well-being in the face of this new technology.[30] As most developing countries do not have the capacity and skills to develop and implement bio-safety regimes, they are all too often grateful to receive the help that the US is offering, unwittingly opening their doors to a barrage of GMOs. Transparent and rigorous regulation is one of the greatest challenges this technology poses for developing countries.

Strategies of resistance

Resistance to GE crops has once again highlighted North–South issues. In the South, this technology has been seen as a new wave of colonialism, where land and cheap labour serve agribusiness and multinational corporations appropriate natural resources with internationally upheld intellectual property rights. In the wealthier countries of the North, much of the resistance has been around the lack of scientific certainty about the safety of the technology and the effects it may have on human health and environment. Organizations and groups resisting GMOs in the North are well aware of the issues mentioned above, and have contributed an enormous amount towards teasing them out. There has also been a fruitful exchange of information and support between the North and South in developing lobbying and advocacy strategies.

North-based groups have used a consumerist focus to great effect in their lobbying strategies. Especially in the EU, consumers have been at the forefront of rejecting GE foods because scientific knowledge about their long-term effects on humans and environment is incomplete. An 'Open Letter to All Governments' from over 700 scientists from 79 countries is indicative of the kind of campaign strategy employed in the EU.[31] In the letter, the scientists

> urge all Governments to take proper account of the now substantial scientific evidence of actual and suspected hazards arising from GM technology and many of its products, and to impose an immediate moratorium on further environmental releases, including open field trials, in accordance with the precautionary principle as well as sound science.[32]

By and large, the public has been convinced of their standpoint.

Outspoken critics of GM crops have thus far been environmental groups, but now others are starting to pay attention – including farmers, human rights and women's rights organizations – as the impacts of these technologies go beyond environmental concerns and touch on women's health, food security and labour rights.[33]

Women's issues and feminist engagement

Most of the work of feminist groups around the environment has been direct work with groups of women, empowering them to resist the commercialization of their environment.[34] Some work has also gone into advocacy. Feminist groups were particularly involved in the 1992 Earth Summit and the 2002 World Summit on Sustainable Development, where they advocated strongly for the inclusion of gender analysis. However, policy-level advocacy has mostly remained at the level of challenging states. Not as much work has been done, within and across social movements, to incorporate these concerns into other issues of people's struggles for life and livelihood.

However, the bio-political issues of this technology also divide women and feminists.[35] Because so much of the resistance to GMOs has been consumer-based, as mentioned in the previous section, feminists have found it difficult to incorporate the larger social and ethical issues into their struggles. In addition, Abergel raises the critical issue that the artificial and perceived division between genetic engineering technologies in food and in health care can further polarize women and feminists. Around food issues, there can be a more coherent collective effort for political action, whereas in health, the problems and solutions are seen more individualistically, leading to difficult choices for women. Some women, for instance, are welcoming new reproductive technologies. There needs to be a visible acknowledgement that the same companies are appropriating, controlling and manipulating genes for both food and health purposes, and that states and other international institutions are complicit in these processes. We need to make more strategic connections across and between groups, in order to resolve these contradictions in our struggles. In particular, the links between feminist and environmental critiques of economic governance need to be made.[36]

Working with South Africa's two major GMO-focused organizations, Biowatch and the South African Freeze Alliance on Genetic Engineering (SAFeAGE), there has been an absence of the strategic involvement of women's organizations. Why? It could be that those working on GMOs have not recognized the value (and necessity) of bringing women's organizations on board, or that women's organizations have not put GMOs high up on their priority list. It may be a combination of the two. Nevertheless, all organizations that fight for women's human rights, even out of the context of agriculture, are part of the struggle, either consciously or not, to improve food security and ensure that research and development is driven by human rights rather than by profits. The efforts of the GMO movement to develop platforms where farmers can make their voices heard, and our drive to bring appropriate technology and services to farmers, link directly to the work of women's groups, through their constituencies of women food producers.

Struggling against globalization

In September 2003 Lee Kyung Hae, leader of the Korean Federation of Advanced Farmers Association, publicly committed suicide on the opening day of the Fifth Ministerial of the WTO. He had distributed a pamphlet about the plight of farmers, saying:

My warning goes out to all citizens that human beings are in an endangered situation. That uncontrolled multinational corporations and a small number of big WTO members are leading an undesirable globalization that is inhumane, environmentally degrading, farmer-killing and undemocratic.[37]

The anti-globalization movement is gaining momentum all over the world as civil society recognizes that the varied social injustices are rooted in an unfair world order where wealth, rather than democracy, has power. This movement is becoming very visible, as people working for land and water rights, clean energy, fair trade and equal rights join forces. Our voices are growing louder. We are calling for democracy and equality: from the grass roots up to the UN and WTO. Each of us contributes to the weight of this movement with our own constituencies behind us, supporting the fight from different angles.

Supporting ecological farming

Ecological forms of agriculture are not capital intensive, and they build on traditional community knowledge while providing varied and healthy food in an environmentally friendly way. They can, however, be very labour intensive, which means that the added responsibilities fall on to the shoulders of women. 'Future research needs to focus particular attention on the demands of low input agriculture on women, and we need to work with women to develop technologies that relieve, rather than increase their work load.'[38] Support for low-input agriculture needs to go beyond appropriate technological support to include the improvement of rural areas so that basic services, infrastructure and education are available. Greater strategic alliances must be made between organizations servicing farmers and women's movements, to support each other in ensuring that women have equal rights and access to necessary services and resources.

Fighting for human women's rights

First, women are the main producers of food in the world; if we want food security, we need to cater for their needs and acknowledge their skill and contributions.[39] Second, we must ask ourselves if women must continue to be the main producers of food by default. Many women around the world continue to be defined and to accept their inherent roles of being 'close to the Earth' and 'nurturers', whose natural function is to ensure the physical and emotional well-being of the family and the smooth running of the home (while financial issues remain beyond their jurisdiction).[40] This characterization may or may not be true, but it certainly serves to keep

75

women in defined gender roles, with no claim to the kinds of power that would allow free decisions or the redefinition of roles in society. A lack of participation in the formal economy often means that women must rely on natural resources for their family's survival, and as a result, they often have enormous skills in and knowledge about utilizing the fruits of biodiversity. In a circular manner, their relationship with the earth is reinforced as an inherent one. The knowledge and skills related to the utilization and maintenance of biodiversity are recognized in the preamble of the UN *Convention on Biological Diversity* (*CBD*), which states 'the need for full participation of women at all levels of policy making and implementation for biological diversity conservation'.[41]

Some of the most important work around issues of GE crops is happening outside NGOs focusing on globalization and farming issues, and is being done within organizations focusing on women's human rights (of course these overlap!). These struggles are not so much about accepting this technology or that, but, more importantly, are about assisting the major food producers of the world to have a voice and more choice in their own lives. Without access to resources such as land, money and education, women will continue to be the invisible natural food producers of the world – whether they like it or not. Their work in the fields and in their homes will continue to go on unacknowledged. Their power to make the choices that claim their rights will remain unclaimed. Those women who want to continue their current lifestyles and maintain the status quo should also have every right to do so, but this should be a matter of choice rather than a *fait accompli*. Feminists need to resolve the contradictions that arise out of different uses of GE, in order to work towards a holistic sense of women's well-being. The control that genetic engineering companies could exercise, over women's choices of both food security and reproductive technologies, may well signify the ultimate patriarchal project.

Notes

1 Universal Declaration of Human Rights: <http://www.unhchr.ch/udhr/index.htm>; International Covenant on Economic, Social and Cultural Rights: <http://www.unhchr.ch/html/menu3/b/a_cescr.htm>; Universal Declaration on the Eradication of Hunger and Malnutrition: <http://www.unhchr.ch/html/menu3/b/69.htm>.

2 World Food Programme (2004), 'Counting the hungry', see <http://www.wfp.org/>.

3 World Food Programme (1979), *Food Aid Policies and Programmes: Role of Food Aid in Strengthening Food Security in Developing Countries* (Rome: FAO), pp. 22–31.

4 A. Shah (2002), 'GE technologies will solve world hunger', see <http://www.globalissues.org/EnvIssues/GEFood/Hunger.asp>.

5 M. Ayalew (2002), 'What is food security and famine and hunger', see <www.bradford.ac.uk/research/ijas/ijasno2/iyalew.html>.

6 M. W. Ho (1998), *Genetic Engineering: Dream or Nightmare?* (Bath, UK: Gateway Books), p. 21.

7 GMOs are the product of the process of genetic engineering. If genes from an unrelated species are used in the process, they may also be called 'transgenic' organisms.

8 Convention on Biological Diversity (2001–04), 'Cartegena Protocol on Biodiversity', see <http://www.biodiv.org/biosafety>.

9 M. Mayet (2004), *Africa: The New Frontier for the GE Industry. TWN Briefings for MOP1 – No. 4*, see <http://www.biosafetyafrica.net/_DOCS/africa_new_frontier.pdf>.

10 B. Lubhoyza (2001), *What is the Impact of GMOs on Sustainable Agriculture in Zambia?* from the Kasasi Agriculture Training Centre and Jesuit Centre for Theological Reflection, p. 6.

11 G. Reardon (ed.) (1993), *Women and the Environment* (Oxford: Oxfam).

12 FAO (2004), 'World Food Day 2004 highlights the importance of biodiversity to global food security', see <http://www.fao.org/newsroom/en/news/2004/51140/print_friendly_version.html>.

13 B. Tewolde (2001), *The Use of Genetically Modified Crops in Agriculture and Food Production, and Their Impacts on the Environment – a Developing World Perspective* (Ethiopia: Ethiopian Environmental Protection Authority), p. 1.

14 FAO (2002), 'Gender and food security', see <http://www.fao.org/gender/en/agri-e.htm>.

15 NIAID (2004), 'HIV/AIDS Statistics', <http://www.niaid.nih.gov/factsheets/aidsstat.htm>.

16 M. A. Torres (2002) (ed.), *The Convention on Biological Diversity: Ensuring Gender Sensitive Implementation* (Eschborn: Gesellschaft für Technische Zusammerarbeit).

17 G. Reardon (ed.) (1993), *Women and the Environment* (Oxford: Oxfam), p. 5.

18 A. E. Stuart Samson (2004), 'Why new technology is a women's rights issue: facts and issues No. 7', see <http://www.awid.org/publications/primers/factsissues7.pdf>.

19 A. Lovins and H. Lovins (winter 2001–02), 'Are genetically altered foods the answer to world hunger?', *Earth Island Institute* 16(4).

20 A. Shah, 'GE technologies will solve world hunger'.

21 Shiva quoted in A. Shah (2002), 'Food patents – stealing indigenous knowledge?', see <http://www.globalissues.org/EnvIssues/GEFood/FoodPatents.asp>.

22 Apoteker quoted in R. Ali Brac de la Perriere and F. Seuret (2000), *Brave New Seeds: The Threat of GM Crops to Farmers* (London and New York: Zed Books), p. 10.

23 E. Pschorn-Strauss and R. Wynber (2004), 'Six reasons why Africa is concerned about genetically engineered crops, briefing 6', in *Genetic Engineer-*

ing in South Africa: Barren Harvest of Fields of Plenty (South Africa: Biowatch South).

24 C. Hope Cummings (2002), 'Risking corn, risking culture', from World-watch Institute, see <www.worldwatch.org>.

25 Ibid., p. 57.

26 Shah, 'Food patents – stealing indigenous knowledge?'

27 D. Gatti (1998), 'Patents, a new form of colonialism', from Interpress Service, see <http://www.oneworld.org/ips2/aug98/20_52_078.html>.

28 D. Glove (2003), 'GMOs and the politics of international trade', in *Democratising Biotechnology: Genetically Modified Crops in Developing Countries Briefing Series: Briefing 5* (Brighton, UK: Institute of Development Studies), p. 1.

29 M. Mayet (2004), Africa: The New Frontier for the GE Industry. TWN Briefings for MOP1 – No. 4, see <http://www.biosafetyafrica.net/_DOCS/africa_new_frontier.pdf>

30 Ibid.

31 Institute of Science in Society (2005), 'Open letter from world scientists to all governments concerning genetically modified organisms (GMOs)', see <http://www.i-sis.org.uk/list.php>.

32 Ibid.

33 Association for Women's Rights in Development, Gender Equality and New Technologies Factsheet #2, Agricultural Biotechnology, September 2004. <http://www.awid.org/publications/primers/agr_bio_en.pdf>.

34 For example, the Green Belt Movement in Kenya and the Chipko Movement in India. Feminist approaches to women's relationships with the environment have, however, been varied; they include eco-feminism (posited by Vandana Shiva and Maria Mies (1993), *Ecofeminism* (Zed Books: London and New Jersey) and Bina Agarwal's 'feminist environmentalism'; see critique of this in: B. Agarwal (1992), 'The gender and environment debate: lessons from India', *Feminist Studies*, Spring.

35 E. Abergel (2000), 'Genetic engineering in agriculture and health: feminist dilemmas and/or opportunities', see <http://www.cwhn.ca/groups/biotech/availdocs/10-abergel.pdf>.

36 E. Charkiewicz (2001), 'Seeking a sustainable alternative', see <www.dawn.org.fj/global/unconferences/ WSSustDevel/ewadiscussionptsnov01.html>.

37 <global.so36net/2004/03/629.shtml>.

38 Reardon, *Women and the Environment*, p. 12.

39 Ibid.

40 A. Salleh (1997), *Ecofeminism as Politics: Nature, Marx and the Postmodern* (London and New York: Zed Books), p. 13.

41 M. A. Torres, *The Convention on Biological Diversity*, p. 4.

6 | 'You'll know what we are talking about when you grow older': a Third Wave critique of anti-trafficking ideology, globalization and conflict in Nepal

SUSHMA JOSHI

My mother and I had explosive confrontations when I was in my teens and twenties. She disliked my hair, my clothes, my make-up, the way I walked, the way I talked, the friends I had – the life I led. Looking back, I realize that her strongest resistance to my lifestyle and my personal identity came from a deeper urge than wanting to change me; it came from the fear that she was failing in her duty as a mother to rear a good daughter who could function in society. 'This is how you should behave' was a constant refrain. My challenge 'Why?' received the definitive reply: 'You'll know what we are talking about when you grow older', which ended the discussion.

I come from Nepal, from a strongly conservative Brahmin family from Kathmandu, and it is in this context that I write. In my community, girls are brought up to be well-educated professionals who marry young in arranged marriages, give birth to two children (one of them being a son), never divorce their husbands, never raise their voices at their elders and live happily ever after within their extended families. More importantly, young women are taught never to challenge their elders. Any deviation from this 'normal' trajectory is a reflection of failure – not just of the woman but of her parents and her family as well.

Especially troublesome to my family was my burgeoning sexual freedom. After studying abroad, I returned to Nepal and decided to live by myself. Soon after, my boyfriend joined me and we lived in sinful (and in Nepal, criminal) unmarried cohabitation. My parents dealt with this extraordinary decision by extraordinary means; they cut off all communication with me for two years. My relationship was never acknowledged and my immoral behaviour was punished by social ostracization. Only after my relationship was over would my parents resume their familial responsibilities.

This strong moralistic foundation of Hindu-dominated society continues to control women's lives in both urban and rural areas in Nepal today. From my own experience, I am all too aware of the mechanisms that continue to operate, even inside seemingly modern and 'feminist' apparatus and institutions, as social controls over women by families and society.

Although the Nepali Constitution guarantees the equality of men and women, discriminatory provisions in the National Civil Code still exist.[1,2] Nepal has signed and ratified many of the international treaties and laws giving rights to women. Unlike some countries that resist even paper reforms, Nepal has been, on a theoretical level, amenable to keeping abreast with international treaties. However, many of these laws remain unimplemented at the grass-roots level.

The *Manusmriti* (the Laws of Manu) is a medieval and patriarchal Hindu text whose influence lingered on in the *Muluki Ain*, Nepal's 1963 Country Code, and in later legal provisions dealing with gender. The *Manusmriti* is written by an author (or authors) who had very clear notions of caste divisions, as well as notions of women's dependence on men. This ideological framework continues to shade the contemporary laws governing relations between men and women in Nepal, both from Hindu and non-Hindu backgrounds, to this day. This is no more apparent than in the anachronistic law that criminalizes as a prostitute a woman who lives with a man outside of marriage. Although this law is rarely used, the fact that it remains in the law books is significant.

Customary practices that elevate boys over girls continue unabated, even though legal reforms in property rights and women's rights have finally been passed by the Nepali Parliament. Even the reformed property laws are less about equality than they are about traditional norms of gender. For example, a daughter who remains unmarried until she is 35 years old is entitled to half of her parental property. However, the Nepali law states the property has to be returned in the case of her marrying.[3] This law assumes that a woman's first and foremost place is in the husband's home under his care. Failure to get married is a socially damning state; and in this pitiful spinsterhood, a woman, in order to sustain herself, is entitled to half of the parental property. This decision, importantly, is based not on the notion of equal rights between boys and girls, but on the charitable notion that a woman beyond 35 years old cannot sustain herself and needs some financial help from her parental home.

Women, even after they obtain legal rights, have a difficult time accessing them.[4] Women fear the legal process, including the justice providers, the courts and the police, all of whom are liable to manipulation and corruption. Cosmetic reforms at the national level mirror the cosmetic reforms that women's rights institutions advocate but rarely implement with full and unconditional support for a woman's dignity and freedom. Women's organizations can actively promote moralistic and old-world values of what women should be like, acting alongside patriarchal forces that bring women back to their traditional gender roles.

The anti-trafficking movement

Nepal experienced a phenomenal growth of NGOs, many of them women's rights organizations, in 1990, after democratization. Funded by donors from Europe and North America, these organizations concentrated on legal reform, abortion rights, property rights, HIV/AIDS and anti-trafficking measures. Anti-trafficking quickly became a 'hot' issue to fund. Organizations headed by prominent women received undocumented amounts of funding from multiple sources. These organizations worked in 'rehabilitation', and were often at the forefront of bringing women and children back from Indian red-light districts by networking with organizations in India who 'rescued' trafficked girls.

Dominated by urban, middle-class, predominantly Brahmin-Chettri women, and fuelled by orthodox, gendered moral ideologies, the movement has been extremely successful in using the language of kinship to push forward its women-as-victims narrative of trafficking. *Cheli-beti* (literally, daughters) is used as a blanket term to refer to all Nepali women living and working in India, regardless of their age. The notion of women as *cheli-beti* has been so successfully disseminated that trafficking, in the Nepali language, is known as *cheli-beti bech-bikhan* (the sale of daughters). This has consolidated and reified the status of women-as-dependent-kin within the nation, blurring any attempts to restructure women as citizens.

The discourse of *maiti* is a defining feature of the anti-trafficking and rehabilitation discourse within Nepal and has major implications for national policy. The term *maiti*, in Brahmin-Chettri culture within Nepal, refers to the natal home: the home territory that girls grow up in before they get married and go off to their husband's home. While *maiti* offers women special privileges, such as love, care and limited financial support, it is also clearly defined as a space where daughters have no formal inheritance or economic rights. The *maiti* is a space further restricted to a woman once she formally leaves it; the leaving is imbued with the assumption that girls leave the home only on the occasion of marriage.

Once the woman is married, she can only come back to her *maiti* over certain festivals and days, for short periods of time, since that space formally belongs to her brothers, and by extension, to her sisters-in-law. It is a space where women can return in situations of extreme desperation – for instance, in cases of desertion or the death of their husbands. This 'coming back' is never a right; it is always a favour bestowed on the woman by her natal family. The woman and her children, if she has any, are always treated as family members with limited rights. Within the hierarchy of the family, where gender and age privileges are paramount, a woman who returns to the *maiti* is usually a social outcast.

81

By framing the return of trafficked women into Nepal within the terms of *maiti*, activists restrict what rights women can expect from their country. Once back on home territory, women have to behave as family members, not individuals with certain intrinsic rights guaranteed by the Constitution.

I sat in on one particularly enlightening session with an activist from a well-known anti-trafficking organization while she recounted the NGO's rehabilitation methods. 'The girls', she said, 'come back speaking foul language, swearing and cursing. We teach them how to act like women.'[5] She had a military authority about her and was clearly used to disciplining recalcitrant girls. My colleague, a foreigner and a man, received her full attention. She told him about the camps they were setting up for women with HIV/AIDS and showed him a display of traffickers, many of whom were family members and individuals of the same ethnic community as the women. She ignored my questions and did not look at me throughout the session. My half-hour with the gender activist left me (and my colleague) shaken and disturbed. I did not feel safe or secure around her, and if my experience was any indication, I doubt that the girls under her authority felt safe or secure either.

Rescuees who are handed over to rehabilitation organizations find themselves physically locked inside buildings with security that rivals that of a brothel. Fear that outside agents – traffickers (including boyfriends and family members) and nosy journalists and photographers – will try to contact the rescuees is one reason for these security measures. The other reason is the fear that the girls, dissatisfied with the meagre livelihood options offered to them (knitting does not make a particularly reasonable or even viable livelihood), might try to run off to rejoin their former profession.[6]

Anti-trafficking organizations are either consciously or inadvertently active in perpetuating myths about girls who are duped and drugged to go abroad.[7,8] This need to portray the girls as completely chaste and innocent victims, who are at the mercy of cruel and merciless men who deceive them due to their naivety, is part of a strategy to perpetuate the mythology of chastity, where young girls never feel sexual desire. Many of the trafficked girls, of course, go over to India with men with whom they have had sexual relationships or who have promised to marry them.

Purity

In 1998, I worked as a translator for two journalists from the *Sunday Times* of London on a child trafficking story. We showed up early at a rehabilitation organization and started to interview a 16-year-old girl. One of the questions the journalist wanted me to ask was if the girl knew the man who took her over to India. The girl nodded. 'Did you like him?' The girl smiled. It was obvious that the man had been somebody with whom she had had an emotional or a sexual relationship. The representative of the rehabilitation organization got agitated after this question was asked. He answered curtly: 'She did not know the man. He was a stranger.' Shortly afterwards, he left the room. A few minutes later, the activist who headed the NGO called the journalist in and gave her a verbal lashing, demanding that we leave the premises instantly. We left the interview unfinished.[9]

Nepal remains the only country in the world where a young girl is still worshipped as a virgin goddess and where the idea of a pure and unadulterated woman has as much weight and mystique as in medieval times.[10] Mythologies of the virgin as being a powerful force in creation and sustenance continue to be favoured by New Age practitioners and feminists of certain backgrounds. In the sections below, I will confine myself to looking at how the phenomenon of trafficking, and the reactions to it, can be understood through the lenses of purity and virginity.

At a Coalition Against Trafficking of Women (CATW) conference in Dhaka in 1998, I heard a young girl tell her story of violence and abuse. The girl was 13 and was accompanied by people from the NGO that had 'rescued' and 'rehabilitated' her from Bombay. In the beginning, the girl was unable to speak; at the encouragement of the head of the rehabilitation organization, she burst into tears and said that she would share her tale of suffering so other sisters might not have to go through the same experiences. Her story, translated from Nepali, was long and complex, involving many incidents and sub-narratives. At the end of her testimony, a participant remarked: 'I did not know that Nepal was such a barbaric place.'

What struck me about this narrative was the emotional resonance of the Nepali details. These were details and themes that rang familiar bells to me from childhood fables: getting lost in forests, being found by millers, being adopted by a kind person, being treated unkindly and driven out of the home by a stepmother. I am not disputing the nature of her sufferings or the exploitative conditions of her childhood. What I found striking was the form of the narrative that she chose to use to represent herself publicly, and the number of cultural themes of oppression and parables of suffering she included. Compared to the stories of other survivors from the US and the Philippines, which were straightforward autobiographical accounts of economic deprivation and familial abandonment that led to a slow slide into prostitution, I found this particular narrative different in two fundamental ways. First, her story was not just hers alone, but a parable of suffering and oppression of all destitute girls. Second, she was very aware of it being a *Nepali* story.

Let me elaborate. A Nepali girl who returns from Bombay is tainted in many ways: physically, sexually, socially and morally. Nepal is seen as the bounded ritual realm of unadulterated Hinduism, with an inner moral world separated from the outer immoral world; crossing the border of the nation implies that the outside taints all such Nepalis. The notion of people defiled by crossing the borders is symbolized by the *pani patiya* mandated by Prithvi Narayan Shah and later Gorkhali rulers; these were 'complicated and time-consuming rites of ritual purification' performed for any Nepali returning from outside the Hindu world.[11] It does not matter, therefore, that a woman left because she was destitute or abandoned, she still has to prove that leaving the inner, moral space was justified. The only way for her to regain a place in a society whose framework is built upon norms of sexual purity is to prove that she suffered from circumstances beyond her control. This can be done only by including large numbers of cultural tropes of women's suffering in the oral tradition. Putting all these parables together also creates a narrative that acts as a warning for other girls who are contemplating crossing boundaries.

Tellingly, the activist who ran the rehabilitation organization had produced a tape of songs that warned women about future consequences if they went to Bombay. A narrative with such resonance acts as a public expiation: only somebody who has suffered so much, and who has come back to warn others about her experiences – one who, in other words, has redeemed herself – can come back into the sacred threshold of the home.

The concept of *cheli-beti bech-bikhan*, appropriated by actors in many locations for their own purposes, has also been appropriated by the state as a Nepali *national* story. It encapsulates all the elements of Nepali's national identity: poverty, destitution and forced migration for the sake of labour opportunities. All these elements create a public image of Nepal to the world and reinforces the idea that bad things happen to Nepali women because the country is poor. This myth allows for an elision that sidetracks people from bringing up issues such as political commitment to change gender discriminatory laws, efforts to make education accessible to girls on a national level, and provisions in the Constitution to ensure equal rights.

In other words, trafficking has become a narrative that binds the nation together with the secure knowledge of our poverty and the inevitability of conditions of exploitation outside the nation. By making the flow of women into India forced, and never voluntary, Nepal manages to re-create the inviolability of the borders. By making the clients into evil, exploitative

Indian men, it reconsolidates the barrier to what is most threatening to Nepal's national identity: the violation of purity.

Kumari: the virgin goddess

The 'Living Virgin Goddess' is indisputably one of the prolific national myths of Nepal. Kumari, the 'Living Virgin Goddess', is extensively photographed, painted, filmed and written about in many languages.[12] She is a familiar symbol, and used as an icon to represent Nepal. Kumari, as the national trope of purity, reinforces certain gender norms within Nepal.

A Kumari is always chosen from the Shakya clan and is usually aged from 5 to 11. She should theoretically never have bled (even a girl who has cut herself is not accepted as a candidate). This girl is confined in the old Kumari Ghar, a safe home which she cannot leave, but from whose window she is allowed to look out and give *darshan*. Every year at Dashain,[13] she receives the king. She is anxiously watched to make sure that she never cries while she is giving *tika*[14] to the king, since a crying Kumari is an inauspicious event, and a sure sign that the king's mortal days are numbered. Just before she reaches puberty, has her period and starts bleeding, the Kumari is replaced by another girl. The Virgin Goddess, once she is symbolically defiled by her period and the permeability of her body, loses her divine status and can no longer represent the nation. Instead, she has to go back to being an ordinary little girl. But not just any other ordinary girl: once fallen from the status of divinity, she is feared and thought to have a mortally bad effect on the men that she may marry. Her fall from divine status imbues her with the power to cause death to men.

The trafficking myth of Nepal cannot be analysed without taking this national myth into account. The Kumari is integral in consolidating and holding together the authority and legitimacy of another human divine: the king. The traditional power structure of the present Shah monarchy has always hinged on the notion of the Virgin Goddess, and the two institutions have always supported and legitimized each other. The king, seen to be an incarnation of Vishnu, is present at every Indra Jatra and at Dashain to watch the procession and get blessings from the Living Goddess. With the advent of the democracy movement, and voices of dissent and treason that would like to do away with the monarchy all together, the position of the monarchy has reached shaky ground where they have to define themselves in more secular terms. Their political authority, while still derived from and tied to divine authority, has had to readjust to the changes in the power structures. Most people who support the king do so because they believe he is the one institution that keeps Nepal from merging with India. The historically friendly ties between the Nepali Congress Party and

85

the Indian Congress Party have provided no security or confidence in the Nepali people that one party will not completely 'sell and eat Nepal'.[15] Many people see the king as the only remaining bulwark between Indian intervention in and encroachment on, and eventual take-over of, Nepali territory and affairs. It is of interest to note here that the notion of 'selling' the country has the same cultural resonance and generates the same outrage as *cheli-beti bech-bikhan*.

Nepal, since the time of Prithvi Narayan Shah down to the Rana regime, has constructed itself as a geographically inaccessible, secluded and closed nation. After the advent of democracy, new political leaders were amenable to opening up the borders, allowing a better flow of trade between India and Nepal. This transitional time of national reinterpretation, where a closed, feudal, political system started to renegotiate with its neighbours, was fraught with anxiety about maintaining Nepal's sovereignty, and the need to maintain its impermeable boundaries.

India and its cultural influences are easily available and consumed at all levels: through Bollywood movies, Doordarshan (Indian state television), goods, education, travel, pilgrimages and shared cultural notions. Prominent voices in Nepal have raised the need for Nepal to maintain its own cultural and linguistic héritage and to create boundaries that cannot be breached. Women, who are the last frontier and who are being infiltrated by Indian men, add another blow to a carefully maintained sovereignty and purity.

The reactions of the Nepali police illustrate this with more specificity. The police, who have been incorporated by women's NGOs and international NGOs into their networks, seized the purity issue with enthusiasm and have been active in promoting anti-trafficking activities through mainstream media. Their involvement has meant that the nuances of trafficking have been reduced to a simple crime: an operation where women are drugged, duped or deceived into going to India. TV programmes that are dramatized versions of police operations are simple narratives of women who are intercepted at the borders and brought back to their homes. The process, while envisioning and re-envisioning national boundaries through the mythic female body, also plays out the national anxieties of attack, adulteration and inundation by India.

Anxieties of cultural and national disintegration, by becoming re-inscribed on female bodies, reinforce the notion of an encroaching India. The discourse of trafficking, then, always looks at trafficking as a *Nepali* problem (it only happens to Nepali girls): never as a phenomenon also shared with Bangladesh, or poorer states within India. The thought of young *cheli-beti*, who by extension are Virgin Goddesses, being violated and desecrated by Indian men is intolerable and morally unjustifiable. The trafficking myth, in this way, gives moral shape to Nepal as a sovereign nation and reinforces its separateness from India.

'Rescue': an unviable strategy

In 1997, I was stopped at the international airport by immigration officials. Although I had the necessary documentation corroborating that I was going on a professional trip, and was accompanied by a male colleague from my office, the border official interrogated me about my activities in Bangladesh. *Timi*, used in informal situations between younger family members and close friends, or as a patronizing form of address to strangers, was the form of address that he used to speak to me. After ten minutes of this, I became angry and raised my voice. The official told me flatly that he was not going to allow me through immigration. When I complained, the head official explained to me that he was doing this for my own protection because '*hamro cheli-beti haru lai hamilay hernu parcha*' ('we have to take care of our daughters and sisters'). He explained that I might be trafficked in Bangladesh and that I could leave the next day if I came back with a male guardian to take responsibility and vouch that I would not get sold (*bechinu*).

When I came with my brother the next day, a higher-ranking immigration official told me that he was letting me through only because he knew my brother on a personal level. After being chastised for using 'foul' language, I was finally allowed to take my delayed flight. The articulation of women-as-kin made it perfectly acceptable for an immigration official to call me *timi*, to take quasi-legal authority to stop me from making any moves to defile my sexual purity, as well as to chastise me for using foul language that is inappropriate for a sister or daughter. Within this framework, it was also acceptable to ask for a male guardian to guarantee my safety, implying that I could cross the boundaries of home only with the full cognizance of my (male) guardian. A Nepali woman still, to this day, cannot apply for a passport without an official form signed by a guardian (father, husband) and attested by a gazetted officer of His Majesty's Government.[16]

It was acknowledged that I could 'sell myself' (*afailai bechnu sakhuhuncha*). However, by the very nature of the transaction, one cannot sell oneself, and therefore it can never be a voluntary act; exploitation cannot be seen as voluntary. By consolidating the multi-faceted nature of people's mobility and reducing complex economic, social and political transactions under one mythical signifier, 'selling' (*bech-bikhan*), the anti-trafficking activists within Nepal have managed to coopt and reduce all issues of migration and labour to a single homogeneous idea.

Surprisingly, I found that many women from socio-economic back-grounds different from my own, and who may have been trafficked, also dislike being involuntarily 'rescued', and try to avoid the same interference in their movements and decisions.[17] My interviews in Bombay showed that many women who were 'rescued' chose to escape and go back to places such as Kamathipura, where they had established emotional and social ties. One young woman told me that women who escape from rehabilitation organizations disguise themselves so they won't be recognized by social service workers and be forced to return to Nepal. Many trafficked women prefer living in India in a neighbourhood where they have established social ties and livelihoods, rather than in detention in an authoritarian rehabilitation organization.

I am not denying the realities of trafficking. In Bombay, I saw women crowded in bunk beds in tiny rooms in brothels. Some of them had run away from home, others had been trafficked by individuals whom they loved and trusted. Some of them had come to terms with their lifestyles; others wanted to do something else. I saw cases of 'hard' trafficking, where a young woman was enslaved inside a small wooden box deep inside the heart of a dark building. A pimp once told me that under-age girls were carted away overnight to Gujarat to avoid police raids. He then showed me his folder of college students who worked as part-time prostitutes and told me that I could look him up if I ever needed work. As a young woman myself, I felt under threat in a place and economy that traded on the dreams and vulnerability of young women who could not speak the language, and who were at the mercy of the 'caretakers' who bought and sold them.

At the same time, I had a hard time reconciling this world of horror with the one that purported to offer a way out – the world of rehabilitation organizations, which in many ways are as limiting for the young women who find themselves 'rescued' within them. The debate, then, is not so much about whether trafficking exists or not. Clearly it does. But do the programmes to stop trafficking really work? Or do they merely hinder women's mobility across states without providing them any another viable alternative to sources of income, employment and livelihood?

A (very small and cramped) room of our own

The primary challenges for young Nepali women, both urban and rural, are visibility, respect and identity. Young women, if they happen to live in urban areas and have access to certain cultural capital, are viewed as citizens to be respected, but this respect is conditional and limited. They can be professionals, but never in high decision-making positions. They can get married and work, but their marriage and children hold primary importance. They can be vocal in public, but always within boundaries. Their mobility is always tied to their respectability. It takes women longer – if ever – to acquire a position in public office. When they get inside public institutions, they rarely get the responsibility that men do. Women's roles continue to be defined as belonging inside the home – a single night's viewing of Nepali news on television, where every seminar, conference and national-level meeting is dominated by men, illustrates this vividly.

Women from rural or geographically inaccessible areas, especially in minority or 'lower'-caste communities, have even more drastic limitations on their rights. Many of them cannot get a signature from a government officer for their citizenship papers, and are effectively cut off from recognition as citizens of the Nepali state.

The missing link: accountable leadership

This is why it is especially problematic when the handful of women leaders who do gain recognition and power use it to push agendas that keep girls and women limited, even if indirectly, to defined social and cultural boundaries. The major thrust of anti-trafficking activists' work has gone into stopping women from migrating, not into making the process of migration safer. When girls and women return to Nepal, the focus is to make them into 'decent' women with bourgeois sensibilities. There is little effort put into making them independent and self-reliant, and little care put into making women feel that they are free. Instead, locks and bars reinforce the notion that women are safest behind closed doors.

Anti-trafficking programmes worldwide obtain significant international funding. These funds continue to increase annually, but there is no public accountability in terms of whether these programmes are effective and little monitoring and evaluation of results.[18]

Despite the fact that anti-trafficking programmes have been active in South Asia for almost two decades, trafficking has not stopped. Due to the lack of hard data, it is difficult to make an informed estimate of how many women were trafficked before, how many continue to be trafficked at present, and whether these numbers have gone up or down. According to news reports and experiences of people 'on the ground', trafficking remains a problem in Nepal. As many as 500 Nepali children from Makwanpur, a central region of Nepal, are in Lucknow, India, where they are forced to work as circus entertainers in dangerous and difficult circumstances. They are at risk of sexual abuse from circus-owners, who are often organized by the mafia.[19] Prosecuting traffickers is difficult with the insufficient justice systems throughout South Asia; out of 254 traffickers arrested in Bangladesh between 2000 and 2003, for instance, only 35 were convicted.[20]

In Nepal, donors supported legal reform to prosecute traffickers. Unfortunately, the Human Trafficking Control Bill, which came out of these initiatives, put the burden of proof on the accused, making it easy to misuse the law.[21] Consequently, most women and men imprisoned for trafficking say they were framed by individuals who had personal disputes with them. Another controversial programme is a border control programme implemented by a well-funded Nepali gatekeeper organization. Women travelling for work are stopped at the border and interrogated. Critics have pointed out that this increases deception on the part of women, and does not ensure a well-informed and safe migration approach.

When the donor community starts to direct women's and feminist movements, two things happen. First, activists and activism become dependent on funding, and donor-driven agendas pass for 'issues'. Second, unaccountable funding leads to a damaging culture of non-transparency, making this *the* model for social change.

Millions of dollars for 'women's rights' are granted in good faith to a few select institutions every year. These funds don't reach a larger constituency for two reasons. First, they are confined to 'projects' limited in scope and effectiveness. Second, donors have not been demanding with requirements for accountability, creating an environment where transparency is seen to be a voluntary component to a project funding proposal rather than a public right. A large proportion of these funds has been siphoned off and misused for private purposes. The pervasive belief that activists are not accountable to their constituents, leading to the violation of public trust, is the biggest obstacle to a larger, united movement for social change.

A changing landscape

Nepal, as a country, has been pressed from two sides: an internal civil conflict that threatens to destroy the ecosystem of an imagined nation on one hand and the pressures of globalization on the other.[22, 23] Conflict, internal poverty and lack of employment force people to migrate outside Nepal at ever-increasing rates. Many villages are empty of men – most of them work outside the country. Migrant men fear returning during festivals, as both the Maoists and the Royal Nepal Army are known to kill, abduct and extort the labourers. The psychological pressures of conflict on both men and women are enormous.

Employment opportunities for women are rare. The traditional male escape route – India, the Persian Gulf, East Asia, South East Asia and North America – is a different experience for women. While men work as guards in Mumbai, women end up working as sex workers. Getting further abroad requires capital out of reach for the poorest. Inevitably, women who cannot find decent work will be, voluntarily or involuntarily, recruited into the ranks of a guerrilla war. Whatever the compulsions and contexts, women, having once moved beyond a private constricted realm into a public space with arguable freedoms, are unlikely to go back to the hearth and field any time soon. The cessation of conflict therefore hinges on ensuring sustainable livelihoods for women.

As fragile threads of 'community' fall apart under these stresses, younger women are increasingly moving away from traditional gender roles. Thousands have already taken their lives into their own hands and have moved into professional and public spheres. While some migrate, others struggle to carve out an identity for themselves in the streets of the capital with fashion, music and MTV. Still others join the guerrilla movement. For all sides, empowerment has come about in their personal and political lives through a new order – a new national as well as global order. The new order limits their horizons on one hand, and broadens them on the other. The women's and feminist movements need to account for these changes, and move away from a static dichotomy where women either remain at home, or are 'trafficked' abroad. An inclusive process of empowerment has to take into account these radical social changes in the lives of women and girls.

Nepal denies citizenship to children of women married to foreigners, indicating in no uncertain terms that a woman's identity after marriage is defined by her husband. If her husband's home is outside Nepal, this is where she belongs. This sense that Nepal is always a natal home and one in which an unmarried girl or woman is only accepted on sufferance has to be challenged and changed. Nepali women can no longer afford to be just *cheli-beti* in their own country. The time for *maiti* is over – the time to reclaim and reinvent the *ghar* (home) has come.

This means active lobbying for equality in all spheres of life, from reform of the Constitution and National Civil Code to broadening the roles of women beyond private life. Nepali women do not constitute a homogeneous group – they come from all geographic regions, religions, castes and ethnicities. And yet, as citizens of the same country, they are ruled by the same set of laws that envision their roles in defined and rigid ways. Legal and constitutional reforms therefore remain crucial tools with which to create equality for all women.

The women's rights movement in Nepal, currently stuck in its 'first wave' phase, also has to grow up and concede a new social reality where young women are mobile and employed in increasingly complex and globalized economies. The notion that a new generation of young women exists and is demanding equality not just with men but also older women has to be 'mainstreamed' into current thinking.

New models, new changes

A fundamental reason why democratic parties in Nepal have ground to a halt is because of their failure to understand public positions as responsibilities rather than lifetime tenure rights. Leadership in such parties comes from a feudal model where older men from high-caste backgrounds have precedence over young people, women and minorities. This is why Nepal has seen some of the most absurd democratic politics in global history. Since democracy was formally proclaimed in Nepal in 1990, there has been a change of prime minister 13 times – with the same handful of men rotating through the post.[24] This model has trickled down to NGOs, with one woman 'owning' and leading an organization with lifetime tenure rights.

A small seed-group of younger activists is trying to create alternative models of social organizations. Young and dynamic leaders who have worked in the traditional NGOs of Nepal have voiced a critique of their monolithic, unaccountable models. New membership-based organizations whose funding sources are open to inquiry, whose accounts can be scrutinized by the public at any time, and where the position of chairperson changes every few years are, to some extent, taking hold.

Another alternative model comes from the villages themselves. The most dynamic work in women's rights at the moment is being done by small community-based organizations (CBOs) in rural and semi-rural areas. Nepal's civil war is fuelled by economic and social inequalities. Most resources are concentrated in the capital, severely affecting other areas. Funding, therefore, must get disbursed to smaller organizations outside the capital as part of a conflict-resolution strategy. This will help to build, strengthen and push issues relevant to specific ethnic and minority communities, issues that do not get considered within a Kathmandu-based NGO. CBOs and their young activists are capable of bringing about long-lasting grass-roots change, and creating a broad-based movement for women's rights.

Ultimately, change will only come with a new generation of women who are able to see their place in a dynamic and newly emerging democracy – one where the rights of all women, regardless of ethnicity, caste and class, will be seen as critical to political change and a just society.

Notes

1 His Majesty's Government of Nepal (1990), 'Constitution of the Kingdom of Nepal', *Himalayan Research Bulletin*, XI(1–3), see <http://www.oefre.unibe.ch/law/icl/np00000_.html>.

2 Forum for Women, Law and Development (FWLD) (2000), 'Briefing paper on optional protocol to CEDAW', and 'Summary of shadow report on CEDAW', see <http://www.fwld.org.np/cedaw.html>.

3 S. Pradhan-Malla (n.d.), 'Challenging Nepal's inheritance law', see the Center for Legislative Development's website for the online publication <http://www.cld.org/wprnilaw.htm>.

4 S. Joshi, 'Waiting for justice', *Nation Weekly*, 15 November 2004.

5 For more on discipline and punishment, see M. Foucault (1978), *The History of Sexuality, an Introduction* (Harmondsworth: Penguin) or M. Foucault (1977), *Discipline and Punish: The Birth of the Prison* (Harmondsworth: Penguin).

6 T. D. Thinley (2002), 'Anti-women-trafficking tactic ignites controversy', *Kathmandu Post*, Friday 26 July 2002.

7 For more on myths: R. Barthes (1957), *Mythologies* (New York: The Noonday Press).

8 J. Frederick, 'Deconstructing Gita', *Himal*, October 1998.

9 The same activist would later call up and threaten the journalists for not paying half of the transportation fare to a field visit, although this financial agreement had never been stated. The journalists were told that the NGO's men would come to seize their photographs and negatives if they did not pay the stated price. The journalists took the threats seriously enough to take refuge in the British embassy. Because the NGO was being funded by Prince Charles, the embassy staff advised the journalists to keep the case quiet.

10 C. Dunham and D. Haber (2003), *Kumari: The Virgin Goddess* (New Delhi: Roli Books).

11 M. Liechty (1997), 'Selective exclusion: foreigners, foreign goods, and foreignness in modern Nepali history', *Studies in Nepali History and Society* 2(1): 5–68.

12 C. Dunham and D. Haber, *Kumari*.

13 The National Festival of Nepal: a 15-day harvest festival around September–October that celebrates the nine Durga goddesses and also brings together the family as a social unit of meaning.

14 A sticky preparation of vermilion, rice and yogurt put on the forehead as a blessing.

15 *Bechyara khaidincha* is a colloquial phrase literally meaning 'he/she will sell and eat' the specified object, often used to indicate cunning.

16 The term 'gazetted' is used in many post-colonial countries to denote an officer on the government's official gazette's lists – i.e. a senior bureaucrat.

17 Women resent their drop in income levels after rescue. In addition, there is competition between NGOs to 'rehabilitate' the most number of women. See Thinley, 'Anti-women-trafficking tactic ignites controversy'.

18 USAID provided $15 million for anti-trafficking activities in 36 countries in 2003, an increase of more than 50 per cent over USAID anti-trafficking funding in 2002 (USAID, March 2004, 'Trafficking in Persons: USAID's Response').

19 T. Pokhrel (2004), 'Indian circuses: a nightmare for Nepali minors', see <Worldpress.org>.

20 USAID, 'Trafficking in Persons'; USAID (2003), 'Combating trafficking

in women and children in Bangladesh, Cambodia and Nepal', see <http://www.usaid.gov/locations/asia_near_east/features/trafficking11_03.html>.

21 His Majesty's Government of Nepal (n.d.), 'Human Trafficking (Control) Bill', see <http://www.fwld.org.np/trafbill.html>.

22 The Maoists have been waging a People's War for a one-party republic in Nepal since 1996. The armed guerrillas stage mass attacks on police stations and army barracks, bomb state buildings, and execute political opponents. They abduct children from schools to attend their indoctrination programmes, and use children as soldiers and to carry and plant explosives. The Royal Nepal Army has retaliated with torture of suspected Maoists, extrajudicial killings, and 'disappearances' of civil society dissidents. This dirty war has claimed an estimated 12,000 lives in nine years, although the figures are probably much higher.

23 B. Anderson (1983), *Imagined Communities* (London: Verso).

24 http://www.answers.com/topic/list-of-prime-ministers-of-nepal. The last count was in February 2005.

7 | From orphaned china dolls to long-distance daughters: a call for solidarity across borders

INDIGO WILLIAMS WILLING

In recent times, border crossings for all types of women from physically, culturally and economically vulnerable regions of the 'Third World'[1] have become commonplace, yet are often made without free decision. For many of us who have experienced such a transition, our bodies are not only moved across space and time but are also transformed symbolically – from being 'local' to being 'foreign'. Under this transition, our racial and cultural backgrounds are brought forward as embodying 'differences', which are then intersected and subordinated along with our gender. Dynamic forms of transcultural activism have emerged from such disorder and displacement. New communities are being developed, new alliances made. Perhaps most importantly, new voices are being heard, strategizing so that healing, affirmation and resistance can be shared.

Transnational adoption refers to the process whereby an orphaned child from one nation-state is placed in the care of adoptive parents living in another. This form of adoption has offered a complex, but concrete and even compassionate, solution to addressing many instances of child poverty and homelessness within the orphan's birth country. However, to date, transnational adoption has also been troubled by charges that it is a self-interested, imperialist and even self-congratulatory practice of the elite, which has been sustained by a range of problematic economic, social and cultural dynamics that need closer examination.

The practice of transnational adoption first became common when thousands of war orphans were flown from Korea in the 1950s and Vietnam in the 1970s to be adopted into families living in Australia, Europe and North America. According to a migration study, transnational adoption is now 'a phenomenon involving over 30,000 children a year moving between over a hundred countries'.[2] The practice largely involves the removal of orphans from communities in Asia, Africa, the Caribbean and the Pacific Islands to comparatively wealthier ones in the West.[3, 4] One of the most striking disparities in transnational adoptions is that communities in the most vulnerable regions of the world continue to be broken apart, while communities in affluent and powerful regions are being enriched by the other communities' losses.

The US is the main recipient of transnational orphans, receiving up to 75 per cent of the orphaned children adopted abroad. They have facilitated the adoption of 'more than 139,000 children ... internationally in the last ten years'.[5] The number of immigrant visas issued to orphans coming to the US for adoption in 2003 alone was 21,616, with the leading source of orphans being China.[6]

Some adoptive parents in the US have begun to raise their concerns in response to the uneven power relationships between the sender and receiver countries of orphans.[7] C. Register, a mother of two adopted Korean daughters, argues that 'wealth does not entitle us to the children of the poor'.[8] She acknowledges:

> International adoption is an undeserved benefit that has fallen to North Americans, West Europeans and Australians, largely because of the inequitable socio-economic circumstances in which we live. In the long run, we ought to be changing those circumstances.[9]

Feminists within the transnational adoption community have also begun to critique the practice:

> The simplistic assumption that a poor child in a developing country will have preferred a life in a rich country is misguided, imperialistic, and overlooks the sacrifice and loss – not only to the sending country, but to the child.[10]

My understanding of transnational adoption is based, to a certain extent, on my own personal experiences. In 1972 I was adopted from a Vietnamese orphanage by white parents living in Australia. Today, I am a young woman dedicated to helping transnationally adopted individuals recognize and reconcile their cultural backgrounds, as well as address some of the key issues inherent in this form of adoption.

With this background, I examine the more hidden and problematic processes that underpin the practice of transnational adoption, with a particular emphasis on China, Korea and South East Asia. I explore the emerging politics of identity and agendas of young female activists from the transnational adoption community who are united by issues specific to adoption, but who are also beginning to develop a sense of solidarity over concerns that are connected to broader issues of sexism, racism and cross-cultural relations. An exploration into the hopes and actions of these young women can offer insight into how the personal and political tactics of 'Third World feminists' and 'women of colour'[11] can influence emergent communities and address new sites of political struggle for human rights today. My exploration moves beyond the needs of adoptive parents and brings forward less publicized issues of displacement, discrimination and complacency that can trouble the lives of orphaned children, adoptees, their parents and communities of birth.

The politics of transnational adoption

While it is true that some children are orphaned through the death or disregard of their birth parents, the presence of these orphans' birth parents and a range of complex cultural connections are often erased and made invisible through a number of confronting realities. One of the most alarming sources of orphans has been identified as the AIDS epidemic, which at the end of 2003 was responsible for 'an estimated 1.8 million orphans living in South and South-East Asia'.[12] Along with disease, natural disasters also play a role in creating orphans. The tsunami disaster of 26 December 2004, which affected a large section of Asia, is the most recent example and was responsible for creating thousands of orphans. While interest in adopting these children by communities outside Asia was initially high, a number of NGOs and international bodies, such as UNICEF, sent out a message of discouragement based on apprehensions about trafficking and the difficulties of displacement that occur with transnational adoption.

A deeper analysis of transnational adoption reveals some of the more problematic attitudes among some adoptive parents and the negative impact this can have on the children they adopt. One of the existing attitudes that hinders more responsible and respectful transnational adoptions is based on beliefs that orphaned females from Asia are like abandoned rag dolls in need of rescuing from imaginary backgrounds consisting of only abject poverty and savagery. Derogatory beliefs such as these are shaped by discourses that position the sending countries of the orphans as culturally and morally inferior. For example, Eng, a scholar of Chinese heritage, observes that transnational adoption is often explained and legitimized through 'generalized narratives of salvation – from poverty, disease, and the barbarianism of the Third World'.[13] As a result, a number of transnationally adoptive parents come to assume that orphans are naturally 'better off' in countries outside regions labelled and lumped together as being part of the 'Third World'.

Hubinette, a Korean adoptee, argues that much of the discourse used in adoption narratives sends out a clear message: 'Life in the West is best, and that people in the West have the right to adopt children from non-Western countries in the name of paternalistic humanism and developmental thinking.'[14] He also argues that if orphans are pressured to feel grateful for being 'rescued' through adoption, they are unable to reflect critically on being 'stripped of name, language, religion and culture, only retaining a fetishized non-white body, while the bonds to the biological family and the country of origin are cut off'.[15]

Mohanty offers a tactic that can be transferred to revise culturally ignorant or arrogant attitudes in transnational adoption participants. She states that while the West responds to 'Third World' poverty and instabilities, it 'cannot avoid the challenge of situating itself and examining its role in such [a] global economic and political framework'.[16] Roy challenges the US to balance its endeavour to 'rescue' orphans from some of the most troubled regions in the world with the knowledge that 'since the Second World War, the United States has been at war with or has attacked, among other countries, Korea, Guatemala, Cuba, Laos, Vietnam, Cambodia'.[17] These two endeavours seem to contradict one another in a most fundamental way.

Another process that serves to legitimize the removal of orphaned children, while denigrating and obscuring the complex causes of their availability, is based on the simplistic attitude that they are unwanted by the countries they are born into. In the context of adoptions from Asia, there is often an assumption that females are destined to be unwanted in an unchangeable and uncompassionate society.[18] Such gender bias existing in a number of locations does require critical debate with an urgent need to focus on the status of women. But some adoptive parents, and the adoption agencies that serve their desires, can also conflate and exploit this gender bias to legitimize their own needs while failing to engage in any actions that combat this gender discrimination.

The ability of transnational adoption to offer a small solution to child poverty and homelessness is not in dispute. But the fact remains that it offers no means of prevention. Transnational adoptions are made readily available by the severe neglect and lack of political will in governments, and other bodies of power, to put a range of support and protection mechanisms in place so that marginalized and economically disadvantaged families can remain bonded.

Transnational adoption also falls short of being an ideal solution to child welfare, as it can endanger the children that it is ultimately designed to assist. In 1992, Dr M. Babel, a human rights advocate and a participant in the Expert Meeting on Protecting Children's Rights in Inter-country Adoptions and Preventing Trafficking and Sale of Children, issued a warning that rushes to adopt children can 'put a very strong pressure on governments and institutions in Third World countries, obliging them to respond quickly ... without always having the necessary infrastructure and administrative mechanisms to proceed properly'.[19]

While pressure to rush adoption procedures might be humanitarian in nature, they are vulnerable to being driven by market forces. Gerow, an industry analyst, claims that Marketdata Enterprises of Tampa, Florida placed a US$1.4 billion value on adoption services in the US, with a projected annual growth rate of 11.5 per cent in 2004. One side-effect of such growth is that 'when money is as central to a human service as it is in adoption practice, money not only drives the process, but it also shapes the results'.[20]

An investigation by *Time* magazine in the early 1990s reported that:

> Every year, unscrupulous baby brokers in Asia, Latin America and now Eastern Europe hand over hundreds of children to North American and West European parents willing to pay large sums for a healthy child – and ignore evidence that the infant was obtained illegally.[21]

In other words, children were being trafficked into adoption for profit. At the same time that *Time* reported the 'baby brokers' and illegal adoptions that were occurring, the Hague Convention on Protection of Children and Co-operation in Respect of Inter-country Adoption and the United Nations Convention on the Rights of the Child (also referred to as UNROC) became formalized to combat such abuses.[22, 23]

UNROC set out guidelines that deem inter-country adoption to be a last resort for children if they cannot be placed for adoption or in foster homes in their country of origin, or if they cannot otherwise be appropriately cared for in that country. The terms of the Hague Convention on Protection of Children and Co-operation in Respect of Inter-country Adoption deem that a child is only available for adoption overseas 'when an inter-country adoption is in the child's best interests, and ... the necessary consents to the adoption have been given freely and without inducement'.[24] What is important to note is that a number of countries have not ratified the Hague Convention: including the US. Zo Randriamaro also notes that many of these commitments and human rights treaties lack effective institutional mechanisms for implementation and monitoring at the national and local levels.[25]

In the local context, connections between the rights of marginalized, disadvantaged women and transnational adoption must be made more explicit. The agency of women, fighting to keep their children within their families and communities, needs to be given wider recognition. Alternative care that exists for homeless children and single mothers outside the state-run systems of foster care programmes and shelters mostly exist in the form of non-profit projects, which are designed to care for orphans within their own communities. The Community Health Education Society (CHES) in India, run by commercial sex workers, is one such project.[26] CHES and similar cooperatives demonstrate some of the ways in which women are empowering themselves to secure their children and communities, but these are largely under-funded and lack widespread support. Many vulnerable women also lack the awareness that these, and other options, exist.[27]

I am not against transnational adoption as a small-scale and short-term way to assist children in need of material, medical and emotional care. However, I strongly feel that it is the projects that are developed through culturally respectful and women-focused approaches that offer the best long-term solution. Thus the struggle to create a new world, where the lives of children remain truly enriched and ultimately uninterrupted by family separation and community displacement, is clearly a feminist agenda being led by strong women within the most vulnerable regions in the world. What cannot be stressed enough is the fact that to underestimate or remain indifferent to these agendas and struggles is to be complicit with their subordination.

From a migration of china dolls

A number of racist, sexist and culturally loaded processes have permeated the experiences of many Asian females. In fact, 'Orientalist-thinking'[28] and Euro-centric discourses have objectified many of these orphaned Asian females as china dolls. In the context of transnational adoption, such hegemonic processes simultaneously privilege the actions and cultural backgrounds of adoptive parents, while silencing the cultural, emotional and spiritual losses of the children who join their families.

Throughout the twentieth century, and even today, the female 'china doll'[29] is one of the most evocative Western tropes used to reify the 'essence' of the women and girls from China, Korea, Japan and South East Asia.[30] Hurdis, a Korean adoptee, used this term to describe the racism and sexism experienced from friends and relatives who pressured her to be a 'good, cute little Asian'.[31] Such pressure made her feel that she was unable to speak about the losses and pain she felt in being removed from Korea, as well as being treated differently from her white adoptive family. As she matured, she felt silenced and marginalized by white males who stereotyped her as exotic and inferior. As I began to read more works by Asian feminist authors, I came across works by other transracially adopted females who also used the term 'china doll'. Each one similarly employed, and sometimes recast, the term to draw attention to how their non-white, Asian female identities are stereotyped and subordinated. For example, McKee created 'dolly rage'[32] to challenge the china doll stereotype that she was regularly labelled with. She also felt that regardless of her being Korean, the china doll stereotype allowed people to imagine that her 'Asianness' was indistinguishable from Vietnamese, Japanese or Chinese. In other words, the term is used to authorize and reproduce the mistaken assumption that all Asian females are the same.

The contested concept of femininity is at the centre of these accounts. China dolls are expected to possess innate attributes that make them beautiful, quiet, fragile and submissive, thus positioning them as objects of desire, control and domination. An example of the implications of such stereotyping is found in a study conducted in Sweden of 86 adopted girls between the ages of 13 and 18. The findings revealed that 20 per cent of the females who were adopted from overseas had experienced unpleasant sexual experiences connected to low self-esteem and subordination, which left them open to situations of abuse compared to 6 per cent of the adopted Swedish females interviewed.[33]

Transnational adoption of Asian females does not always expose them to situations of sexual abuse, but it can expose them to other variations of marginalization and racism. R. Frankenberg explains that for multi-racial children with white middle-class parents:

> Given their economic upward mobility and the stratification of US society by race linked by class, the family's class and their racial or cultural identities were now in contradiction with each other: they could either live among their economic or their ethnic peers, but not both.[34]

Children who were adopted from overseas locations including China, Korea and Vietnam into other Western countries are reported to have experienced similar dislocations through being settled into homogeneous neighbourhoods consistent with the background of adoptive parents rather than the children.[35, 36]

Unless adoptive parents have a deep understanding of and regularly practise their child's birth culture or surround their children with people who do, there is significant pressure to aspire to assimilate at the expense of their own cultural background. It is easy for this to happen within adoptive homes. But the ability to 'fit in' is limited once the child leaves their home to begin school. This is where physical differences become apparent and start to matter to their peers.

The adopted Vietnamese experience

My own personal struggles and activities illustrate some of the issues raised above; they also demonstrate some of the ways in which positive change can happen. To begin with, I can recall many instances from my own childhood where people would mistakenly assume that I would behave in 'exotic' ways, which were totally foreign and demeaning to me, because I was 'Asian'. My physical appearance attracted name-calling, cultural stereotypes and even threats of violence. My encounters with racism became so regular that there was a time when even being called 'Asian' or 'Vietnamese' seemed inescapably pejorative.

What made this situation all the more painful was that my adoptive family, who have always loved me like I was a biological daughter, were unable to help me find effective ways to recover from racist abuse and fight back. As a result, I began to internalize these racist views and refused to recognize my own cultural background. The anxiety I felt towards all things from Vietnam and Asia, including the people, became an instinctive response to the china doll stereotypes previously mentioned. But the deeply rooted tension I felt about my cultural background was also the result of my cultural dispossession.

My sense of belonging was challenged on a regular basis as outsiders asked me: 'Where are you from?' I would always struggle to find an answer to this question that I felt comfortable with. The only thing I knew about Vietnam was that it was a land of war, poverty and orphanages and I was afraid to be associated with it. I found that this made me an object of pity in the eyes of those who asked. I wanted to be seen as equal. Throughout my adolescent years, I spent a great deal of effort trying to avoid being identified as Asian, after seeing pitiful or murderous Vietnamese characters in the Hollywood Vietnam War movies that were popular in the 1980s. And yet, underneath it all, I was becoming desperate to find ways to feel more positive about my Vietnamese ancestry. Unfortunately, every book and film on Vietnam that I came across was limited to presenting Euro-centric accounts of the Vietnam War that portrayed the Vietnamese people as silent victims, sexual objects or barbaric killers.

General references about the Vietnamese having any 'worthy' cultural attributes were absent from my childhood and adolescent knowledge about Vietnam. Positive portrayals of Vietnamese women, such as the stories about the Vietnamese warrior heroines Lady Triệu and the Turng sisters, along with the other important Vietnamese characters and achievements, were also unknown to me.[37]

It was only when I left school and moved to a multicultural part of the city to study at university that I was able to meet other Vietnamese and Asian people. To my surprise, I found that I was unable to learn my birth language or culture easily. All my life I had been surrounded by people who told me I was 'Asian', and now I was confronted by the fact that I was unable to 'perform' this 'Asianness' on demand.

When I visited Vietnam for the first time in 2001, I felt even more strange and awkward. I was embarrassed that I was unable to speak Vietnamese and felt culturally different from the people of my birth land. I wanted to feel an instant connection, but I had to accept that it would take time. My own ideas about Vietnam and its people, filtered through my Western upbringing, were seen as racist, laughable and even pitiful by other Vietnamese people. My own cultural ignorance and arrogance about Vietnam showed itself in how I interacted with situations of poverty, discussions of the Vietnam War, or the 'American War', as it was known in my homeland, and a variety of other cultural differences.

After reaching out to other adopted Vietnamese people, I realized that I was not the only person who was unable to reconcile easily with their cultural history. Meeting other transnationally adopted people through a variety of different networks[38] helped me to discover that my reality was unusual, but not unique. Along with providing a sense of belonging, these meetings have also assisted Vietnamese adoptees to have the confidence to reconnect with their cultural background. Anne (pseudonym), a female Vietnamese adoptee, offers insight into some of the reasons why she once rejected and is now reclaiming Vietnamese ancestry into her identity. She recalls: 'When I was a child, saying I was born in Vietnam was like confessing a defect.'[39] She feels she is now able to talk about her heritage partly because she has built a sense of resilience to racism after meeting other adoptees and going to Vietnam in 1994. She was eager to assert that: 'I [now] feel much more proud of my background, I even insist on talking about it.' However, she revealed some disappointment in her interactions with non-adopted Vietnamese. 'As we are adoptees we are not considered fully Vietnamese.'

Our transforming sense of identity is a work in progress rather than automatic. Our cultural differences from the people who share our birth culture are repeatedly identified by members of my community as being a main source of tension. The most obvious is the language barrier. We are limited by our lack of ability to speak our mother tongue. This means we are dependent on others to meet us on unequal terms by having to speak to us in English, or by using translators. This can be as impractical as it can be painful. We are often denied a chance to communicate with other Vietnamese people in a deep and meaningful way. We are denied the opportunity to connect with Vietnamese literature, poems, films and media reportage. The challenge that lies ahead is to mentally return to the state of a child and relearn Vietnamese culture and language, starting from the basics.

Language barriers can be overcome with time. A deeper challenge that we face is finding ways to align our personal sense of connection, and emerging sense of politics, with those of our natural mothers and others in our homeland. Our struggles to reconnect with them after being raised in a different culture and country are further exacerbated by the false notion that forms of cultural belonging and solidarity must equate or be reduced to 'a complex whole' based on 'homogeneity, coherence and continuity'.[40]

This notion is contradicted by contemporary conflicts and shifting alliances that occur between the diverse ethnic, political and religious groups in both our homeland and the diaspora. Furthermore, if we consider these and other instances of cultural disorder across all regions, then we are pushed to recognize that no cultural identities can be easily reduced to any one true essence or neatly located within clear boundaries. As individuals who are transnationally adopted, we need not avoid or feel ashamed by the fact that there is something distinctively different about our own sense of identity that makes us a part of, and sets us apart from, others. Identity and belonging are constructed through complex relationships, not innate attributes.

Our physical differences from people who share our adoptive parents' background, and cultural differences from those of our birth culture, can result in our experiencing a disturbing sense of unrequited ethnicity. Yet as we navigate our way through others' expectations that we seamlessly fit within our birth or adoptive cultures, our struggles to do so prove to us, and to others, how flexible, unfixed and strategic all such identities really are. The next challenge that lies ahead for my community is to identify further what new space we wish to occupy, what new world we wish to create and who we want to join us on this quest.[41]

Stepping outside the doll's house: strategies for creating a new world

Transnational adoptees' efforts to be reconciled with, and assist in protecting the rights of the communities who share their birth culture can be strengthened through sharing their struggles and successes with other culturally diverse activists. For the adopted female activists, this includes sharing our particular concerns and challenges with women from indigenous communities, the homeland and the diaspora, in the hope that we can learn from and support each other. Without such exchanges we are denying ourselves the opportunity to understand the broader issues of sexism, racism and cultural discrimination that profoundly affect women, and their children, across the globe.

For example, works by numerous feminist writers from across the globe have already begun to outline paths of resistance through new ways of thinking and expanding our analysis.[42] This will no doubt assist transnationally adopted women to further develop our own political agendas. In addition, academia is just one area where women can initiate new alliances and share strategies of resistance to, and recovery from, hegemonic forces. This work can offer transnational adoptees a range of effective intellectual tools to deconstruct racist, Euro-centric and sexist representations that denigrate and subordinate our own cultural backgrounds and identities.

Many of the women with whom we interact are white middle-class women. Such women may be our mothers, schoolfriends, neighbours, teachers or work colleagues. This is because of the racially privileged networks we have been exposed to over our lives. The majority of individuals who publish research about adoption are also white women.[43] While their own insights into adoption issues can be equally valid and informative, some fail to acknowledge that many, now mature, transracial adoptees also have a valid and informative opinion about who they are, what they feel and what they need, from their own perspectives.

However, we must be mindful of not re-creating a world constructed through binaries and polarities of 'us and them'. We want collaboration. While a hierarchy of race privilege in the West does distance our means to psychologically, socially and culturally connect evenly with white women, this equally diverse cultural group, which is also open to transformation, can offer us strong and strategic allies in our fight against racism and other forms of oppression. Rather than seeing the white cultural backgrounds of the women we know as a factor that can dissolve our relationships, we need to encourage them to enter into new discussions on how they can use their own ethnicity as a means to promote dynamic social changes from 'inside' their current location of racial and structural privilege.

So, what are the main changes that young women who are transnationally adopted aim for, using the tools of feminism and a rights-based framework? What new world do we want to create? One is a world in which no woman and/or family is physically, financially, socially or culturally coerced into giving up their child. Gender-focused human rights groups can raise public awareness about such situations, in our home bases and in realms suitable for gaining international attention, such as in conferences, the media, on websites and in publications. We can also pursue activities that force governments in our homelands to take responsibility for their most disadvantaged citizens, instead of allowing them to be displaced and dispossessed, by getting involved with adoption policy forums, councils and governing bodies.

Such changes are rarely made suddenly. Returning to the limited but concrete viability of transnational adoption, the practice still remains an option for dealing with the millions of children around the world who are left homeless and without enough support or stability to provide them with safe shelter. Overseas adoption is sometimes the only alternative for the survival of a number of these children. Accepting this reality, we must aim to ensure that adoption does not become a profitable industry that is based on meeting the needs of traffickers and their unethical and/or unknowing clientele. It must be based on meeting the needs of the children, and not caught up with the 'supply' and 'demand' of a market-driven endeavour. The procedures that allow adoptions to take place must be strictly guarded and closely scrutinized by the international community, and support must be given to those who are locally involved as gatekeepers.

Finally, we need to send out a clear message that the act of transnational adoption carries with it serious long-term responsibilities. Adoptive parents must ensure that their adopted child's right to remain in contact with surviving biological relatives and the cultural background of their birthplace is sufficiently maintained and respected. People who adopt children from overseas can achieve this only by working together with people who share the birth culture of their children. The benefits of this are two-fold. First, it can assist with maintaining orphans' sense of connection to their homeland. Second, it can bring diverse groups of people together, uniting them through a common purpose.

Conclusion

In summary, the strategies I have proposed do not set out to create a world where different types of people are divided and antagonistic towards each other. What I hope to have introduced is a quest that can bring a diverse range of people together to create a world where differences and diversity are respected. The ever-expanding networks and activities, process of identity, and sense of home and homeland in transnationally adopted females are undergoing radical shifts and transformations. While not without challenge, this new stage in our history is opening us to new forms of empowerment and belonging that previously seemed out of reach. We are no longer as vulnerable to pressures to assimilate into our host culture or revert to static and reified cultural stereotypes of our homeland culture in order to make sense of our lives. Instead, we are capable of creating a new world where our experiences can be shared with other women across borders; one day, it is to be hoped, bringing the different places and people of our past, present and future together in such a way that we can not only survive, but thrive in solidarity.

Notes

1 The terms 'Third World', 'Asia', the 'South' and 'developing countries' are all deeply problematic as they homogenize diverse peoples and regions

that often may have little in common with each other, while subordinating their status, as they are set in contrast, and positioned as lower than regions deemed to be part of the 'First World', 'North' and 'West'. Such terms also fail to acknowledge the complex relationships, intense flows and multiple transformations these regions may share with each other. Despite the contested nature of these terms, they are sometimes used to offer convenient markers of cultural identity, geographical location, political alliances and position in global wealth distribution.

2 P. Selman (18–34 August 2001), 'The movement of children for intercountry adoption: A demographic perspective', paper presented at the International Migration – Macro: 24th IUSSP General Population Conference, El Salvador, Brazil, pp. 1–20.

3 L. D. Hollingsworth (1999), 'Symbolic interactionism, African American families, and the transracial adoption controversy', *Social Work*, 44(5): 443.

4 T. Volkman (2003), 'Special trans-national adoption issue', *Social Text*, 21(1): 1–109.

5 Ibid.

6 USCB (2004), 'CB04-FFSE.12: Special edition – National adoption', US Census Bureau (USCB), accessed 17 January 2005, see <http://www.census.gov/Press-Release/www/releases/archives/facts_for_features_special_editions/002683.html>.

7 The terms 'sender' and 'receiver' countries are often used to describe the migration patterns of moving orphans from the 'Third World' to the 'West', which is typical in transnational adoption.

8 M. S. Serril (21 October 1991), 'Going abroad to find a baby', *Time*, 138(16): 86–9.

9 Ibid.

10 S. Cox (3–5 November 2002), 'International adoption: problems and solutions, testimony of Susan Soon-keum Cox', House Committee on International Relations, Accessed 1 October, 2004, see <http://wwwc.house.gov/international_relations/107/cox0522.htm>.

11 The terms 'Third World feminism' and 'women of colour' were both developed as a means to describe and make distinct women activists whose agendas fall outside the main focus and concern of Western feminism, which has predominantly looked at the specific needs of women with white racial and cultural backgrounds. Taken from R. Frankenberg (1999), *White Women, Race Matters: The Social Construction of Whiteness* (Minneapolis: University of Minnesota Press).

12 J. Fredriksson, A. Kanabus and R. Noble (2004), 'HIV/AIDS orphans statistics', Avert Organisation, accessed 7 January 2005, see <http://www.avert.org/aidsorphans.htm>.

13 D. Eng (2003), 'Transnational adoption and queer diasporas', *Social Text*, 21(3): 1–37.

14 T. Hubinette (2003), 'Adopted Koreans and the development of identity in the "Third Space"', *Adoption and Fostering*, 27(4): 1–9.

15 Ibid.

16 C. T. Mohanty (1999), 'Feminist scholarship, colonial discourses', in B. Ashcroft, G. Griffiths and H. Tiffin (eds), *The Post-Colonial Studies Reader* (London: Routledge), pp. 259–68.

17 A. Roy (2004), *The Ordinary Person's Guide to Empire* (London: HarperCollins).

18 K. Miller-Loessi and Z. Kilic (2001), 'A unique diaspora? The case of adopted girls from the People's Republic of China', *Diaspora*, 10(2): 243–60.

19 V. Altman (1995), 'Baby trafficking or inter-country adoption', *Signposts to Asia and the Pacific: Australian Centre for Independent Journalism* (ACIJ), accessed 21 August 2003, see <http://www.signposts.uts.edu.au/articles/Australia/Children/333.html>.

20 M. Groenig (2002), 'The complexity of adoption ethics', *Adoption in Society and Ethics*, accessed 10 July 2002, see <http://www.neo-vox.net/~bcadoption/articles/ethics/ethics.htm>.

21 M. S. Serril (21 October 1991), 'Going abroad to find a baby', *Time*, 138(16): 86–9.

22 Hague Conference on Private International Law (1995), 'Convention on Protection of Children and Co-operation in Respect of Inter-country Adoption', see < http://hcch.e-vision.nl/index_en.php?act=conventions.text&cid=69>.

23 National Youth Advocacy Service (n.d.), 'UN Convention on the Rights of the Child', see <http://www.nyas.net/unroc.html>.

24 THC (1993), 'Hague Convention of 29 May 1993 on Protection of Children and Co-operation in Respect of Inter-country Adoption', Hague Conference on Private International Law.

25 Z. Randriamaro (2004), '"We, the women": the United Nations, feminism and economic justice', *AWID Spotlight*, 1(2): 1–12.

26 World Bank (2001), 'Spotlight on India's AIDS control efforts: grassroots projects the key to success', media release of the World Bank Group.

27 Altman (1995), 'Baby trafficking or inter-country adoption'.

28 E. Said (1991), *Orientalism* (New York: Penguin).

29 The term china doll is thought to have first appeared in the literary work of the author P. Loti, a Frenchman, to denote passive, Japanese females he developed a fetish for during his travels in the early part of the twentieth century. Since then, feminists have noted that the term has gained popular use to refer to any Asian female who is imagined to be childlike, compliant and appealingly exotic. Taken from P. Loti (1901), *Madame Chrysanthème* (London: Routledge).

30 It is useful to note that various tropes are used to reify and subordinate females from Island nations, South Asia, Africa and Latin America, where transnational adoption is also practised. This chapter focuses on a particular region of Asia, but the hegemonic practices involved are transferable across the globe.

31 R. Hurdis (2002), 'Heartbroken: women of color and the Third Wave', in D. Hernandez and B. Rehman (eds), *Colonize This!* (New York: Seal Press), pp. 279–92.

32 K. McKee (2001), 'The Other Sister', in V. Nam, *Yell-oh Girls: Emerging Voices Explore Culture, Identity and Growing Up Asian American* (New York: HarperCollins), pp. 142–4.

33 K. Berg-Kelly and J. Ericksson (1997), 'Adaptation of adopted foreign children at mid-adolescence as indicated by aspects of health and risk-taking – a population study', *European Child and Adolescent Psychiatry*, 6(1): 199–206.

34 Frankenberg, *White Women, Race Matters*.

35 Hubinette, 'Adopted Koreans and the development of identity in the "Third Space"'.

36 M. Sarup (1996), *Identity, Culture and the Postmodern World* (Edinburgh: Edinburgh University Press).

37 I. Williams Willing (2004), 'The adopted Vietnamese community: from fairytales to the diaspora', in Special Edition 'Vietnam Beyond the Frame', *Michigan Quarterly Review*, 43(4): 648–64.

38 I first began to meet other Vietnamese adoptees by using the internet. I developed a website and e-group in Australia called Adopted Vietnamese International <www.adoptedVietnamese.org>, which was launched in April 2000 on the twenty-fifth anniversary of the end of the 'Vietnam/American War'.

39 Williams Willing, 'The Adopted Vietnamese community: from fairytales to the diaspora'.

40 H. R. Wicker (2000), 'From complex culture to cultural complexity', in P. Werbner and T. Modood (eds), *Debating Cultural Hybridity: Multicultural Identities and the Politics of Anti-Racism* (New Jersey: Zed Books), pp. 29–45.

41 H. Bhabha proposes that more open, fluid and often contradictory forms of identification and solidarity can be played out in a 'Third Space' that is loosely situated 'in between' any polarities based on notions of 'us' and 'them'. He explains that within this space: 'affiliation may be antagonistic or ambivalent; solidarity may only be situational and strategic: commonality is often negotiated through the "contingency" of social interests and political claims'. Taken from H. Bhabha (1996), 'Culture's in-between', in S. Hall and P. du Gray (eds), *Questions of Cultural Identity* (London: Sage Publications), pp. 53–60.

42 A non-exhaustive list of some of these feminist writers, in no particular order, includes G. Anzaldua, a female Chicana activist and writer, G. Spivak, a female academic born in India, and L. T. Smith, a Maori female academic from Aotearoa New Zealand, who have detailed strategies on how to cope with border crossings, shifting identities and situations of being marginalized.

43 For example, S. Patton (2000), *Birthmarks: Transracial Adoption in Contemporary America* (New York: New York University Press); and R. J. Simon and H. Altstein (2000), *Adoption Across Borders: Serving the Children in Transracial and Inter-country Adoptions* (Maryland: Rowman and Littlefield).

A call for solidarity across borders

8 | www.coming? Imaginings on a world of wealth and well-being[1]

ANASUYA SENGUPTA

Nafsa woke up to the smell of fresh kapi. Vishwa must be up, she thought – and ready to leave for work. Unis and Vasudhi were both out on assignments; Unis was healing someone in Europa, while Vasudhi was researching an article for her Wiser. Luckily it was Nafsa's week off – she had just returned from a vibrant new town in Latina, where she had been working on the construction of a Community centre – and she had time enough before she checked where she was going to next, and what she would be doing there. She lay in bed for a minute, working out dates in her head. If this is Tuesday ... it must be the B-time next Wednesday, she calculated. The WWW always factored in hormones. So next week would be a less gruelling task: perhaps some transcription work out of home, or an easy knitting job. Repetitive tasks with minimal need for sustained intellectual effort were always a stress-reliever when the body decided to have its lunar letting of blood, and adequate rest was something that the WWW not just appreciated, but insisted upon.

She walked into the shower, calling out as she did, 'Warm and lavender-tinged this morning, Rei.' Which it was. Wonderful how Rei processed the simplest wishes in the most magical of ways – although SHe still needed language of some kind or the other for activation. Nafsa suspected, though, that there would soon be a morning when she would walk in and be treated to a super-delicious soaking just the way she had thought of it in her head – Rei was definitely working on subliminal messaging.

A process that Vishwa had worked out to perfection. A hot cup of kapi, some lightly scrambled eggs and warm idlis were waiting for her, as she walked into the foodroom. Vishwa was half-way through his own breakfast, and scanning the information pages. She kissed him on her way to her own console. 'Any news on the WWW Council's latest updates with Rei?' she asked. 'The Mystory archives of the pre-Council times?'

'Well, you're the one who's going to be discussing them later today,' he replied. 'Your Wiser session with Cathy is scheduled for about an hour from when you finish eating. Aren't you discussing times of mal-wealth with her? What did they call it then?'

'Poverty,' she exclaimed. 'And what kind of Wiser am I, who forgets to check in with Rei while soaking? SHe must have realized – was my meeting schedule transmitted in on your information page?'

'Yes,' Vishwa said. 'Along with pictures of Unis smiling at his healee, and Vasudhi complaining about missing us. But you better get Moving soon; I charged your mobility card for you. It's waiting at the door.'

Nafsa escalated down to the street level and walked into the nearest Move-Around. She flashed her card in, and closed her eyes as it flew quietly towards the WWW Centre near their home. Sun machines were such a comfortable way to travel, she thought. Although the street Move-Abouts were more interesting – they went slower, and you could chat with friends on another street, and watch the children as they played in the nearby Commonspace. But if Cathy had checked in with Rei, she would know Nafsa was on her way, and would probably soon be at the centre herself. As a Wiser, Nafsa enjoyed their Mystory conversations – the past was always fascinating, and collective memory was what had made this a gentler, happier world. The Council asked every person to take regular Mystory classes – and a Wiser's role was to share information on the Mystory times they had researched the most; with great support, of course, from Rei's processing systems.

Cathy was waiting for her at the entrance to the WWW Centre. As Nafsa gave her a hug, Cathy called out to Rei to open up the Chatspace. A side wall slid up immediately, and Nafsa and Cathy walked into a comfortable room with an array of single and shared consoles. They chose a shared console facing each other, and asked Rei to turn on the archives.

'So what do you understand about mal-wealth?' Nafsa asked. 'And what do you want to know from me and Rei?'

Cathy thought for a moment. 'Well, you know I've been trying to understand how the WWW was begun – and what is so different about our World of Wealth and Well-being. Why is it so different? I suppose the Mystory of mal-wealth is part of the difference ... '

'Yes,' Nafsa replied. 'Certainly, the ways to understand and remove mal-wealth were very much part of the Mystory of the WWW. But remember that it was only about 300 years ago that the Council was formed – and its centres were set up all over worldspace soon after. For about 350 years before that, humankindness had been trying to understand what they called "poverty" ... What it meant, how to measure it, how to remove it ... '

'Perhaps then we should be looking at the Mystory of around 200 pre-Council?' Cathy quickly asked. 'Because it would tie up with that fascinating Mystory you and I were exploring some time ago – the Femstory, "feminism" ... Do you remember?'

Nafsa laughed, 'Oh, of course I do! You were my Wiser for that one; you

111

were obsessed with the stories of women and men who had completely changed peoplestyles ... changed the ways they lived, the ways they treated each other and finally changed the ways everyone else lived too ... Thank kindness they did, it sounded like a very strange worldspace then. I know you'd have loved to have been part of that Mystory, but I'm very happy where I am now. My well-being would have dropped by a hundred flash, if I'd even Moved past a world like that! I think you're correct, though, the two Mystories come together at some point. It would have been natural that they did meet, wouldn't it?'

Just at that moment, the consoles beeped at them disconsolately. Rei was starting to feel left out of this conversation ...

Perhaps you would like to flash straight into the 200 pre-Council archives? The archives could display some of the Mystory sources behind understanding mal-wealth, and then you could discuss the Femstory links to it.

'That sounds excellent, Rei,' Cathy grinned. 'Thank you for steering us past chat time and into Mystory time!'

The vocabulary and language of poverty (from the archives 200–325 pre-Council; 1880–2005 AD)

Poverty is both reality and myth. People's perceptions of who is 'poor' and who is not have varied over socio-cultural time and space. There are numerous words for the poor in every world language. In Persian, for instance, there are more than 30 words for the poor; every language in Africa has at least three to five words for poverty. In the Middle Ages, there were over forty Latin words covering the range of conditions encompassing the concept of poverty (Rahnema 1997 AD).[2]

'It's quite strange,' said Cathy. 'Why was being "poor" so difficult to understand? Surely peoplekindness could have expressed how they felt? Was it their peoplestyles that didn't help them? I mean, everyone now knows when their well-being count changes ... '

'I think it was a complex problem,' Nafsa replied. 'Like that pre-Council game that Vishwa told us about the other day? The jigsaw ... Lots of pieces that needed to come together for the worldspace to be seen ... Most importantly, they didn't have Rei to help with worldspace perception. Everyone understood how they lived differently, but they couldn't always communicate it to each other. There was a story I read which talked about how in a little inhabitation in pre-Council times, that very few people visited, nobody understood what being "poor" was. And then when there were more visitors, there was also more of the outside worldspace that came in to that inhabitation, and their peoplestyles changed. They wanted things they didn't have ... and suddenly, ten years after they said they didn't know "poverty", they were pleading with visitors to help, talking about how they were "so poor" ... '[3]

Cathy looked upset. She walked across from the console to the food panel at the side of the Chatspace. She knew Nafsa loved kapi at all times of the day, and asked for one of those, along with her own calming favourite, a sanguina. As she was waiting for them to be beeped through, she turned back to listen to Nafsa, who was reading out from Rei again.

According to normal usage, poverty is '[t]he state of one who lacks a usual or socially acceptable amount of money or material possessions' (Kanbur and Squire 1999 AD: 5).[4]

Cathy walked back to the consoles, sipping her sanguina. She gave Nafsa the kapi, and then stared at her own console. 'So some people understood what mal-wealth was about ... It meant not having enough wealth. That's what "money" and "material possessions" meant, didn't they?'

Nafsa smiled. 'The pre-Council jigsaw was a very complicated game, Cathy. Most people then didn't understand wealth the same way we do. They thought having or not having money, meant being or not being, "poor". And yet, money was different across worldspace, different across units of inhabitation. One unit of money didn't mean the same thing to everyone. Think about it in our worldspace – very few peoplekind even use the word "money" any more. Our WWW cards measure costs of Options and Opportunities – and that, for us, is the closest we come to the pre-Council system of money, or income and expenditure. The costs and the entitles of worldspace Options and Opportunities measured against our individual work and leisure rhythm cycles are what we call wealth, and Rei helps us calculate and distribute this justly. But there were very few people who were starting to see it that way then ... '

'But Nafsa, didn't they have any ways to understand mal-wealth then? I mean, the way Rei helps us to measure our wealth helps us improve our well-being counts ... Wouldn't that have been the same then? Trying to understand how to measure "poverty" would have helped peoplekind with strategies to reduce it?'

'You're a wise woman, Cathy! That's exactly what was important, then – the way you named, or "defined" "poverty", gave you a particular way to create strategies to reduce it.[5] The only problem was that there were so many different namings, so many different definitions, that no one really agreed on what to do or how to do it!'

The measurement of poverty and strategies of poverty alleviation (from the archives 200–325 pre-Council; 1880–2005 AD)

While there is worldwide agreement on poverty reduction as an overriding goal of development policy, there is little agreement on the definition of poverty. [Among others, there are] four approaches to the definition and measurement of poverty – the monetary, capability, social exclusion and participatory approaches ... [E]ach is a construction of reality, involving numerous judgements, which are often not transparent. The different methods have different implications for policy, and also, to the extent that they point to different people as being poor, for targeting ... Empirical work in Peru and India shows that there is significant lack of overlap between the methods with, for example, nearly half the population identified as in poverty according to monetary poverty [but] not in capability poverty, and conversely. This confirms similar findings elsewhere. Hence the definition of poverty does matter for poverty eradication strategies (Ruggeri Laderchi, Saith and Stewart 2003 AD: 1).[6]

Nafsa was explaining this archive to Cathy. 'It may seem strange to us now, but back in the pre-Council years, it was practically impossible to agree on how to measure poverty. Humankind didn't know what concerns to include in its definition, whether this definition would apply across cultures and nations, whether to rely on perception or statistical data, and finally, what it was that really separated the "poor" from the "non-poor" – were there some kind of disjunctures that made this more visible?'

Cathy grew excited. 'Oh, but surely they looked at both individual and humankind perceptions? After all, that's what Rei helps us do – consolidate our individual perceptions into a larger worldspace mapping of wealth and well-being.'

The consoles beeped happily. Rei was clearly delighted to have SHe's presence acknowledged.

Nafsa laughed. 'Well, Rei is an extraordinary creation of the Council's Techno-Wisers, Cathy. About three hundred pre-Council years ago, it would have been difficult to imagine a process in which every single humankind was able to flash his or her perceptions of well-being into Rei's analytical consoles, and have that mapped against the Council's wealth and well-being counts. That's the knowledge that's now stored on our WWW cards, and that's what allows us to work and rest, to live according to a justice of options and opportunities.'

'You mean there was no idea-image of justice then? How did they live with kindness?'

'Of course they had idea-images of justice! They had had them for a few thousand pre-Council years, but they weren't able to agree on it for all of worldspace, exactly like their idea-images of poverty. They didn't know whether to measure mal-wealth for an individual humankind, or for their homeunit, or for a Commonspace inhabitation ... or for what geographical location ... They also didn't have Rei's capacities for measuring different aspects of wealth or mal-wealth across worldspace and consolidating these counts and they certainly weren't sure for what moments or periods of time they should be measuring these changes.'[7]

'Were homeunits like those we have now?' Cathy asked. 'Because I remember that was one of the inner Mystorys of the Femstory – how people lived in homeunits, that they called "households", and whether they shared the homeunit justly.'

'Now that's what I call a Wiser winder, Cathy! I can't remember exactly how they defined the homeunit then, but I'm fairly certain that it wasn't both choice and bloodline, as it is now. I think it was only bloodline, and only two people were allowed to be Parents. Most often, one man humankind, and one woman humankind ... Certainly, a homeunit like yours or mine, with three or four Parents, and Children by both choice and bloodline, would have seemed very strange to them ... '

Rei flashed at them. A reminder that Cathy's 'Wiser winder' was definitely winding them away from the Mystory of the moment.

The monetary approach to poverty measurement [is] a set of techniques and methodologies, adopted mostly by economists, based on the identification of poverty with a shortfall in a monetary indicator and the 'objective' derivation of a poverty line (Ruggeri Laderchi 2000 AD: 3).[8]

Cathy sipped her sanguina, again thoughtful. 'Does that mean that this approach was based on how much below a poverty line a personkind was, and that the line was measured in terms of wealth?'

'Well, wealth in the pre-Council days: money wealth. They measured it either as earnings, or what they called consumption, how much you spent of these money earnings. You can imagine that this was limitative in many ways; it was based on individuals, not humankindness as a whole, it assumed that measuring spending and earnings in money terms could apply similarly across different kinds of individuals, with some adjustments in their data ... But I suppose that in pre-Council times, money value was one of the few ways to measure wealth of other kinds – well-being as we understand it ourselves.'[9]

'And who were economists, Nafsa?'

'Ah, that's a whole other Wiser session, Cathy, and I'm not sure I'm the one who can chat with you about them! They were Techno-Wisers, I think, but only about issues around money ... I'm not very sure, though, we should ask Vasudhi when she Moves home ... Once humankindness stopped seeing wealth and well-being as being only about money, they lost much of their importance ... '

The relevance of economic performance is that it may be a means to an end. That end is not the consumption of beefburgers, nor the accumulation of television sets, nor the vanquishing of some high level of interest rates, but rather the enrichment of mankind's feeling of well-being. Economic things matter only in so far as they make people happier (Oswald 1997 AD: 1815).[10]

'Before you ask, beefburgers were a kind of food, and television sets were the pre-Council Parents of Rei's consoles! I think the reason Rei's flashed this to us, is for us to remember that not all economists were limitative in their idea-images; not all of them agreed about this monetary measurement of poverty. So there were other idea-images, some of which led to the creation of the Council itself ... For instance, there was one whose knowledge was quite important in the way peoplekind began to understand well-being, a little like we know it today. He described what he called capabilities ... '

[Sen's] capability approach calls for people to have the largest possible set of valuable functionings among which people can then choose a life they have reason to value. Among the basic capabilities are the ability to be lead a long life in good health, be well nourished, educated, housed and adequately clothed, and integrated into the community (Klasen 2004 AD: 5).[11]

'So for this Techno-Wiser, poverty was the failure to achieve basic capabilities.[12] He felt that well-being was not based on the fulfilment of desires, measured through consumption, because it didn't consider the physicalities of the individual personkind. Instead, he said, well-being was the process of extending the choices of all peoplekind.'

'So rather than focusing on means, like having money for food, the capability idea-image looked at ends, like being nourished ... [13] Is that what it was, Nafsa?' Cathy asked excitedly. She was beginning to see how this had led to the worldspace she now inhabited.

'Yes, exactly. It looked at a range of different ways to make all human-kindness less poor, from both money earnings, as well as services like better health, food, learning ... And those who believed in this approach started seeing mal-wealth as we see it now – not just about peoplestyles in terms of money, but also political and cultural peoplestyles ... '

'But it feels as though both these idea-images still looked at the individual peoplekind, Nafsa. Didn't they see them also as group inhabitants, like we do now? Like you said before, Rei analyses both together ... '

Rei sent a spark of starworks across the consoles, with a couple of meteor tails writing out 'Thank you ... ' as they blazed past. Depending on who was heading the Council on which day, SHe's sense of humour was either extremely subtle and ironic, or rather exuberant and Child-like. As Nafsa and Cathy smiled at each other, they both knew exactly who was at the Council headcentre today!

The European Union defines Social Exclusion as a: 'process through which individuals or groups are wholly or partially excluded from full participation in the society in which they live' (European Foundation 1995) (from Ruggeri Laderchi, Saith and Stewart 2003 AD: 20).[14]

Nafsa looked at this archive for a little while, trying to understand how best to explain it to Cathy. 'Do you remember when we discussed world-space as divided over time, into geographical units called countries, rather than our virtual units of WWW centres that are also mapped on to a few Community cultural centres at a time? Well, a particularly large unit in pre-Council Europa wanted to describe how poverty affected both poor and non-poor countries; some people in non-poor countries could also be described as "poor", they said, because they could not participate in all activities and enjoy all opportunities of that country ... So you were correct in that the previous two approaches we were archiving were both based on individual humankind. But you can see that this is different, can't you?'

'Yes, like saying that if a Community centre couldn't access a WWW unit, they would all be "poorer" than those of us who can ... Is that correct, Nafsa?'

'Precisely, Cathy! Not that the Council would accept that ever happening in present-time, but in some ways, that is exactly what did happen to the poor in pre-Council days. They couldn't access their councils, or governments, in the same ways as others. And often, certain groups of peoplekind were "excluded" all together ... like people who were Elder, or Dif-Abled ... '

'Can you imagine Vasudhi not being able to access the Council because she has limited out-sight?' Cathy grinned. 'She's one of their most important members when she's not away on work! And all the sensory clothes she wears that Rei is so proud of creating ... We should send Rei back in time to make certain no one feels "excluded" in any way – I'm sure SHe would make sure the councils worked for everykind, not just some peoplekind!'

'Hmm ... before Rei starts showering us with actual starworks in SHe's happiness, let's move on, shall we?' asked Nafsa. 'Rei, could you flash us any archives on the last approach we wanted to discuss? The participatory ways of measuring mal-wealth?'

PRA (participatory rural appraisal) is defined as 'a growing family of approaches and methods to enable local people to share, enhance and analyse their knowledge of life and conditions, to plan and to act' (Chambers

www.coming?

1994 AD: 57). Participatory Poverty Assessments (PPA) evolved from this methodology.[15]

'This approach came out of a well-intended attempt to make certain that those who were "poor" participated in the decisions made about understanding their peoplestyles in order to measure how poor they were ... So many of the People-Changes in the pre-Council times were brought from outside the communities, that this approach made people the centre of their own Mystories of change ... '

'But Nafsa ...' Cathy looked surprised. 'Weren't the people themselves the Councillors, like we have now? Didn't they all get a chance to be part of these ... "governments", like our Councils? I mean, that's why Rei randomly chooses us to be on the Council, because each of us has a Vision for our Communities, and we get Opportunity to express how we feel. And Rei and we work together to discuss with our Communities what People-Changes we all might need, and how we must act upon them.'

'In pre-Council times, Cathy,' Nafsa replied, 'there were many more levels of Council than we have now, but the most important level was not at the Community level of the WWW centres as it is for us, it was at the Country and Inter-Country levels of the WWW centres. People disremembered that the further you are from your communities, the less you remember their needs ... Now, of course, our virtual units mean that Rei is in constant scan with all the WWW centres in worldspace, and it is only a few Wisers and Councillors who need to be at the worldspace WWW Council, and even they keep Moving between their own Community headcentre and the worldspace Council.'

'Coming back to the "participatory" approach, Nafsa, wasn't it necessary to have both in-sight and ex-sight to measure mal-wealth? It's again what we do with Rei – we flash in our own counts of wealth and well-being, and Rei analyses that against the Community counts and the other WWW centre counts ... isn't that so? Is it possible for us to have an entirely correct view of our own and our Community well-being without this process?'

'That's an excellent point, Cathy, and one that the Wisers of pre-Council times had to think about a lot. Another issue was that in those days, Communities were much more unequal than they are now, and so not all peoplekind had Opportunity to participate. And really, was it Techno-Wisers from outside who did these "assessments" or the Communities themselves? Who analysed the information, and what did it mean for People-Change, the process they called "policy"?[16] It was an important step, though, in pre-Council times, to return to the Communities ... '

'Umm ... can we return home now, Nafsa? This is a lot of Wiser-session to process, and we still have the Femstory to discuss. I need to do a little more archiving on that, considering it's my area of interest ... '

'Fine, Cathy, check in with Rei or me tomorrow, and we can decide when to meet. Don't dream about mal-wealth!'

'I have other things to dream about, Nafsa,' Cathy said wickedly. 'Flash you tomorrow!'

Feminist perspectives on poverty (from the archives 200–1100 pre-Council; 1105–2005 AD)

As Nafsa was soaking in her orange-sprinkled and cool shower the next morning, Rei flashed three times, and activated a voice connection to Cathy.

'Are you in your shower right now, Nafsa? Didn't you think a sight of you would energize me for the day?' Cathy laughed.

'It might energize you, my Witty one, but it would probably drop my well-being by a few counts!' Nafsa replied. 'Are we meeting again today?'

'Yes, please ... Rei and I have a little surprise planned for you. I was working on it all day yesterday, after our session. See you at the Centre!'

A few hours later, Nafsa was sitting at a console in the WWW Centre, looking across at Cathy expectantly. 'And what's this little surprise, Cathy? Rei's been sending smilies and laughies across the screens and the walls all the while I've been waiting for you.'

'Well,' said Cathy, looking uncannily like the holo-images Rei was flashing by at that very moment, 'we've looked at a few concepts of mal-wealth in pre-Council times, and we'd promised to link it to the Femstory that I'd been working on. So Rei and I decided to put the two together in a rather Creationary way ... let us introduce you to Akka!'

'I can introduce myself, thank you, Cathy,' said a lilting voice from somewhere behind Nafsa. 'After all, having come through unlikely worlds and eighty-four hundred thousand vaginas,[17] give or take a few thousand, I'm sure I can speak this strange language you use these days. Besides, Kannada was the language of my tongue, only Cathy and Rei have transformed it into the English you understand ... '

Nafsa nearly slid off her console seat while it was spinning round to see where the voice came from. Just behind her, almost Her-size, was the holo-image of a naked woman with long hair streaming down her back.

'What Cathy and Rei have done, as I understand it, is to have created an Arti-Intel woman – whatever that means – comprising the thoughts of various feminists through the pre-Council ages, to help you understand how they understood their worlds of poverty and well-being. Quite clever, I must say ... If the monster my daughter had created had even a little

119

of the intelligence you've poured into me, her story on that silly creature would not have eclipsed my writings on women.[18] Hmmph!'

Nafsa looked entirely bewildered. Cathy, on the other hand, was smiling delightedly. 'Sorry, Nafsa, because Akka's a Creationary collage of various Femstories through pre-Council times, she does tend to jump from being one woman to another. It's a little confusing, but I need more time to work on her. For now, we'll try and get her to concentrate on the mal-wealth story. Akka, can you think about 200 pre-Council and tell us about how issues of poverty were seen by Feminists of that time?'

Before Akka could answer, Rei, clearly not willing to be left out of the conversation, had flashed another piece from the archives.

'Feminization of poverty' has come to mean not (as gender analysis would suggest) that poverty is a gendered experience, but that the poor are mostly women (Jackson 1996 AD: 491).[19]

'The answer, my friend, is blowing in the wind ... ' Akka sang. 'Oops, sorry both, memories carry me away. And the answers are always being lost in time. You want to know the connections between gender and poverty? There were so many to make, and so few to make them! And the real revolution ain't about booty size ... '[20]

As Akka trailed off, humming another song, Cathy looked at Nafsa.

'Sorry, Nafsa, Akka really does seem to be a bit on the wild side. I suppose too many Feminists do spunk up the broth ... '

'Don't worry about that, Cathy. I think Akka's a lot of fun, actually, let's keep her in Rei storage for other Wiser sessions! But here's a question for you, this time. I understand what Akka means by gender and its complexities, Cathy ... I mean, we archived all that during my Wiser sessions with you, but surely it's strange that the pre-Council times didn't appreciate the Femstories enough? That they didn't make the connections easily?'

'I suppose that's why we believe so strongly in Memory, Nafsa, knowing that if every peoplekindness remembered the past-times, they would treat each other with dignity and gentleness. And I suppose that's also why the Wiser sessions are considered so important by the Council, so that we keep making the connections between issues and events, processes and outcomes, consequences and well-being. I guess we should look at the pre-Council time of the late twentieth century and early twenty-first century in the same way. As far as I can understand, there was slowly growing to be a literature of the connections between gender and poverty, but the interlinkages were still not adequately analysed at the time.'[21]

'That's true, Cathy. I'm beginning to remember my past-time archiving in this area. As Rei displayed to us, rather than looking at how gender differentiates the social processes leading to poverty, most people concentrated on looking at whether women suffered more than men, in numbers or in intensity ... "Policy" analyses, what we now call People-Change, equated female-headed households with poverty, made certain assumptions about female disadvantages in well-being within this household, and posited a positive relationship between "investing in women" and poverty reduction.[22] I suppose the feminists questioned easy assumptions, and asked difficult questions. And out of some of that questioning, came the ways in which we understand well-being today ... '

Akka suddenly spoke up, quietly, seriously. 'My dears, the moment of change is the only poem.[23] Only when we ask the difficult questions can we make the complex connections. Does studying less make a girl poor, or being from a poor family mean that she will study less than her brother? Why are there more young girls dying than young boys? Is a poor older man more at risk of dying early? Is a women alive with illness for much of her life? Do men and women die different deaths, for different reasons?'[24]

Both Cathy and Nafsa were silent for a moment. Then Cathy said, 'Yes, Akka, it takes courage to change. But look at the pre-Council approaches to poverty. Surely peoplekind realized that only a combination of these approaches would make sense of mal-wealth? That even then, it was so much about culture and context and community that it would be difficult to make worldspace judgements based on Commonspace experience? Was that also what the Femstories were able to add to the Mystory of mal-wealth?'

'I'm sure that was true,' Nafsa added. 'After all, the Feminists were able to use their own Mystories and their Techno-Wisdoms to analyse all four approaches, and make further contributions to ways in which to reduce mal-wealth in those times. They looked at how understanding the gendered nature of poverty changed the way resources were distributed, including who owned land, how ways and kinds of work and trade needed to change, and how all this affected the way homeunits were run. They analysed the different ways in which the poor, both men and women, coped with difficult times, and how new networks of friendship and solidarity were created ...[25] And with all this, it was about ways in which to understand peoplekind's freedoms and well-being.'

In mainstream economics, freedom is often seen only as 'negative freedom', i.e. the freedom from interference, but for the poor, women in particular, 'positive freedom' – the capability to be and to do – is equally, if not more, important, to the ways in which they understand well-being.[26]

'That's an interesting archive from Rei, Nafsa. I suppose that's how we began to build the Council too ... a worldspace built on Options and

www.coming?

Opportunity, the ability to be and to do ... It did begin with pre-Council dreams, didn't it?'

Akka laughed. A lovely full-throated laugh. And her voice turned husky. 'Yes, my friends. I am always learning to unlearn. The words of a friend of mine ... And listening to the two of you, and hearing about this strange wonderful whimsical life that you live, I have hope for the women of my many pasts. I, who once felt that if you live long enough, every victory turns into a defeat,[27] now see that victories can even lead to happiness. Un autre monde, c'est possible, n'est-ce pas?'

Across Rei's console screens and across the walls of the Chatspace, starworks and smilies accompanied these words: *Without leaps of imagination, or dreaming, we lose the excitement of possibilities. Dreaming, after all, is a form of planning.*[28]

Notes

1 This world could not have been created without the references of Caterina Ruggeri Laderchi, and the conversations with Ashwin Mathew. Any shortcomings in its imagination and analysis are, naturally, mine.

2 M. Rahnema (1997), 'Poverty,' in W. Sachs (ed.), *The Development Dictionary: A Guide to Knowledge as Power* (London: Zed Books), pp. 158–76.

3 Ibid.

4 Merriam-Webster's *Collegiate Dictionary* (1995), quoted in R. Kanbur and L. Squire (1999), 'The evolution of thinking about poverty: exploring the interactions', unpublished paper.

5 Ibid.

6 C. Ruggeri Laderchi, R. Saith and F. Stewart (May 2003), 'Does it matter that we don't agree on the definition of poverty? A comparison of four approaches', Queen Elizabeth House Working Paper Series, No. 107 (Oxford).

7 Critical issues around the different definitions and measurements of poverty include: spaces of deprivation, i.e. different definitions capture different 'spheres of concern'; the universality of the definitions; subjective or objective measurements of poverty; discrete poverty lines; units of measurement of poverty; the aggregation of indices; and the time horizons of measurement. For a clear explication of these issues, please see ibid.

8 C. Ruggeri Laderchi (December 2000), 'The monetary approach to poverty: a survey of concepts and methods', Queen Elizabeth House Working Paper Series, No. 58 (Oxford).

9 'For economists the appeal of the monetary approach lies in its being compatible with the utility-maximizing behaviour assumption that underpins micro-economics, i.e. that the objective of consumers is to maximize utility and that expenditures reflect the marginal value or utility people place on commodities. Welfare can then be measured as the total consumption enjoyed, proxied by either expenditure or income data, and poverty is defined

as a shortfall below some minimum level of resources, which is termed the poverty line' (Ruggeri Laderchi, Saith and Stewart 2003: 7). See n. 6.

10 A. J. Oswald (1997), 'Happiness and economic performance', *Economic Journal*, 107: 1815–31.

11 S. Klasen (2004), 'Gender-related indicators of well-being', WIDER Discussion Paper No. 2004/05, p. 5 (Helsinki: World Institute for Development Economics Research). The details of this approach can also be found in A. K. Sen (1985), *Commodities and Capabilities* (Amsterdam: Elsevier Science Publishers). For a critical appraisal, see P. Dasgupta (1993), *An Inquiry into Well-being and Destitution* (Oxford: Clarendon Press).

12 A. Sen (1993), 'Capability and well-being', in M. C. Nussbaum and A. K. Sen (eds), *The Quality of Life* (Oxford: Clarendon Press), pp. 30–53.

13 A. Sumner (2004), 'Economic well-being and non-economic well-being: a review of the meaning and measurement of poverty', WIDER Research Paper No. 2004/30 (Helsinki: World Institute for Development Economics Research).

14 Ruggeri Laderchi, Saith and Stewart, 'Does it matter that we don't agree on the definition of poverty?'.

15 R. Chambers (1994), 'The origins and practice of PRA', *World Development*, 22(7) (Montreal).

16 The institutionalization of participatory methods includes the scaling up of the PRAs by the World Bank as complementing their poverty assessments, as well as the multi-country exercise, covering 23 countries, which was the background to the WB 2000/1 *World Development Report*, called *Voices of the Poor*. In addition, the Poverty Reduction Strategy Papers (PRSPs) are purportedly prepared through a participatory process of member countries, involving domestic partners as well as external stakeholders, including the World Bank and the International Monetary Fund. Yet 39 organizations and regional networks in 15 African countries agreed at a meeting in Kampala, May 2001, that PRSPs were 'simply window dressing' (Ruggeri Laderchi, Saith and Stewart, 'Does it matter that we don't agree on the definition of poverty?').

17 Akka Mahadevi (*akka* is a honorific that means 'elder sister' in Kannada) was a visionary poet of the twelfth century AD, in south India, whose *vachanas* or verses in Kannada challenging social norms continue to be sung into the twenty-first century. One of her most famous *vachanas* begins with these lines: 'Not one, not two, not three or four, but through eighty-four hundred thousand vaginas have I come. I have come through unlikely worlds, guzzled on pleasures and pain ... ' translated by A. K. Ramanujam, excerpted from S. Tharu and K. Lalita (eds) (1995), *Women Writing in India, Vol. I* (Delhi: Oxford University Press), p. 80.

18 Mary Wollstonecraft (1759–97) wrote various classic texts of liberal feminism, particularly *A Vindication of the Rights of Women* (1792). She married William Godwin, author of *An Enquiry Concerning Political Justice and Its Influence on General Virtue and Happiness* (1793). She died a few days after the birth of their daughter, Mary, who later married Percy Bysshe Shelley, and wrote *Frankenstein, or the Modern Prometheus*, and other novels. See <http://www.philosophypages.com/ph/woll.htm> and <http://www.literature.org/authors/shelley-mary/frankenstein/>.

19 C. Jackson (1996), 'Rescuing gender from the poverty trap', *World Development*, 24(3): 489–504.

20 An excerpt from Sarah Jones's song 'Your revolution', originally a poem: <http://www.sarahjonesonline.com/press/VillageVoice.html>.

21 S. Razavi (September 1998), 'Gendered poverty and social change: an issues paper', United Nations Research Institute for Social Development (UNRISD) Discussion Paper No. 94 (Geneva).

22 Ibid., p. 1.

23 Adrienne Rich: see <http://www.wwnorton.com/introlit/poetry_rich5.htm>.

24 See Razavi, 'Gendered poverty and social change', for an explication of issues including gender disadvantage in sex ratios, complexities in the adjustments required for gender and age differences in nutritional and morbidity factors, and poverty as a cause rather than an outcome for gendered access to education. See also G. Sen, A. George and P. Östlin (2002) (eds), *The Challenge of Equity* (Chicago: MIT Press).

25 S. Baden (1997), 'Economic reform and poverty: a gender analysis', Report No. 50, prepared for Gender Equality Unit, Swedish International Development Cooperation Agency (Brighton: Institute of Development Studies).

26 I. van Staveren and D. Gasper (July 2002), 'Development as freedom – contributions and shortcomings of Amartya Sen's development philosophy for feminist economics', Working Paper No. 365 (The Hague: Institute of Social Studies).

27 Simone de Beauvoir: quoted at <http://www.brainyquote.com/quotes/authors/s/simone_de_beauvoir.html>.

28 Gloria Steinem quoted at <http://womenshistory.about.com/cs/quotes/a/qu_g_steinem.htm>.

9 | Reflections on the World Social Forum as a space for alternative engagements[1]

MARÌA ALEJANDRA SCAMPINI

Everything has been globalized except our consent.[2] All over the planet, the rich get richer while the poor are overtaken by debt and disaster. The world is run not by its people, but by a handful of unelected executives who make decisions that affect everyone else. Without democracy at the global level, the rest of us are left with no means to influence these processes except to shout abuse and hurl ourselves at the lines of the police who defend the high-level and impenetrable gatherings and decision-making processes.[3]

For a minute, imagine with me a world where we, the people, are not reduced to resisting 'coercion'. Where we have the necessary and recognized means and mechanisms to hold the global and international powers accountable. Where we, the people of the world, have the opportunity to influence decisions that impact our lives, our livelihoods and our environments. Where we can come together in our quests for social justice and create collective actions to make this 'better world' possible. Where we can effectively make the connections between the local and the global. Where we can act differently, navigating and reflecting in the middle of ongoing confrontation between old and new. Where we can act differently, aspiring to coordinate and join together in the wide multiplicity and variety of social practices that are challenging global hegemonies. Imagine the World Social Form (WSF) as a space where we can construct and realize our alternative engagements and methods for social justice and gender equality.

In the current global order, it is no secret that people are feeling hard done by. There is a desperate search for alternative proposals to challenge, to resist and to create new politics that will overthrow hegemonic economic models. In January 2001, the first WSF in Porto Alegre, Brazil, provided an opportunity to start a process where people from a range of different social movements could come together in a democratic space to debate, share proposals and experiences, and link their agendas for organizing around social injustices. With the theme 'Another World is Possible', the WSF presented an opportunity for plurality, diversity and recognition of the different struggles that we face, as we strive to challenge the powers that are impeding the realization of social justice. For once, people and movements had the opportunity to identify their role in making this change happen. As Sergio Haddad says:

> The great novelty of this process is that civil society is the protagonist, as seen by the massive public presence of social movements and civil society organizations that bring with them the voices of agents for social change – peasants, indigenous communities, women, men and many others. In this way a new political culture is built, where diversity of voices, non-hierarchy, collective building of alternatives are all marks of new models of constructing authority and social change.[4]

Increasingly, the WSF seems to be attracting young women, who want to engage with different forms of activism and engagement.[5] From Seattle to Geneva, from Porto Alegre to Mumbai, young women have found themselves involved in active resistance in multiple movements. In contexts of feeling powerless, young people have identified the WSF as an important vehicle for confrontation between new and old ways of organizing and resisting, where they can engage with different forms of political leadership and challenge the hierarchies within organized movements. The WSF is one of the few spaces where there is an opportunity for inter-movement dialogue and the coexistence and coordination of different ways of protesting. It also allows for diverse proposals from movements, organizations, networks and campaigns aimed at using the forces of transformative radical movements in the construction of another social order.

As young people approach the WSF with their hopes and dreams for social justice, they experience the tensions of being part of multiple movements, perhaps not realizing initially that there are common threads between all the different struggles and issues, and that we are all in a state of learning and unlearning. I myself speak from the privilege of having been part of all five WSFs held so far; I am a witness to the changes in different social struggles and how the WSF has evolved over time with the changing dimensions of struggles. This chapter, therefore, attempts to outline the aspirations of young feminist women who, in shifting contexts, look for ways to find relevance, solidarity and support for making change happen. I attempt to present how these old and new methods of political action open a historic possibility of moving from a platform of resistance to one of transformation in the face of dogmatic neo-liberal thought, and how the WSF can provide both these platforms. As Gigi Francisco said,

> We are in the WSF to engage in liberating cultural translation of our visions and alternatives. We are here because we continually seek spaces and create moments, albeit briefly, to live out our individual self-consciousness

because we have not found our authenticity in a world system that has been so constructed and structured on domination and hegemonic control. And we are here to contribute to the specific project of interlinking differentiated struggles and resistances so that together we can each locate tactical and strategic trajectories for multidirectional critique, mass actions and alternatives.[6]

Promoting inter-movement engagement

In our current context, it is very important to have a vision that allows us to imagine that another world is possible: a world that includes everyone. Our work cannot end with vision, though; it has to follow through with strategies and proposals on how to achieve our aim. There is no doubt that today we exist in a context where there are political risks in action as well as inaction. The commitment to react in the face of new challenges and new players has brought us as a movement to relate to the public and private sectors and to rethink the nature of actions necessary to ensure that our demands are met. In local processes we have learned to work with the state and to challenge it, and to work in international alliances to challenge new actors in the complexity of global governance. Spaces open before our eyes, and new demands are created while the old ones remain. The challenges are enormous and many affect, for example, the way organizations act in campaigns, networks and coalitions and their increasing commitment to flexible and non-hierarchical structures.

Across movements, in our engagement, we are cognizant of the pluralities, diversities and conflicts that exist. There is a sense among many young women that there are tensions between the global agenda and specific agendas (for example, feminist agendas), as if one has to choose one agenda over the other. We may have been born in different places and times, but today the fact that we live in a world of dogmatic thought unites us. Work on specific issues and analyses of how certain facts affect us specifically, as women in different contexts, supports a feminist vision of society. Building a broader agenda, however, is possible only if it involves a collective creation of this other world(s). Eccher and Fernández explain:

> One sure and non-negotiable thing is that this other world or worlds must have justice and equality in gender relations. One of the things we have learned from feminists is that creating alternative proposals ... [has] not necessarily include[d] a gender analysis of the present reality.[7]

This point is reinforced by Anderson, who states that

> gender equity and justice are an essential condition for real change. It

127

is not a slogan; and we cannot continue to talk about a more just and equitable distribution of economic, national, regional and global resources – without incorporating an analysis of the distribution of wealth across gender, race and ethnicity, among other things, within the socio-economic variable.[8]

Thus feminist (especially young feminist) engagement is essential if we are to ensure that the broader social justice agenda is representative of feminist concerns.

At the 2005 WSF, in discussions among feminists, issues concerning the difficulties and problems that continue to exist in spaces where different movements coordinate and interact were raised. At one of the feminist workshops in Porto Alegre two feminists were interviewed about this issue:

> Irma van Dueren: Feminists have always tried to influence the agendas of progressive social and political movements to change their perspectives. However, we know that there is still a long road ahead to make inclusion of the feminist perspective a reality ... We don't want the WSF to become an event dominated by men: feminist leadership and alliance-building are necessary ... This challenge is complex. We don't want to have a nominal presence and we are tired of superficial references to gender.

> Ana Irma Rivera: Generally, women's voices are not present in economics or finance. I understand that these issues are identified as masculine, not only the voices but also the content. The problem of the lack of women will not be resolved simply with the inclusion of women in the discussion of economics and finance; it is also necessary that these issues are viewed with a gender perspective.[9]

The inter-movement dialogues are a clear example of the challenge of trying to transform other groups' perspectives of feminisms, diversity and gender. There has been progress in these dialogues in the sense of recognizing differences and the need for the space to do so. However, it should not end here. It is not enough to have men and women of different ages, races, genders, ethnicities, sexual orientation, education and economic situations to present at the WSF; the discourses and debates should create the space for us to engage openly and honestly about these issues and the resulting actions. In our engagement, I believe that we must be able to recognize that we have different scars on our bodies, and from these, we see the world, and interact in it, differently. Dialogue should not, however, be an end in itself; there is a need to intensify and build on this dialogue so that we can move beyond 'talking' to implementing our collaborations outside the WSF space.

128

Women's experiences, acquired in the various years of struggle in the global arena, have allowed us to advance towards more coordinated work in terms of strategies, networks and alliances on specific activities. In these years of meetings, we have reflected on participation in different spaces on different levels, recognizing advances in our visibility, influence and achieving greater equity in women's participation. Feminists, in particular, have been organized and recognized to make crucial contributions to the evaluation of processes and interventions.[10] We have also reflected on obstacles, limitations and challenges.

At the WSF, one of the key objectives for feminist and women's movements is to ensure that feminists are present in all of the official spaces of engagement and, by implication, that a gender analysis is inherent in all the actions related to the Forum. Despite this, feminists are aware that the Forum is also a space where new and old forms of discrimination persist and co-exist. There are new and old practices that seek ways to share, confront and translate their implications, challenges and ways of being and doing. The relationship between translation and change is an integral part of the Forum. It is important that new generations of young women and feminists become part of these processes and efforts to ensure that the WSF can be a model for 'another world'. The lesson to be learned from these experiences is that there is diversity and complexity in our movements and at the same time we enter into processes of coordination, as well as power struggles. Colleagues who were part of the Forum's International Council explained, at the Feminist Dialogue in 2005 in Porto Alegre, that there had been an increase in the participation of women from the first Forum, leading to greater visibility and responsibility in organizing panels on two of the five basic issues: human rights and democracy, and civil society and political power at the third and fourth WSFs.

The participation of feminisms in the WSF offers us another space to think about coordinating methods locally, nationally and globally. It is interesting to see how the struggles translate on different levels, as well as to analyse the different obstacles and challenges at these levels. In these new dynamics of participation, young women have the opportunity to provide greater analyses on stumbling-blocks of feminism itself, by expressing our concerns within alliances or working towards the interlinking of these alliances with other movements.

Sylvia Borren explains:

I believe that the moment has come for many of us (more of us than currently do) to take serious responsibility in giving form to our world on the micro, middle and macro levels. In other words, to take a step forward for feminism, the feminist movement and feminist leadership, to concern ourselves not only with women's way of life but also the quality of the lives of men, women and children more generally, to concern ourselves in finding solutions to the tensions and conflicts in the world, to assume leadership in organizations, to seek ways of making our lives and our world more inclusive and diverse.[11]

Constructing alternative ways of acting

Tensions exists around the Forum's capacity for making proposals, its size, and issues of representation and participation, as well as the ever-present manifestations of globalization and the perpetuation of power struggles. These are all part of the process that makes the WSF the vibrant, challenging and engaging space that it is. As Boaventura de Souza explains:

A great effort of reciprocal recognition, dialogue and debate are necessary to promote practices against hegemonies, combining among others the environmental, pacifist, indigenous, feminist and worker's movements in a non-hierarchal way and with respect for the identity and autonomy of each movement.[12]

Therefore, if we are to construct alternative ways of acting, it is important for us to recognize that the frameworks we use to interpret ourselves and others, and from which we plan our actions, are not unique or static. The WSF, for example, is a space where different interpretative frameworks co-exist (not without tensions), which can accompany and promote debate among us, challenging dogmatic thoughts and suggesting alternative roads. In the face of current challenges, we should ask ourselves: what are people's capacities for resistance and adaptation? We have learned that even in the most adverse situations, people resist, respond and adjust to the situations by negotiating, creating alternatives, interacting with others and showing affection, rage and pain – individually and collectively. Today we are witnessing this resistance and capacity for adaptation continuously. It presents the opportunity and the possibility of acting differently. We face this challenge within and outside of the movement.

Young feminist women noted in the Feminist Dialogues of 2005 that they perceive the women's movement to be inactive and stagnant. Yet it is important for young feminists to recognize that the movement has been fluid, and like any other social movements has had to modify its ways of being and acting. Movements broaden, diversify and transform. Movements create and re-create their discourses. The ways in which groups develop their methods of resistance vary. The new complexity of global governance has forced social movements to move towards different places of intervention and to various forms of coordination among groups. Under other circumstances, this may not have occurred. However, in the light of the state of the world today, joining together is a necessity in order to find common causes and methods of action that allow us to build our 'better world'.

The recognition of diversity and plurality makes it clear that, rather than consensus on where our commonalities converge, we need a clear explanation of our individualities and how to combine agendas from different groups – respecting autonomy yet striving for coordinated efforts for common goals. We must advance our analysis of flexible, democratic and participative ways of acting and collectively organizing that acknowledge differences in a positive way. Interactions of younger and older feminists can strive towards this with a dialogue of respect and an ongoing explanation of our differences. The feminist movement initiated the inter-movement dialogues to advance an emancipating proposal – one that integrates and articulates the public and private, along with the subjectivities and powers of class, race, gender, sexual orientation, and so on, in order to create new democraticizing political identities. But at the same time we must address this challenge within ourselves and our own movements, recognizing diversities: especially in the case of young women.

In the debates on tolerance at the Feminist Dialogues, some voices admitted to feeling less feminist than others, and therefore finding fewer opportunities for adding their visions to the debates. A tolerant space is one that gives equal opportunities to its participants to express and formulate proposals and visions. The incorporation and recognition of diversities, beyond the surface level, continues to be a challenge within the feminist movement. It is not enough to promote participation on the surface: we must work towards honest engagement in easing the tensions that continue to cause difficulties in the movement. It means overcoming a hierarchical and even, at times, dogmatic vision of the struggle of 'us' against 'them'. It is not accepting but rather celebrating diversity through translating the varied experiences of the world in a spirit of intelligible reciprocity: without endangering identity and autonomy, without reducing them to hegemonic entities. This translation within feminisms is still a challenge. Young women must be part of the process, through careful reflection and evaluation.

The WSF shows itself to our young eyes as a space of permanent tension, where we must learn to revalue militancy and social commitment, while exercising patience to deal with disputes, being open to the influence of other movements, resisting the temptation of eliminating contradictions and not falling into an dictatorial and fundamentalist role ourselves. As to the future, uncertainty does not scare us; we live it. What is true is that we will have to face new challenges within the ever-evolving WSF process. The way we do this will determine whether the Forum and different levels of participation will continue to catalyse the energy of a large part of the global movement, while calling on a diversity and plurality of people. Young feminist women have an opportunity to unite in the face of this challenge. The invitation has been extended to us, and we must continue to make progress in learning how to combine new and old ways of acting in dialogue with other movements and generations.

Young women taking on the challenges from within feminist movements

One of the most remarkable elements of the new cycle of protests that has appeared in the last years throughout the world is the new generation of militant youth and their role in the majority of large international mobilizations.[13]

As young women, as young people, we are part of a wide range of diversities. We come to the WSF with what we have learned, as well as with our dreams and our questions. Many of the people we meet in these spaces saw the beginning of this process, while we are working hard to make space to infuse the WSF and its initiatives with our own energy and visions. We are united by the fact that we grew up and were educated under neo-liberalism; everyone in one way or another suffers from the growing strength of right-wing and fundamentalist groups. In laughter, drama, confessions and debates there is a clear feeling that our goals are inhibited and that there is a lack of renewal in the movement.

For us, the WSF is a space to unlearn the ways of doing and acting politically within the neo-liberal system and to learn from, and create, other social practices. On our own, we may not have been capable of realizing how some of our actions exclude others; the WSF can be a mirror for reflecting upon ourselves. Progress in learning this at the WSF comes from recognizing that we are part of a women's movement, as well as other movements that advance in different ways. As young women, we are critical and reflective of our feminist identities and how this informs our interactions with others. We are also cognizant of the potential for us to bring about a unique fundamentalism for achieving social justice. We must leave our ghettos of identity behind. As we engage at the WSF, we make efforts to rescue, recognize and explain diversity, and we also see within it the potential for fragmentation. However, we know that if we want to achieve another world, we must first achieve other ways of organizing within and without the women's movement.

132

We must begin from the recognition that there can be many ways of being 'feminist'; each expression of this identity is a response to the needs and concerns of women in different regions, societies and historical moments. We must recognize that as young people we are joining a political movement that expresses the concerns of women from different regions and with different lives. It is therefore naive to think of, or even strive for, one homogenous 'feminism'. As a political movement, we can assume different issues, objectives and methods, but what should unite us is the common vision that we are all fighting to end gender subordination and create equal opportunities.

Within the feminist movement, there is a need for inter-generational dialogue that leads to renewal and recognizes and learns from past struggles and achievments. This is imperative if we want to claim our place within the movement. That being said, we also have to understand and address power relations outside and inside feminist movements. It is important to recognize that the politics of the feminist movement are also about power, which can, and many times does, replicate the patriarchal power structures that are the same as those we are fighting against. Although it is sometimes important to point out that we are 'young', just as important is the need to be compatible with a plural and democratic vision of feminism. In this way, young feminist women must demand the right to say and give meaning to their identities, while participating in a collective effort discussing common meanings, priorities and life goals.

There remains the challenge of joining, connecting and translating ourselves with and within other movements. It is critical that we expand the debate about the feminist movement as a political agent by entering into the WSF process. We must position ourselves as agents of political change and/or occupy this place responsibly with *informed* proposals and debates. As young women, we join these processes in a non-linear way and have the potential to promote interconnecting multiple agendas.

The age of consent

We have responded to the age of coercion with an age of dissent. This is the beginning of the battle. It is time to invoke the age of consent.[14]

As a young woman who has been at all five WSFs, I marvel at how the Forum has evolved, how it has changed the interpretations of those who attend it and how it has influenced my own activism. Among images of Chè Guevara, songs that 'another world is possible', and while passing through the inter-movement dialogues, I am inspired by the opportunities presented by the WSF to create another world. Thus far, however, young feminist women have not participated directly in formal debates and decision-making on the nature, form and continuity of the Forum. We are still on the peripheries of the formal structures, such as the International Council, that help create the WSF. But our perspectives are shared indirectly through our representatives at the International Council (senior feminists, for instance), or directly in spaces within the Forum. In the formal space of the 'Youth Camp', there is a clear and legitimate participation of youth, who have their place on the International Council; we can use this space strategically. However, it is important that we promote the participation of young women at all levels. As young women, we want to expand the discussions beyond the WSF, so that we can, in the framework of democracy and solidarity with other social movements, promote women's issues as issues of political interest for men and women of all generations.

Finally, the problem of young feminist women is just that: our age is considered a problem. Stressing the importance of this category of 'young women' also creates a void: a void related to how young women process these situations. We need to remember that this categorization is transient. One day we will no longer be young, but we will continue to be black, poor, immigrants, Indians, lesbians, rural ... The heterogeneity of young people is the same as that of the movements in which we participate.

Notes

1 This chapter was orginally written in Spanish and was translated by Nicole Lisa.

2 G. Monbiot (2003), *The Age of Consent: A Manifesto for a New World Order* (London: Flamingo).

3 Ibid.

4 S. Haddad (2003), 'The World Social Forum as a place for learning', *Convergence*, XXXVI(3–4), see <http://www.scielo.bv/#back1>.

5 In 2003, 30,000 young people, mostly women, participated in the Youth Camp. At the Feminist Dialogue in Porto Alegre in 2005, the majority were between 20 and 35 years old.

6 G. Francisco (2003), 'Inaugural speech at the women's conference of the Asia Social Forum: January 2003', in *DAWN Informs*, see <http://www.dawn.org.fj>.

7 C. Eccher and M. C. Fernández (2003), 'A journey full of hope', *Convergence*, XXXVI(3–4): 91.

8 J. Anderson (2002), 'Permanent education for macro and micro-economy: women's political and social assets', in REPEM Training Workshop Series, p. 91, see <http://www.repem.org.uy>.

9 Taken from: L. Celiberti and V. Vargas (2003), 'Feministas en el Foro', *Rev. Estud. Fem.*, 11(2): 586–98.

10 G. Sen (1997), 'Globalization in the 21st century: challenges for civil society', UvA Development Lecture 1997, University of Amsterdam.

11 Taken from Celiberti and Vargas, 'Feministas en el Foro'.

12 Ibid.

13 J. Antentas (2001), 'La Jeunesse face à la globalisation', *Contretemps*, no. 2: Seattle and Porto Alegre, and *Gênes: Mondalisation capitaliste et dominations imperials* (Paris: Ed Textuel) (trans. from French).

14 Monbiot, *The Age of Consent*.

10 | Rooting out injustice: discussions with radical young women in Toronto, Canada

JENNIFER PLYLER

A few years ago, while at a women's rights conference, I attended a workshop entitled 'Taking on the WTO'. I was excited at first to be participating in an explicitly feminist discussion on how to challenge more effectively the global powers forcing neo-liberalism and imperialism on us, but my enthusiasm quickly dwindled. As each panellist spoke, it became clear that their focus was more on how to increase the number of women in positions of power within the WTO than to formulate strategies on how to dismantle it. This was disappointing since, as a young woman engaged in struggle against imperialist globalization, I knew that simply gaining power within capitalist superpowers would never satisfy me.

When the question period began, I approached the microphone and directed my question to the person I felt was the most radical speaker on the panel. 'Wouldn't it be more strategic to unify our efforts to tear the WTO down rather than divide our efforts between reformist and radical camps?' The panellist answered my question with a chuckle, 'Well, when I was 20 I had no problem with running around in the streets and getting arrested, but I have different priorities now.' Numerous older women in the audience laughed. This response did not answer my question, nor did it even begin to address whether efforts to reform dominant institutions are effective or whether it is simply easier to work within them because it requires less sacrifice. What it did do was embarrass me in front of a lot of older feminists and make me feel isolated and unwanted. The existence of a divide among women's rights activists seemed threatening and real. Unless action is taken to recognize and show solidarity with the visions, analysis and action of young radical women on the frontline of struggles, we may start finding ourselves not only on opposite sides of the fence at anti-globalization protests but also on opposite sides of the fence within our efforts to transform our own communities.

In Toronto, Canada, there are young women building radical movements of action and solidarity that challenge injustice head on. These young women, who epitomize the slogan 'think global, act local', are leading new and militant struggles against the forces of imperialism, colonialism, racism, sexism and poverty. They are organizing within their communities not only for justice and rights but also for survival. This chapter aims to introduce you to a few of these women, the organizations they lead and their perspectives on social change. It also aims to document their struggles, their sacrifices and their raging spirits.

Facing realities in Toronto, Canada

Today in Toronto someone will die on the streets, someone will be deported to a place where they face torture and many children will go to school with nothing to eat. By the end of the week, at least one woman will be beaten to death by her partner.[1]

Yesterday was the first snowfall of the season, but many families will not be turning on their heat. Since our hydroelectricity was privatized a few years back, many people simply cannot afford to pay the bills.

Over the past quarter of a century, while the IMF and World Bank have been forcing poor countries around the world to adopt neo-liberal structural adjustment programmes, Canada, largely voluntarily (but also with some 'help' from the United States), has been choosing to do the same, resulting in public policy and laws that ensure growing inequality and injustice. As a result, human rights such as health care and education are beyond the means of many in Canada. The elimination of rent control in the province of Ontario is forcing many into sub-standard, crowded housing. Or worse: on to the streets. Over 30,000 people are homeless in Toronto, the majority being women, youth, psychiatric survivors and indigenous peoples.[2]

At the same time, Canada is a global leader in pollution, energy consumption and environmental exploitation. The Canadian government has yet to ratify the Kyoto Protocol to curb greenhouse gas emissions. In addition, it continues to export its hazardous waste to poor countries around the world and to use its political power to block the adoption of international law that would ban such practices.[3] Here in Canada, the consequences of environmental destruction are borne most heavily by indigenous communities, undermining livelihoods, health and community survival. Members of Grassy Narrows and Whitedog (both indigenous communities located in Northwestern Ontario) continue to face the economic and health consequences of mercury poisoning, which resulted from the corporate dumping, prior to 1970, that contaminated the water supply and wiped out the local fishing economy.[4] In addition, Grassy Narrows is currently in a stand-off with the Canadian government. They are demanding the preservation of their remaining boreal old-growth forest, their traditional lands and their cultural heritage from being further destroyed by the practice of clear-cutting.[5]

Half of the women in Canada have been assaulted either sexually or physically.[6] One-quarter of the women in Canada will be sexually asaulted[7] in their lifetime: one woman every six minutes.[8] Forty per cent of disabled women in Canada have been raped, abused or assaulted.[9] For women without citizenship status in Canada, reporting a rape will more often lead to the woman being deported than the rapist being convicted.[10] Nine out of ten of the rest of us will not report gender-based violence to the police, either because we feel ashamed or because we do not believe that the police can really protect us.[11]

Over 500 indigenous women in Canada have 'disappeared' or been murdered in the last 20 years.[12] In the ongoing spirit of Canadian colonialism, indigenous peoples in Canada continue to be brutally discriminated against in terms of health care, housing, employment and access to education, to name but a few examples. This has created a situation where the average life expectancy for indigenous peoples is five to seven years less than the national average, while the youth suicide rate is six times as high.[13] Although indigenous people constitute less than 4 per cent of the Canadian population, they represent 17 per cent of the men and women currently incarcerated nationally.[14]

Since 11 September 2001, the reality for many immigrants and refugees in Canada has gone from bad to worse. Although Toronto is one of the most culturally diverse cities in the world, racist backlash and xenophobia continue to affect our everyday lives. Half of all recent immigrants in Canada are living in poverty.[15] In the name of 'security', and in favour of maintaining friendly relations with our US neighbours, substantial changes have been made to Canada's immigration laws. These changes are closing our borders to people in need of protection, forcing families apart and many refugees to live underground rather than be imprisoned or deported back to persecution. Targeting of South Asian and Muslim men by immigration authorities is leading to climates of fear within these communities. Individuals without immigration status who have taken public stands in defence of immigrant rights have been particularly targeted. Prisons for immigrants and refugees (and their children) are being built; international human rights laws are continuously undermined.

The Canadian Crown Corporation, which is owned by the government, makes 70 per cent of its profit through the sale of weapons and weapon components to the US.[16] A popular radical anti-war slogan goes 'Bring the war home!' Clearly, with all the injustice communities in Toronto are facing, it's already here.

And so is resistance.

Liisa, Farrah, Rachel and Rafeef are all young women activists and community organizers in Toronto, fighting back against the injustices taking place in our city. Their community work is diverse and intersecting, addressing issues of occupation, political prisoners, poverty, capitalism, anti-racism and immigrants' rights. I met with each of these young women to hear about their journeys to activism, the groups they work with, the action they take, the challenges they face and the wins they've had in defending rights and contributing to change. I also asked them about feminism: how they define it and how it has influenced their ideas and actions.

Liisa: the 30 June Committee

Liisa, a student activist at York University in Toronto, is a leading organizer around issues of occupation and war. She describes her upbringing and explains how it politicized her and defined her relationship with the state.

Liisa: I grew up with my mom and my brother after my mom left my father, who was abusive. My mom has a permanent disability. And so surviving was a constant financial struggle because she couldn't work full-time. Eventually she had to go on Ontario disability support. We grew up in poverty with a single mother who was constantly trying to make ends meet, constantly coming up against the Ontario government not giving us enough to buy winter boots, groceries or pay the rent. I became politicized at a young age, as I was exposed to what it's like for a woman trying to get away from an abusive situation and then trying to survive economically without enough support from the Ontario government.

Beginning in her teenage years, Liisa became active in advocating on behalf of her mother's case to gain disability benefits from the Canadian government. She describes trying to get enough support to survive from the government as 'a huge battle' and says, 'I think that's when I stopped having any faith in electoral politics or any faith in the government as it stands.' She was also inspired to become politically active through the strength that her mother, and other survivors of abuse, demonstrated to her.

For the past several years, Liisa has been active on her campus around anti-war and human rights issues. Last spring she became involved in a coalition that brought together activists working against the occupations in Iraq, Palestine and Afghanistan to organize a demonstration marking the day that US forces were 'supposedly' going to hand over power to the interim Iraqi government. This coalition named itself the June 30th Committee. With the goal of achieving more than symbolic actions against US foreign policy, the June 30th Committee aims to raise awareness about Canadian involvement in the occupation of Iraq.

Liisa: It was definitely a different anti-occupation organizing experience than I've had in a long time because we started off with having a very anti-imperialist and anti-capitalist analysis. We wanted to draw out Canada's role in imperialism and Canada's role in the occupations.

The June 30th Committee organized a day of action in response to the Canadian government's indirect involvement in the Iraq war. This day drew attention to the fact that although the Canadian government had publicly declared that it would not send troops to the US-led invasion of Iraq, this has not stopped Canadian corporations from profiting from the war through military contracts and weapons manufacturing at the expense of lives and autonomy in Iraq.[17] The action included setting up pickets and an aggressive march through Toronto's financial district. The day was notable in that young women were both the primary organizers and the primary decision-makers.

Liisa: The day challenged both the state and our own structures at the same time. I think confronting the state in such a harsh way and being able to do it with young women was a really inspiring and empowering moment.

The June 30th Committee has been a strong (re)mobilizing force amongst anti-war and anti-occupation activists in Toronto. It has opened a space for increasing radical analysis and action. It continues to organize direct action against war-profiteers throughout the city.

Farrah: Project Threadbare

Farrah was active in the anti-globalization movement when she was in high school. When she started university, she knew she wanted to become politically involved in the university setting but, as a young woman of colour, found few opportunities to do so.

Farrah: The only groups that were politically active on campus were mostly white-dominated spaces that were organizing within a Christian framework. This work wasn't really based on systemic change or actions against the state; it was more service-type stuff that was available to become involved with at the time, and I felt very frustrated.

Since 11 September 2001, Islamophobia[18] and xenophobia have been on the rise throughout Canada, including Toronto. On 14 August 2003, a joint investigation by the Royal Canadian Mounted Police (RCMP) and Citizenship and Immigration Canada (CIC), called 'Project Thread', led to a pre-dawn raid targeting 24 South Asian Muslim men who were held without charges and on unsubstantiated terrorist allegations that were later dropped. The targeting of these men, and the damage done to their lives and reputations as a result of the accusations, has had a paralysing effect on South Asian and Muslim communities in Toronto. Everyone is wondering 'Who could be targeted next?'

When Farrah came across a poster advertising a public forum that read: 'Being Pakistani is not a crime', she decided to attend. The forum was organized by a group called 'Project Threadbare', a joint initiative of mainly South Asian men and women whose aim is to expose the injustices done to the 24 victims of the Project Thread investigation and win their release from detention. Farrah began organizing with this group. She and numerous other young activists of colour began providing legal and jail support to the detainees. They were able to secure the bonds and release of many of the detainees, but many others had been pressured by detention authorities to sign consent forms authorizing their deportation and were subsequently deported back to Pakistan straight from jail. As part of their campaign, Project Threadbare also undertook educational and awareness-raising initiatives, such as pickets, delegations and letter-writing campaigns, to educate the Canadian public about the victims of Project Thread and about the targeting of South Asians and Muslims in general.

The campaign reached a point where one of the ex-detainees, Fahim Kayani (a man who had become active in the Project Threadbare campaign since his release from detention), was informed by CIC that he was going to be deported. This was despite the grave risk of persecution he would face in Pakistan as a result of the unfounded Canadian terrorist allegation, and despite Canada's international responsibility to provide protection to those at risk of torture. Faced with the news of Fahim's pending deportation, members of Project Threadbare decided to intensify their actions.

Farrah: We were at a point in our campaign where we were going to lose the heart of the coalition – we were going to lose our leading organizer – and we were absolutely furious. In a meeting, we decided that we had to step up our action, and though we realized that we wouldn't necessarily be able to stop Fahim's deportation, we were determined to send a message to CIC that it would not be 'business as usual' at their offices while they continued to deport these men without apology and without any kind of compensation for trauma they were put through. A group of us, acting outside of the coalition, organized an occupation at the minister of citizenship and immigration Canada's office. This action was a very emotional response to the minister, who had been attacking not just the men targeted by Project Thread but also other leading non-status organizers working to challenge Canadian immigration policies.[19] The people who participated in the occupation were all young women and men of colour in the city: of Arab, South Asian, First Nations, West Indian and Iranian decent. It was the first action of its kind, where young people of colour challenged the state in such a direct way.

Despite their efforts, Fahim was deported back to Pakistan, and all the young activists who participated in the action were arrested and are now facing criminal charges. However, those involved have set an example of how young activists of colour can work together to gain power and push for radical change.

Farrah: The action built trust, understanding and commitment within the group of people that participated in the occupation, and we continue to work with other young activists of colour around issues of immigration. We have since developed a commitment to working in our own communities trying to mobilize other young people to get involved in the same kind of work. Through this, we aim to start raising these issues and making people see how it affects not only their communities, and non-status people in those communities, but also how we can concretely challenge racist attacks through our ongoing activism.

Rachel: Ontario Coalition Against Poverty

Rachel is a 20-year-old woman who has lived in Toronto her entire life. She describes her parents' involvement in union organizing as central to helping her understand how people can resist injustice in Canada.

Rachel: I grew up in downtown Toronto in a very mixed neighbourhood in terms of class and race. This has had a huge impact on the way that I see things. One would have to have blinders on not to notice that there is a lot of injustice going on: in both Toronto and the rest of the world.

Neo-liberal welfare reform has been a rising trend in Canada for several decades. The eight years of Conservative rule in Ontario (from 1995 to 2003), led by Premier Mike Harris, and the social service funding cuts that his government enacted, have contributed to an ever-widening gap between rich and poor. With promises to decrease the budget deficit and lower taxes, the Harris government slashed social welfare programmes, including health care, education, social assistance and housing (among many others) to a state where they are shadows of their former selves. In the face of the destruction of social welfare programmes, increased levels of resistance and popular mobilization arose and many Canadians began making the connections between what was happening in Ontario and the impacts of capitalism and neo-liberalism in the rest of the world.

In 1990, a group called the Ontario Coalition Against Poverty (OCAP) emerged to defend poor and working-class people against the violence of capitalism and welfare reform. Since then, OCAP has carved out a reputation across North America for its aggressive and radical actions in support of poor communities. Although best known for organizing militant demonstrations against government spending cuts, the bulk of OCAP's work revolves around providing direct-action casework to poor individuals, resisting the institutions that keep them poor. This work includes preventing evictions, gaining social assistance money and fighting deportations.

Rachel became involved in OCAP while she was still in high school and explains that 'since then that's where my heart and days have been'. Rachel explains that OCAP believes in the power of poor people to organize themselves and sees its role as providing support to these communities in whatever way is necessary. Unlike many other groups that identify themselves as anti-capitalist, Rachel explains, 'OCAP shows through its actions where it stands, how corrupt the system is and how the system breaks people's backs and then throws them in the trash, instead of just talking about it.'

The casework that Rachel does with poor women highlights the intersectionality between sexism and poverty in Toronto.

Rachel: I was working on a case with a woman who had been abused and beaten by her husband. She left her husband and was living in a government-subsidized social housing project. However, her husband found out where she was living and broke in several times, threatening her and her children. The housing provider who was in charge of the housing project she lived in refused to move her to another location, even though both the break-ins and threats she had received from him were well documented. She was in a position where she was being forced to choose between living in fear for her life or living on the streets to avoid her husband, as she couldn't afford to pay rent at a place that wasn't subsidized. We corresponded with the housing office several times but they refused to do anything about the situation. So we took a delegation to the office of the housing provider, laid the facts of the situation out for them and demanded she be accommodated. A couple of weeks later, the woman was transferred to another apartment.

Rafeef: Sumoud, a political prisoner solidarity group

Rafeef is a Palestinian refugee who grew up in the refugee camps of Lebanon. For her, being politically conscious, particularly around the Palestinian struggle for self-determination, was not a choice, but a given, due to the politically charged environment she was raised in. What was more complicated for her to grasp was the dichotomy that existed within her family and her community in relation to the revolutionary struggle and women's roles.

Rafeef: I think my first feminist moment, when I thought 'something is wrong with this picture', was when I realized that even though I was raised to idolize the women revolutionary fighters, I was never meant to become like them. I was meant to get married, have kids, be a good wife and support my husband. I was taught that these women were important components of the Palestinian resistance, but I was not meant to become one of them because that would mean that I was not a 'good Arab woman'.

Rafeef recalls that after the signing of the Oslo Accord with Israel, there was a sense among Palestinians that their fight was over and people felt 'that there was peace now, and all we had to do was go back to Palestine and build a capitalist economy'. When Rafeef's family moved back to Palestine, she was shocked at the poverty and corruption that was taking root, as well as the conservative elements that were starting to restrict women's freedoms so much more so than had been the case during the first Intifada. It was from this shock that her class-based politics developed and her concept of revolutionary change was altered. She refused to believe that the Palestinian struggle for self-determination could be about the wealth and power of a few select men.

Rafeef decided to come to North America to study: first in the US and then in Toronto. In the past year she has co-founded a political prisoner solidarity group called Sumoud, which means 'steadfastness' in Arabic.

Rafeef: Sumoud wanted to bring out the issue of not only political imprisonment of Palestinians but also the imprisonment of indigenous communities and people of colour in North America. Our aim was to raise awareness about the racism and criminalization of poverty that exists within the prison system. The group envisioned working on issues of how colonialism and imperialism manifest worldwide, not only in Palestine.

One of Sumoud's primary focuses has been a pressure campaign against the International Red Cross. In numerous conflict zones, it is the Red Cross that is responsible for overseeing the treatment of political prisoners and, in the case of Palestinian prisoners, they have largely been complicit in Israel's human rights violations by not taking a public stand against them. When Palestinian political prisoners staged a nationwide hunger strike to demand better treatment in Israeli jails, Sumoud members and supporters organized, in solidarity, a hunger strike across from the Red Cross offices in Toronto.

Confronting oppression in relation to feminism

What Liisa, Rafeef, Farrah and Rachel have in common is a commitment to rooting out and dismantling injustice, exploitation and inequality in all their forms. While all four of these young women hold strong commitments to gender equality (and challenge gender injustice in the work they do), each of them, to varying degrees, holds 'feminism' at arm's length. At the end of the day, this is largely because feminist movements and organizations have failed adequately to address, in their analyses and actions, the multiple oppressions that these young women face and are fighting against – be they racism, colonialism, ableism, heterosexism, patriarchy or poverty. In one way or another, all four women expressed the view that a feminist analysis alone would not bring about the social, political, economic or cultural changes they want to see in their communities and in the world.

For Rafeef, creating social change requires both an understanding of how women are affected by multiple forms of oppression, as well as a commitment to challenging power.

Rafeef: Women don't just face discrimination on the basis of being women; we face it on the basis of class, gender, race, histories of colonialism and histories of occupation. We face it at different levels. I don't think that we can step out of this reality and say 'I want to do just feminist work on its own.' That being said, I do think that my work is feminist in that I don't think 'feminist work' means working on strictly women-specific issues in isolation. A lot of women's organizations today are defining their work quantitatively. Their focus is on such things as how many women are going to be in government. If this number rises by 10 per cent then it's considered 'feminist work' because more women have been put in 'positions of power'. However, this is without thinking about who the women are who are getting into power, why these specific women have been chosen, and what this indicates. Are we challenging the power structures, if all we are doing is adding more women regardless of their politics? Is this really challenging the systems or is it just a way of making things look prettier? I think doing feminist work actually means taking feminist theory and applying it to all of the activist environments that we find ourselves in – explicitly feminist or not.

Through her work with Project Threadbare, Farrah feels that putting forth a gendered analysis is something that must be done alongside working within South Asian communities to stop the racism they are facing.

Farrah: It's [sexism] something that I have to work with within my community and it has to be negotiated alongside many other issues of oppression that come up. The systemic targeting of South Asians and Muslims, by Canadian authorities, is responsible for creating severe poverty, and for destroying people's lives. I think, as a woman in this community, it is my responsibility, first and foremost, to work with everyone to challenge these things, and through this process bring forward a gendered analysis.

Liisa explains that, from her perspective, feminism must be both radical and explicitly anti-capitalist in order to stand a chance in dismantling patriarchy.

Liisa: I would define feminism as a movement/struggle against structures of patriarchy, as well as against the institutions that politically, socially and economically sustain sexist structures. The structures of colonialism and the structures of capitalism are beneficial to the structures of patriarchy; they reinforce one another. Colonialism brings out patriarchy and reinforces it. I've chosen not to work in mainstream feminist organizations because I find them very 'NGOish': they are often not explicitly anti-capitalist and I find that they are very academic. They are not taking their politics to the streets, where I sincerely feel that they should be. They are not building bridges with other ongoing struggles. Too much emphasis is being placed on petitioning the government, or lobbying the powers that be, believing that things need to change step-by-step or slowly. I won't accept this slow pace and arbitrary points of focus when people are being bombed in Iraq, when violence against women is on the rise and when my own mother can't afford to pay her rent. I won't accept small steps; I won't accept reformist ideas. I think that is what is so different about organizing in radical organizations. You actually get to start doing work that is challenging the state in an obvious, direct and harsh way. It is empowering to do this. It is especially empowering to do this as a woman who has experienced the powers of poverty and violence. My criticism of the feminist movement at large, particularly in Toronto, is that I don't see it in the streets, except for once a year at the International Women's Day march. I don't think the feminist movement is going to get us very far, or not far enough, if they don't start putting themselves 'out there'.

Challenges and strengths

The organizing that Liisa, Rafeef, Farrah and Rachel are involved with provides examples of dynamic community-based activism. Their insight, leadership and commitment provide a glimpse into the power that young women possess to create radical social change. That being said, it is also important to recognize some of the real challenges politically active young women in Toronto are faced with. All of the local groups discussed above stay afloat on bare-bones budgets collected mainly through fundraising events. None of these groups receives any government or private funding. Liisa, Rafeef, Farrah and Rachel are not paid for the activism that they engage in; they balance their time between community work and finding the means of survival (either through waged employment, scholarships or social assistance), which is a constant concern for them and many other young activists.

The radical nature of their work, and the ways in which it directly challenges the powers that be, is threatening to those who benefit and profit from maintaining the status quo and the inequality and exploitation inherent in it. In addition to being arrested, tear-gassed, pepper-sprayed and beaten by state authorities through the course of their political work, young women activists also face threats and violence from men in far-right political groups. Last year during an anti-occupation rally at York University to commemorate the one-year anniversary of the death of US activist Rachel Corrie,[20] several young Arab women were spat on, kicked and threatened with rape by white men belonging to right-wing pro-Zionist groups.

The organizations that these young women work within are not necessarily safe spaces either. As within our city and communities, sexism is often present within the groups we work with and in the communities where we live; it constantly needs to be rooted out and addressed. To do this, numerous groups have created 'women's caucuses' within their organizations; however, these caucuses have often created more work for women members and reinforce misconceptions that sexism is a 'women's issue' rather than leading to a stronger feminist analysis of the group as a whole. Each of the young women interviewed offered other ideas and strategies for addressing sexism, heterosexism and patriarchy within our activist circles. Within Project Threadbare, Farrah says an important starting point has been educating young men within the group about their responsibility to confront the sexism they witness – be it disregarding women's ideas and opinions or talking too much and taking up too much space. Rafeef calls for procedures to be put in place so that organizations know how to addresses sexist behaviour collectively, instead of letting the responsibility fall on the victims. Rachel points out that women have played very central roles in OCAP's organizational and campaign development; this has helped to ensure that the organization addresses the ways in which poverty impacts women specifically. The need to make more space to address these challenges and develop strategies, as well as learn from women, who have faced similar struggles before us, is very much acknowledged.

In the long run, our ability to dismantle inequality and challenge injustice will depend on our collective ability to confront oppression in all its forms. For older feminists, supporting young women does not only mean making space for them in already existing organizations and movements, nor does it only include efforts to mentor or share knowledge and experience (although these things are both essential and appreciated). Solidarity with young women activists also means giving time, energy and support to the initiatives and actions *they* are leading – whether they are taking place in local community centres, on campuses or in the streets. The ability of feminist organizations to remain relevant to social change will depend on their efforts to support this vital work. Only when the visions, perspectives and leadership of young women are given respect and solidarity will we be able to create movements that are truly transformative.

Notes

1 M. Dauvergne (2002), 'Homistat-2001', *Juristat*, 22(7).

2 Toronto Summit Alliance (2004), 'Issues facing our city: affordable housing', see <http://www.torontocitysummit.ca/urban_challenges/affordable_housing/>.

3 Basel Action Network (2002), 'Environmentalists expose illegal Canadian electronic waste dumping in Asia', see <http://www.ban.org/ban_news/Environmentalists_expose.html>.

4 Canadian Broadcasting Corporation (CBC) Archives (2004), 'Mercury rising: the poisoning of Grassy Narrows', see <http://archives.cbc.ca/IDD-1-70-1178/disasters_tragedies/grassy_narrows_mercury_pollution/>.

5 L. Carter (2003), 'Grassy Narrows fights for their future', see <http://firstnationsdrum.com/Spring2003/CovGrassy.htm>.

6 Status of Women Canada (2004), 'Violence against women in Canada', see <http://www.swc-cfc.gc.ca/dates/dec6/facts_e.html>.

7 According to the University of Victoria Sexual Assault Centre: 'sexual assault is any type of sexual activity, from fondling to kissing, to intercourse, in which one of the partners does not consent – or consents by force, or threat of force. It takes many different forms, such as stranger rape, date rape, acquaintance rape, marital rape, sexual harassment, child sexual abuse, incest, gang rape, etc. In every instance, it is an act of violence which is motivated by the wish to control, to humiliate, and to dominate.' <http://www.uvss.uvic.ca/avp/sexual_assault.htm>.

8 University of Victoria (2004), 'Open resource', see <http://www.uvss.uvic.ca/avp/statistics.htm>.

9 J. Ridington (1989), *Beating the Odds: Violence and Women with Disabilities* (Vancouver: Disabled Women's Network).

10 Women who come to Canada on specialized restricted classes of visas, such as the live-in caregiver visa or the exotic dancer visa, are particularly

at risk of exploitation and abuse from their employers since their staying in Canada is dependent on them keeping their jobs.

11 Ontario Women's Directorate (1998), 'Dispelling the myths about sexual assault', see <www.gov.on.ca/owd/resources/sexual_assault_dispel_myths/sexassa.htm>.

12 Sisters in Spirit (2004), '500 Aboriginal women missing in Canada', see <http://www.sistersinspirit.ca/engmissing.htm>.

13 Health Canada (2004), 'Health care renewal', see <http://www.hc-sc.gc.ca/english/hca2003/fmm/fmm02.htm>.

14 Statistics Canada (1996), 'The justice data factfinder', *Juristat*, 16 (9).

15 A. Jackson and E. Smith (2002), 'Does a rising tide lift all life boats? recent immigrants in the economic recovery', *Policy Research Initiative*, 5 (2), see <http://policyresearch.gc.ca/page.asp?pagenm=v5n2_art_09>.

16 S. J. Kerr (2003), 'Meet Canada the global arms dealer', see <http://www.en-camino.org/june032003kerrcanadaarms.htm>.

17 June 30th Committee (2004), 'A guide to Toronto's war profiteers', see <http://fr.freeshell.org/june30th_factsheets.pdf>.

18 Islamophobia refers to discriminatory attitudes, stereotypes, and fear of Muslims.

19 The term 'non-status' refers to anyone without full legal citizenship or permanent residence status in Canada.

20 Rachel Corrie was a US citizen and a member of the International Solidarity Movement. She was crushed to death by an Israeli bulldozer while attempting to prevent the demolition of Palestinian homes in the Gaza Strip on 16 March 2003.

11 | A human rights instrument that works for women: the ICC as a tool for gender justice

ZAKIA AFRIN AND AMY SCHWARTZ

Ferdousi Priyabhashini was 22 years old and working in a jute mill to support her three children when the war that liberated Bangladesh from Pakistan broke out in 1971. She was brutally raped for seven and a half months by the Pakistani military and their accomplices. In 1999, after 28 years of painful silence, she publicly demanded that the perpetrators of these acts be tried. Ferdousi was not alone. According to the estimates of international aid organizations, about 400,000 women were raped during this nine-month conflict.[1] Rather than punish the perpetrators of these crimes, the newly independent state of Bangladesh did what most governments and the international community have done throughout history: they failed to address grave abuses of women's rights in times of conflict.

The recent establishment of the International Criminal Court (ICC) and the entry into force of its gender-inclusive Rome Statute is hailed by many as the breakthrough in international law and human rights that not only will ensure that women such as Ferdousi have recourse to justice, but also will ensure the strongest instrument yet available for the advancement of women's rights.[2] For the first time, crimes of sexual violence and gender-based persecution are codified with due gravity in international law and can be enforced by the mechanisms of this new court. This automatically fulfils several of the objectives of the women's rights movement as outlined in the Beijing Platform for Action (PFA) and serves to end impunity for such crimes. The enforceability of this statute, coupled with its influence on domestic legal systems, has implications for international and national legal reform that could significantly improve women's rights.

This chapter will examine the achievements of the women's movement as represented by the creation of the ICC and evaluate the extent to which the ICC can further the women's rights agenda. We will show that the ICC represents a significant breakthrough in gender integration in international law and in providing a strong mechanism to enforce women's human rights. We will explain how, despite its limitations, young women activists can use the ICC as an instrument to further women's rights at the national and international levels.

Background

Gender integration in the substance, structure and procedures of the ICC was made possible, in part, by concurrent developments in international criminal law and the human rights field. In 1993, at the UN World Conference on Human Rights, feminist activists claimed that the Charter of the UN (1945), the Universal Declaration of Human Rights (1948), the International Covenant on Civil and Political Rights (1966) and the International Covenant on Economic, Social and Cultural Rights (1966) failed to provide adequate provisions for women's rights. These activists worked to ensure that the separate issue of women's rights was integrated into the human rights agenda through the Vienna Declaration. The Declaration on the Elimination of Violence Against Women by the UN General Assembly and the establishment of a thematic mandate and special rapporteur on the elimination of violence against women in the UN Commission on Human Rights soon followed.[3] When, in 1995, the Beijing Platform for Action of the Fourth World Conference on Women pushed international lawmakers to account for violence against women within its jurisdiction, the UN system unequivocally identified gender-based violence during armed conflict as a serious threat to women's rights.[4] Considering that the world has witnessed more than 250 horrific regional and internal armed conflicts since the Second World War and that these conflicts have a combined death toll of between 70 million and 170 million, there is no doubt that the problem of armed conflict directly affects the rights of a vast number of women.[5]

The Platform for Action called on all relevant international institutions to take strong actions to deal with this urgent issue by mainstreaming gender into policies and programmes that address conflict.[6] This represented a strong push for transformation in international humanitarian law. The Hague Convention, the Geneva Conventions and Optional Protocols, as well as the Nuremberg Charter, provided for the protection of women in armed conflict only in terms of their relationship with others, for instance as pregnant women, mothers or valued property of men or family, but not as legal persons themselves. This meant that crimes of sexual violence, which bear the characteristics of torture, persecution and disregard for bodily integrity that are recognized as 'grave breaches' of human rights in other cases, are not ascribed due gravity in international law. As a result, rape is not 'prohibited' as an unacceptable breach of international standards of human rights; rather it is an expected crime committed in times of war from which women should be 'protected'. The conceptualization of rape as a crime from which women should be protected, rather than a prohibited grave breach of international law, implies that crimes of sexual violence are not considered to be premeditated, unacceptable acts of torture, genocide or persecution, but are unfortunate and inevitable by-products of war.[7] The inferior treatment of crimes of sexual violence and the lack of gender sensitivity and balance in the composition of the prosecutors, investigators and courts that have dealt with war crimes in the past are blamed for the dearth of prosecutions for acts of violence against women in times of war.[8]

Crimes of sexual violence against women in the conflicts of the former Yugoslavia and Rwanda generated considerable publicity for the horrific and systematic abuse of women's rights in war. This added pressure to the PFA's calls for crimes of sexual violence against women to be addressed seriously. Modest improvements were made to this effect, as the statutes of the International Criminal Tribunal for the Former Yugoslavia (ICTY) in 1995 and the International Criminal Tribunal for Rwanda (ICTR) in 1998 codified rape as a crime against humanity. Despite this improvement, rape was still not considered to be a grave breach of human rights. A small group of women who served as legal activists, investigators, advisers, prosecutors and judges in these tribunals sought to change this disparity in international law by investigating and prosecuting crimes of rape as forms of torture, inhumane treatment, wilful killing, enslavement and other grave breaches of international humanitarian law.[9] This groundbreaking jurisprudence, which included the first international investigation of rape as a war crime and the first conviction for rape as a breach of international law, enabled women's rights activists to secure an invaluable foothold in international law that could open possibilities for further legal advancements for women's rights.

After more than 47 years of periodic deliberations, in 1998 negotiations began in Rome to create the treaty and statute for the first permanent international tribunal that would have jurisdiction over the gravest violations of international humanitarian and human rights law.[10] Feminist activists knew that this new instrument could offer strong mechanisms to advance women's rights. To advocate for a gender-integrated mandate for the new International Criminal Court, feminist activists formed a powerful lobby. The Women's Caucus for Gender Justice (WCGJ) in the ICC, a compilation of more than 200 women's organizations from every region of the world, presented several important provisions and additions to the Rome Statute that would help achieve the strategic objectives of the Beijing Platform for Action. The policy of gender integration throughout the UN had made most governments aware of the importance of the provisions proposed by the WCGJ, and they generally supported WCGJ advocacy. Arguing that such inclusion offended their religious standards, a strong opposition presented itself from mostly North American anti-choice groups, the Vatican and a handful of Islamic states, who were determined to keep provisions for women's rights out of the statute. Since the Rome Treaty Conference was committed to producing the statute through consensus, the few states that supported the opposition strategically used this condition to try to prevent gender integration into the provisions. While the efforts of this opposition almost prevented the inclusion of the most important gender aspects of the statute, a more restrictive definition of the word gender than that used within the UN system was finally accepted by all parties.[11]

Achieving women's rights goals

Although conservative pressures caused major obstructions in the negotiations, gender integration in the Rome Statute was successful; in 1998, when 120 states voted to adopt the statute, the provisions, procedures and structural imperatives of the ICC that would further protect and uphold women's rights in times of conflict were codified in international law. When the statute entered into force in 2002, major deficiencies in international law related to gender-based crimes were finally overcome, and several important objectives of the Beijing Platform for Action were automatically fulfilled.[12]

In the Rome Statute, the PFA's call for the international community and its judicial instruments to recognize gender-based persecution, rape, sexual slavery, trafficking in women, enforced prostitution, enforced sterilization, forced pregnancy and other forms of sexual violence as war crimes were realized. For the first time, these crimes of sexual violence are included in the definitions of war crimes, crimes against humanity and even acts of genocide.[13] Crimes of trafficking in women and gender-based persecution are considered to constitute crimes against humanity. This allows the possibility of prosecuting those responsible for trafficking and those responsible for discriminatory policies, such as the sexual apartheid imposed by the Taliban in Afghanistan. Additionally, the statute recognizes and outlaws gender as a basis for persecution.

Until the adoption of the Rome Statute, women's rights in international law were characterized by stereotypical concepts of femininity and the 'place' of women in the private sphere.[14] Feminist legal scholars noted that the jurisdiction of international law includes public activities such as politics, economics and intellectual pursuits, hence crimes of sexual violence that have not been articulated to be within the public sphere are not dealt with in major international legal conventions.[15] The Rome Statute clearly articulates sexual violence, dismantles inadequate notions of 'honour' and 'family', and squarely places international legal mechanisms in the 'private' domain of women's sexuality. The Rome Statute represents an important reconceptualization of women's experiences as requiring legal recognition. This could lead the way for the further dismantling of the patriarchal structure of international law.

In addition, the ratification process of the Rome Statute makes significant contributions towards improving national legal frameworks in terms of gender-based violence. Since the ratification of treaties requires that domestic laws and procedures conform to the treaty provisions, states that ratify the Rome Statute must introduce legislation for its implementation. In this way, crimes that are prohibited in the Rome Statute must also be prohibited in domestic law. Gaps in a national criminal code related to the prosecution of gender-based violence, including procedural mechanisms, will have to be resolved in domestic laws. Such changes can significantly enhance the capability of domestic legal systems to define and process crimes of gender-based violence in times of peace. This process is upheld through the principle of complementarity, which stipulates that the court has the jurisdiction to intervene if a state is unwilling or unable to prosecute crimes identified in the Rome Statute. To avoid such interference in their domestic affairs, states have added incentive to conform their legal systems to the provisions of the Rome Statute.

At the individual level, the PFA thoroughly outlines the need to ensure access to justice and reparations to women who are victims of violence.[16] To this end, the ICC has set up several procedural mechanisms to ensure victims and witnesses can face the judicial process without additional harm or trauma, including the provision of counselling and psychological support and guaranteed confidentiality at all levels with the possibility of testimony in closed hearings. The court also does not require corroboration to prove crimes of sexual violence, nor can personal sexual conduct be considered as evidence. The Victim Protection Unit will help ensure that witness rights and interests are protected in every step of the trial. In addition, the court is able to provide reparations to victims of gender-based and other crimes.[17]

Structurally, the PFA calls for international judicial bodies to strive for gender balance and to promote women's participation in all decision-making levels.[18] The Rome Statute sets provisions for 'fair representation' of men and women in the selection process of the judges for the court, in the Office of the Prosecutor and all other organs of the court.[19] The court must endeavour to hire candidates with legal expertise on violence against women or children.[20] Additionally, the Rome Statute requires legal advisers on sexual and gender violence to ensure that the court has the capacity to investigate and prosecute gender-based crimes properly.[21]

Overall, the Rome Statute provides a powerful response to the PFA's call to work towards the elimination of violence against women and to end the impunity of perpetrators of violence against women. International law is no longer silent on sexual violence and, by implication of the ratification of the Rome Statute, many national legal systems can no longer ignore such crimes. If case law is applied to enforce these legal reforms both at the international and national levels, possible perpetrators will receive a strong message that there are significant consequences for crimes of gender-based violence.

A human rights tool

As a tool for women's rights, the ICC differs considerably from other international human rights instruments. A human rights declaration or document, such as the Beijing Platform for Action, sets guidelines and standards for promoting and protecting human rights. However, such instruments have no inbuilt legal mechanisms for enforcement. Although the ICC is designed as a court with a criminal code, it is a mechanism that can be applied to promote, protect and enforce human rights. Until now, no other human rights instrument has had tools other than ethical, national and diplomatic pressures to compel the compliance of states and to deter individuals from committing abuses of women's rights. While other human rights instruments have mechanisms to deal only with violations by states, the ICC represents new possibilities for the international enforcement of human rights as it has the jurisdiction to prosecute individuals directly.

As mechanisms to prosecute for gender-based crimes are included in the Rome Statute, it provides stronger legal enforcement of women's rights than any other human rights tool. The statute not only enshrines specific measures to protect women from violence and punish perpetrators in international criminal law but also provides structural mechanisms to ensure the court is capable of applying these instruments. Even CEDAW and its Optional Protocols (OP), with relatively complete guidelines and strong mechanisms to compel states to protect and promote the rights of women, lacks the international legal structure to enforce compliance. Although CEDAW's OPs provide a case-based review mechanism for violations of women's rights, the presiding body, the Commission on the Status of Women (CSW), can recommend courses of action to reprimand those in violation; they have no real power to sanction states in this regard. The establishment of the ICC also means that national governments can be called to account for neglecting to address violations of women's rights.

Unlike the CEDAW OPs, the ICC does not require that all national legal mechanisms are first exhausted before bringing a case before its court. If the ICC deems a state to be unable or unwilling to prosecute specific cases of gender-based crimes, those can be brought directly before the court

155

without the prolonged and possibly traumatic effort of first attempting to use an incapable domestic legal system.[22] Furthermore, unlike CEDAW and the PFA, the explicit purpose of the Rome Statute is not to advance women's rights, rather it contains such possibilities within its broader provisions for reform. Since its implications for the advancement of women's rights are less obvious, opposition forces that categorically oppose the implementation of international women's rights treaties may not have the automatic impulsion or sufficient support to resist the national adoption of the Rome Statute. Similarly, governments that are reluctant to integrate women's rights treaties because of the difficult politicking it may involve might find the Rome Statute a less controversial means by which to enact reforms that will benefit women. In this way, important laws for women's rights could be adopted without the usual obstructions.

Young women's activism and the ICC

The success of gender integration into the Rome Statute is widely attributed to the advocacy of women's rights activists in the negotiation of the Rome Statute.[23] The ICC openly encourages NGOs and advocacy groups to take an active role in ensuring that the court is an effective instrument for human rights.[24] Young women can play a critical part in strengthening the ICC as an instrument for women's rights by pushing the court to apply its important substantive, structural and procedural gender-related provisions.

Activists need to ensure that women are aware of the ICC and the applicability of its mechanisms and statute. Also, by using their networks to disseminate information on the ICC, the Rome Statute and national obligations, women's groups can complement the ICC's upcoming campaign to educate women on ways they can approach the court.[25]

The effort of Women's Initiatives for Gender Justice (WIGJ) to ensure that the ICC realizes its provisions both in its internal structure as well as in its substantive work provides young women activists with a model for effective advocacy. WIGJ engages in campaigns to inform qualified women all over the world about key positions within the court, which has led to a significant increase in the number of women applicants.[26] Its lobbying efforts have helped ensure that seven of the 18 judges appointed to the ICC are women and that several strong women candidates applied for the position of the deputy prosecutor, the head of the Prosecution Division.[27] Ms Fatou Bensouda, from Ghana, a woman with relevant legal qualifications and a commitment to gender issues, was finally elected to the position.[28] WIGJ also provides gender-legal advice and training to the staff of the ICC.[29] WIGJ has identified that the senior position of gender legal adviser in the Office of the Prosecutor, as provided for in the Rome Statute, is necessary to ensure that gender-based crimes are properly identified and prosecuted. To ensure that this crucial position is adopted, advocates need to lobby the court, or push their governments to pressure the court.

Women's groups can also mobilize to pressure the US and other states to ratify the Rome Statute, and young women can support advocacy groups that are currently engaged in such efforts.[30] In those states that have ratified the statute, activists can push their national governments to change laws, procedures and structures to better protect women's rights. Although state parties that have ratified the Rome Statute are required, by international law, to make the necessary reforms, as yet only a handful of the 97 relevant countries have made the necessary implementation legislation, and none of these has taken the required steps to reform their legal systems.

Activists can apply pressure on their governments to adopt procedures, laws and structural changes related to issues of gender-based violence by using the recognized and binding provisions of the Rome Statute to argue for reform. They can undertake studies, training and information campaigns to educate their governments, the public, lawmakers and law practitioners on how to conform their domestic legal systems to the statute. Such tactics could be applied to broaden the definition of rape, to develop protections for victim's rights, to improve the rules of evidence and procedure, including the prohibition of personal sexual conduct being used as evidence in trials related to sexual violence, or for reform of national reparations mechanisms. Women's rights activists in Chile, Ecuador and Argentina have applied such strategies and WIGJ plans to undertake a global campaign to this effect.[31]

In those states that have passed implementation legislation for the Rome Statute, legal activists can reinforce or initiate legal improvements by developing relevant case law. Such precedents can convey that crimes of violence against women are taken seriously. Again, this will help to end domestic impunity for violence against women.

The ICC provides an example of how gender integration in composition, administration, procedures and recruitment can be operationalized in a major institution. Young women can translate the applicability of this example to pressure national legal systems and other private and public, national and international bodies to adopt effective gender integration in their composition and hiring procedures.[32]

Jurisprudence can also be applied within the ICC to deal with a variety of other issues important to women activists. Cases related to indigenous rights could be brought before the court under the laws regarding genocide. Violence that targets lesbian, gay, bisexual, transgender and inter-sex

157

people could be brought before the court through the provisions for persecution of identified groups.[33] Cases related to the deliberate transmission of HIV/AIDS as a weapon of war or cases related to persecution of persons living with HIV/AIDS in times of conflict could be tried to develop such jurisprudence. Systematic targeted violence against women in a country without domestic laws dealing with violence against women could also be brought before the court as systematic persecution.

The ICC also offers strategic openings for broad national reform that is not necessarily related to sexual violence. For example, reparations mechanisms in the ICC can lead to reforms of domestic inheritance laws. If a woman from a state that provides few inheritance rights to women is awarded reparations in the form of goods, property or land, a legal precedent can be set for inheritance rights. Related case law can then be applied to develop these rights. Such creative uses through procedural mechanisms could also be applied to family, civil and customary laws.[34]

Limitations of the ICC for women's rights

Although the Rome Statute and the ICC offer groundbreaking opportunities to apply and advance women's rights, it has several limitations that activists should recognize. While it may be early to evaluate the effectiveness and limitations of the ICC, as the court has only been in existence since 2002 and has yet to execute a trial, several assessments can still be made based on its structure, procedures and substance.

Perhaps the ICC's most obvious flaw is that it will never be able to provide justice to women such as Ferdousi. The ICC will accept referrals related only to crimes committed after 1 July 2002, when the court came into existence. As a result the innumerable cases of wartime sexual violence and persecution that occurred before this date, such as the rape Ferdousi endured in 1971, cannot be investigated or tried in the ICC. Considering the number of armed conflicts that have occurred in the last 50 years alone, the ICC fails to provide a means to enforce the rights of, possibly, tens of thousands of women who suffered grave crimes. If the international community fails to address this vast gap in the enforcement of women's rights, there is the risk that these women will never be accorded due justice.

Since 1 July 2002, the court has been working on three main referrals from the Democratic Republic of Congo (DRC), the Central African Republic (CAR) and Uganda. As these cases have not yet come to trial, no convictions for gender-based crimes have been made. The examples of the ICTY and ICTR, where many convicted perpetrators of war crimes of sexual violence remain unpunished, indicate that these instruments can still fail to some degree despite adequate legal infrastructure.[35] It is possible that despite the new provisions, procedures, structure and composition of the court certain mechanisms could still fail to accord women due justice. Advocates must monitor the court to ensure that perpetrators of gender-based violence are properly prosecuted and punished with the new mechanisms of the ICC and that all due procedures are invoked to provide fairness to victims.[36]

Although the ICC has stronger mechanisms than previous human rights instruments to address violations of women's rights, these may prove inadequate. In terms of its capacity to investigate and prosecute cases, the court could receive more referrals than it has the resources or capability to process in a timely manner. While it may be too early to tell if this will occur, a significant backlog of cases could undermine the credibility of the court as an effective and appropriate tool for resolution and redress. If bringing a case to the ICC drags out an already uncomfortable process, and allows for a longer period before perpetrators are prosecuted and punished, those who have endured crimes of sexual violence may experience frustration at the lack of resolution of their case. This could discourage those who have suffered and witnessed grave crimes from engaging with the court.

Another limitation of the ICC is the lack of support from the United States. The US has not ratified the Rome Statute and in 2002 took the unusual action of 'unsigning' the Rome Treaty. As a member of the UN Security Council and the current global superpower, the refusal of the US to participate in the court severely undermines the legitimacy, strength and capability of the ICC. Due to the resolve of the American government to prevent the ICC from gaining strength as an instrument for international justice, the UN Security Council, of which the US is a member, cannot effectively use the ICC as an official organ. This diminishes the ICC's importance as a central tool of international governance.[37] The refusal of the US to ratify the Rome Statute and its 'unsigning' of the treaty sends the message that, as the world superpower, it does not take such grave breaches of human rights seriously, and that the American government considers itself and its citizens morally and legally immune to international law. US non-participation deprives the ICC of strong multilateral backing and allows the US to directly, or in partnership with other states, undermine the ICC for strategic political purposes.[38]

The lack of US support is partly the result of conservative, even fundamentalist, pressures that threaten to reverse global and national advancements in women's rights. In the current political climate, any efforts to implement the Rome Statute in the domestic sphere, or to further reform international law, are likely to be met with such opposition. As conservative forces can mobilize considerable political clout, women's rights activists must be careful in using the Rome Statute to open up debate and mechanisms for change, at both the international and national levels. Such efforts for progress could be hijacked and result in regression.

At this time, few women know about the court and what it offers in terms of redress for crimes at the international and national levels. If women who are affected by conflict are unaware of their rights and the relevancy of the court to their experience, then the ICC is not reaching all those who could use its procedures. Unless this gap in the ICC's accessibility can be overcome, the mechanisms of the ICC will not be relevant to many women who deserve redress for violations of their rights. Similarly, if prosecutions related to gender-based crimes are not widely publicized, would-be perpetrators of such crimes will not receive the important message of deterrence.

At the national level, the Rome Statute is also limited as an instrument for advancing women's rights. Although there are stronger incentives and more complete legal frameworks to compel states to conform to the Rome Statue than there are with any other human rights treaty, states seem as inactive in implementing the Rome Statute as they have been with previous human rights commitments. While governments are aware that the principle of complementarity could result in ICC intervention in domestic affairs, this is an unlikely scenario in the short term; therefore, states are willing to take on the risk of delaying implementation. As a result, important changes to national structures in terms of protecting women's rights have not been adopted. Since there is no way to sanction governments under international law for failing to implement ratification obligations, as with other instruments for human rights, the national enforcement of the Rome Statute will have to rely on pressures from non-governmental sources. It could be argued that, at the national level, the Rome Statute has not yet proved its capability to be a stronger instrument for domestic legal reform than other human rights instruments.

The ICC is further limited as an instrument for women's rights by its inability to address all the distinctive experiences of women in conflict. Although the Rome Statute makes efforts to do so, women's experience of refugee camps, treatment by peacekeepers, starvation, loss of physical shelter and vulnerability to economic sanctions are not explicitly dealt with in the provisions of the statute or anywhere else in international humanitarian law. The specific ways in which the girl child experiences armed conflict is also not addressed in the statute. As feminist legal scholars have argued, an entire redraft of all international humanitarian conventions is required, in addition to more comprehensive enforcement mechanisms, before all aspects of women's rights issues related to armed conflict will be comprehensively and properly addressed.[39]

Although the Rome Statute and the court can be used in strategic ways to address a variety of women's rights issues, their scope is not comprehensive. Many women's rights issues and gender inequalities that are not related to sexual violence or conflict-based persecution cannot conceivably or directly be addressed through the court. Even with the existence of the court, other practical and legal strategies, reforms and procedures remain necessary to respond to violations of women's rights and to advance gender equality.

Feminist legal scholars Dianne Martin and Mark Drumbl have further illustrated the inadequacies of the ICC as a comprehensive tool for the promotion of women's rights.[40] They explain that, as a criminal court, the ICC is a mechanism that can enforce a basic set of human rights, but only after those rights have been violated. Moreover, this enforcement is based on a retributive justice system, which is focused on individualized guilt and punishment, but will not have power to transform the underlying structural causes of gender-based violence in society. If gender-based crimes of violence are treated as individual transgressions that are adequately addressed through 'reactionary' punishments, then it sanctions the international community to conceptualize and deal with violence against women as a simplistic problem, and not as a complex structure of social inequalities that requires a comprehensive response. The supremacy of a retributive justice system that assigns guilt and punishment to members of certain groups can serve to create tensions and further divide societies, thus diminishing the incentive for women to come forward.

We must also recognize the limits of the ICC to act as a deterrent for crimes of gender-based violence. The punitive criminal justice model adheres to the notion that if individuals fear retribution they will rationally choose not to commit crimes. This 'rationality' is not likely to apply to the violence committed due to 'non-rational impulses' in times of conflict.[41] In war-torn societies, where an atmosphere of conflict and hysteria exists, fear and prejudice may distort rational decision making. Individuals may not consider that committing war crimes, crimes against humanity and acts of violence are legally or morally wrong. In such an environment the distant prospect of eventual prosecution through an international court is unlikely to be a strong deterrent from committing crimes of sexual violence and persecution against women.[42]

In addition to all these limitations, the ICC could be considered inherently limited as a tool for women's rights as it represents nothing more than a new addition to a growing pile of declarations and treaties that have been proven incapable to actually improve the lives of women.[43] Critics that espouse this view assert that the women's rights movement has invested too much of its energy in reforming and applying international human rights instruments with the hope that such reform will lead to corresponding national legal change to protect the rights of women. The lack of genuine progress in improving the lives of women through national legal reform is indicative that the application of these tools has not been successful.

The way forward

It may be too early to determine whether the limitations of the Rome Statute will prevent its power as an instrument for human rights. It is also too early to be sure whether its potential for advancing women's rights will be harnessed and strategically applied. There is no mistaking, however, that the ICC and its statute offer new possibilities for enforcing and advancing women's rights that were not previously available. It has opened new avenues for women activists to engage in strategic advocacy for gender justice at the local and global levels. Young women activists are becoming increasingly experienced in applying multi-level advocacy strategies, and are well equipped to engage in and strengthen advocacy efforts related to the applications of the ICC.

While we must be careful not to present the ICC as a satisfactory or complete instrument for furthering women's rights, it can be used as a strong component of a comprehensive approach. If we seek to get rid of structural inequalities and discrimination against women, we must combine punitive and reparative justice with transformative and restorative legal, educational, economic, political and social remedies.

Conversations with the ICC's deputy prosecutor, Fatou Bensouda, as well as with Brigid Inder of WIGJ and Mariana Rodriguez, a young woman activist with the NGO Coalition for the International Criminal Court (CICC), conveyed the sense that the ICC and women's rights advocates alike are determined to make the court hold true to its substantive, procedural and structural commitments to gender justice.[44]

Activists throughout the world are beginning to explore the possibilities of using the Rome Statute to advance women's rights.[45] The conviction of ICC personnel and activists that this instrument will offer possibilities for strategic advocacy gives the impression that the ICC can and will be used to invoke important changes for women's rights in the years to come.

While women such as Ferdousi, who suffered crimes before July 2002, may never directly gain justice through the ICC, she continues to encourage other Bangladeshi women to break their silence on the sexual violence they endured in 1971. The Rome Statute not only provides the framework and momentum that may enable Ferdousi, and countless others like her, to gain justice, but it also creates unprecedented opportunities to protect, enforce and advance women's rights at present and in the future. Young women activists must act now to ensure that this court lives up to its promise as an instrument for women's rights, and we must harness its full potential to further our goals for justice and gender equality.

A note from Zakia Afrin

As we were writing this chapter, the Bangladeshi Community in the San Francisco Bay area arranged a fundraising event for nine of the 'Women of 71'. These women were among the 200,000 Bengali women who were raped by the Pakistani army during Bangladesh's War of Independence. Every year as Bangladeshis remember the women who were victims of brutal crimes against humanity, we shed tears and try to heal their wounds with financial promises. This is all we have done so far. While this war is known in Bangladesh as one of the most horrific attempts at genocide in modern history, there was no trial, no punishment and no apology. Writing this chapter has been an emotional venture on my part. Had the International Criminal Court (ICC) been instituted in 1970 the outcomes and post-war healing process of the Bangladesh War for Independence may have been different. I believe that through the ICC no other nation will have to bear the pain induced by the failure to punish criminals who shake the conscience of humanity.

Notes

1 Adhunika (2005), 'Ferdousi Priyobhashini', see <http://www.adhunika. org/heroes/priyobhashini.html>.

2 WHRnet (2003), 'An interview with Brigid Inder', see <http://www.whrnet. org/docs/interview-inder-0408.html>; B. Bedont and K. Hall Martinez (1999), 'Ending impunity for gender crimes under the International Criminal Court', *Brown Journal for World Affairs*, VI(1): 65–85; Human Rights Watch (2002), 'International justice for women: the ICC marks a new era', see <http://www. hrw.org/campaigns/icc/icc-women.htm>.

3 WHRnet (2005), 'Human rights systems', see <http://www.whrnet.org/ docs/humanrightssystems.html>.

4 United Nations (1995), 'The Beijing Declaration and Platform for Action, Report of the Fourth World Conference on Women, UN Document A/Conf 177/20' (New York: United Nations), see sections 145d and 145e.

5 M. Cherif Bassiouni (1996), 'Searching for peace and achieving justice', *Law and Contemporary Problems*, 59(4): 5–7.

6 United Nations, 'The Beijing Declaration and Platform for Action', see section 143.

7 J. Gardam (1997), 'Women and the law of armed conflict: why the silence?', *International and Comparative Law Quarterly*, 46(1): 74.

8 J. Gardam and H. Charlesworth (2000), 'Protection of women in armed conflict', *Human Rights Quarterly*, 22 (1): 9

9 WHRnet (2003), 'An interview with Brigid Inder', see <http://www. whrnet.org/docs/interview-inder-0408.html>.

10 Although the Rome Statute was not negotiated until 1998, preparations for the ICC were undertaken periodically since 1951. At this time the first statute for a permanent international criminal court was drafted by a special UN General Assembly (GA) committee to fulfil a provision of the Genocide Convention of 1948. The consideration of the draft statute was postponed, however, as the definition of aggression had not yet been decided. This definitional problem prevented further progress on the statute until 1989, when Trinidad and Tobago pushed for resuming preparations for the draft statute. The *ad hoc* tribunals of the ICTR and ICTY reinforced the notion that a permanent court was necessary and in 1994 the GA established a preparatory committee (prepcom) to create a draft statute to submit to a diplomatic conference. This committee met from 1996 to 1998 and finalized its draft in April of 1998. At its fifty-second session the GA resolved to convene the United Nations Diplomatic Conference of Plenipotentiaries on the Establishment of an International Criminal Court, which was held in Rome from 15 June to 17 July in 1998.

11 The Rome Statute, Art 7 (3), defines gender as 'the two sexes, male and female, within the context of society. The term "gender" does not indicate any meaning different from the above.' See the Rome Statute at: <http://www.un.org/law/icc/statute/romefra.htm>.

12 As provided for in the treaty, the Rome Statute would enter into force provided 60 states ratified it. By July 2002 60 countries had ratified the treaty. As of today, 97 countries have ratified the Rome Treaty. The US has not. For a list of states that have ratified the treaty see <http://www.hrw.org/campaigns/icc/ratifications.htm>.

13 United Nations, 'The Beijing Declaration and Platform for Action', see sections 145d, e.

14 R. Coomaraswamy (1998), 'Report of the Special Rapporteur on Violence Against Women, its causes and consequences', Commission on Human Rights, fifty-fourth session, E/CN.4/1998/54, 26 January 4, see <http://www.unhchr.ch/Huridocda/Huridoca.nsf/TestFrame/c90326ab6dbc2af4c125661e0048710e?Opendocument>.

15 Gardam, 'Women and the law of armed conflict', pp. 65–6.

16 Although the use of the term 'victim' has clear connotations of powerlessness and lack of agency that should be challenged by feminists, we have chosen to use the term in this chapter to refer to those who have endured violations of their human rights because that is the terminology used to describe such subjects within the Rome Statute and most international legal documents. It should be recognized, however, that this term is problematic as it stems from patriarchal notions of power and benevolence that is part of the flawed structure of international law that needs to be reformed by feminist legal scholars and policy-makers.

17 See the Rome Statute at: <http://www.un.org/law/icc/statute/romefra.htm>. Articles 68 and 69.

18 United Nations, 'The Beijing Declaration and Platform for Action', see sections 142b, c, 144 c, 190 PFA.

19 Ibid.

20 See the Rome Statute at: <http://www.un.org/law/icc/statute/romefra. htm>. Articles 44(2) and 36(8).

21 Ibid. Article 42(9).

22 D. Sullivan (2004), 'The Optional Protocol to CEDAW and its applicability "on the ground"', see <http://www.whrnet.org/docs/issue-cedaw1. html>.

23 Unpublished interview (February 2005) by Amy Schwartz with Mariana Rodriguez Pareja, Spanish Information Services Coordinator, CICC.

24 Human Rights Watch Backgrounder (2004), 'The International Criminal Court: how nongovernmental organizations can contribute to the prosecution of war criminals', see <http://hrw.org/backgrounder/africa/icc0904/>.

25 Unpublished interview (February 2005) by Amy Schwartz with Fatou Bensouda, deputy prosecutor, ICC.

26 WHRnet, 'An interview with Brigid Inder'.

27 Ibid.

28 'The Deputy Prosecutor', International Criminal Court, Office of the Prosecutor, see <http://www.icc-cpi.int/otp/otp_bioProsec&l=en.html>.

29 WHRnet, 'An interview with Brigid Inder'.

30 Many advocacy organizations that push for ratification of the Rome Statute in the US and around the world include: the American Non-government Organizations Coalition for the International Criminal Court (AMICC), see <http://www.amicc.org/>; the Coalition for the International Criminal Court (CICC), see <www.iccnow.org>; Human Rights First, see <http://www. humanrightsfirst.org/international_justice/icc/icc.htm>; USA for the ICC, see <http://www.usaforicc.org/>; Coalition for International Justice, <http://www. cij.org/index.cfm?fuseaction=homepage>.

31 Oxfam (2002), 'Gender justice in South America', see <http://www. oxfam.org/eng/programs_deve_samerica_gender.htm>.

32 Also see Human Rights Watch (2002), 'International Justice for women: the ICC marks a new era', see <http://www.hrw.org/campaigns/icc/icc-women.htm>.

33 WHRnet, 'An interview with Brigid Inder'.

34 Unpublished interview (February 2005) by Amy Schwartz with Brigid Inder.

35 L. R. Jefferson (2004), 'In war as in peace: sexual violence and women's status', see <http://hrw.org/wr2k4/15.htm>.

36 Ibid.

37 Global Policy Forum (2005), 'The ICC in the Security Council', see <http://www.globalpolicy.org/intljustice/icc/crisisindex.htm>.

38 Human Rights Watch (2004), 'US Congress tries to undermine War Crimes Court', see <http://hrw.org/english/docs/2004/12/08/usint9794.htm>.

39 Gardam, 'Women and the law of armed conflict', p. 77.

40 M. Drumbl (2000), 'Punishment goes global: international criminal law, conflict zones, and gender (in)equality', *Canadian Woman Studies*, 19(4)

(Downsview); D. Martin (1998), 'Retribution revisited: a reconsideration of feminist criminal law reform strategies', *Osgoode Hall Law Journal*, 36(1): 151–88.

41 Martin, 'Retribution revisited', p. 162.

42 M. Drumbl, 'Punishment goes global'.

43 See D. Tsikata (October 2004), 'The rights-based approach to development: potential for change or more of the same?' *IDS Bulletin*, 35(4): 130–3.

44 Unpublished interview (February 2005) by Amy Schwartz with Mariana Rodriguez Pareja, Spanish Information Services coordinator, CICC; unpublished interviews (November 2004, February 2005) by Amy Schwartz with Brigid Inder; unpublished interview (February 2005) by Amy Schwartz with Fatou Bensouda, deputy prosecutor, ICC.

45 Oxfam, 'Gender justice in South America'; WHRnet, 'An interview with Brigid Inder'.

12 | Cyber girls: hello ... are you out there?

KRISTY EVANS

Often when I engage in conversations about technology, especially with feminists, I am faced with negative responses. Most people are cynical, and feel that technology is elitist – reserved for the small minority of people who have access – and developed and implemented in a patriarchal, capitalist system that is inherently exclusive. This has some truth in it, as millions of women still do not have access to internet and communication technologies (ICTs), and much of the software and operating systems must be 'bought' from corporations in order not to violate copyright and individual property rights.[1] If we stop for a second and think of who is excluded, we will realize that the very people whom we are campaigning 'for' and whose 'rights' we are fighting for, via internet activism and organizing, are the people who do not have access to this critical mode of communication and information. How do we reconcile this and what exactly does this mean for our work?

Despite the cynicism, there is still cause for optimism and celebration. The possibilities of communication methods and styles via the internet are infinite; every day more and more ICTs are being created, which are breaking down the boundaries of the current information systems and structures, and allowing for greater participation in internet communication and activism. Currently, there are a wide variety of innovative methods for communicating over the internet and in virtual spaces. The goal of this chapter is to explore some of the existing technologies and their potential to be used in feminist activism. While email, websites and chat rooms are some of the older communication technologies, blogging and text messaging are some of the new technologies that will assist feminist organizing and work in the existing ICT infrastructure. Free and open source software, the Creative Commons, and a variety of other technology projects and movements have come into the virtual sphere. There is much enthusiasm amongst those engaged with social justice activism via (and for) the internet, as these technologies encourage creativity and challenge the existing structures of internet use and communication, as well as the hierarchical systems in which we work, in a very explicit way.

Feminists using internet communications differently

Almost every organization that has access to ICTs has a website. And in turn, almost everyone working for those organizations has an email address to communicate both with each other, and with the outside world. This mode of communication goes further, of course. As many free email services are offered via the internet, most people worldwide, whether they belong to an organization, a corporation or a school, have an email account through which they can communicate.[2] Chat rooms and chat technology have also been utilized extensively to have ongoing 'conversations' over the internet, at work, for personal conversations with friends, or for discussing topics of interest with strangers.[3]

There are many examples of feminist organizations utilizing websites, email and chat technology as a part of their daily work.[4] This technology has allowed the access, dissemination and engagement of a wide array of ideas, information and communication exchange that would have not been otherwise possible. For example, the Association for Women's Rights in Development (AWID) currently has over 5,000 members from all over the world. It has over fifteen staff, working from three different country offices, as well as individual staff members working from their home countries.[5] The internet, including email communication, the AWID website and chat technology, has made the dissemination of AWID's work to its members possible, and has allowed for daily 'virtual' engagement of staff members from diverse working environments and identities.

List serves (and mailing lists, as they are also known) have impacted on the dissemination of information and messages in a substantial way. This type of technology consists of the ability to send an email message to a large number of people all at the same time. Using AWID as an example again, this allows the dissemination of information three times per week to all its members. This can be done to a lesser extent through individual email addresses, but there is a limit to the number of people to whom you can send a message at one time. Therefore, it is necessary to obtain specific computer programmes to enable mass mailing to people, hence limiting this technology to those people who can afford to pay for it.

Some of the newer ICTs that have become available over recent years consist of 'easier-to-use' and more individualized communication technologies. 'Blogging' is one example of this. It has taken off among social justice activists all over the globe. For example, 'in December 2004, it was estimated that Iranians maintained 300,000 blogs online with around 75,000 of them written in Persian from inside Iran'.[6] 'China's biggest blogging service provider blogcn.com reports that the number of subscribers increased from 10,000 in June last year, to more than 500,000 in December 2004.'[7] The advantage of blogging is that it is an internet technology that allows individuals an easy and accessible way to create individualized 'mini websites' in a matter of seconds.[8] This opens up significant possibilities for feminists all over the globe to 'find' each other and exchange information as well as engage in dialogue with each other. Blog sites offer a different world for young women. They offer a virtual world that is easy to access and navigate, which can be utilized for creative, personal as well as career-related endeavours. Blog sites can be created in a very personal manner, where some parts of the sites can be for creative expression, personal experiences and thoughts, as well as debates among people who are interesting in accessing the site. This technology is also useful as it can feed into a system called 'Rich Site Summary' or 'Really Simple Syndication' (RSS) that 'lets you know when a website [or blog site] has been updated'.[9] Therefore, instead of having constantly to go to a blog site or website to see what has been 'updated', the updates come straight to you through the RSS system.[10] This has significant implications and opportunities for social justice organizing and mobilizing efforts, as it revolutionizes information dissemination and exchange.

With cellular phone technologies expanding rapidly throughout the world, especially in developing countries, these present a whole other terrain of virtual communication and organizing.[11] As many countries have 'pay as you go' technology, this allows people who cannot afford or do not 'qualify' for cell phone contracts to be able to obtain cell phones and use them as they can afford them. Text messages (SMSing) are a quick (and cheaper) way of communicating cell phone to cell phone(s). Sending a text message from one cell phone to the other allows people to coordinate, organize and express themselves without actually having to 'talk' to the other person. This has interesting spin-offs for social justice work. Rochelle Jones explains in her article 'HIV/AIDS and mobile technology: SMS saving lives in Africa' that South Africa has created a new mobile phone software system called Cell Life, which provides virtual infrastructure where there is no actual infrastructure.[12] She explains one of the many uses of this new system:

> The new system allows doctors and caregivers to manage an information database containing a patient's treatment history, from remote locations using SMS. When they visit a patient they are able to report on side effects, check pill counts against data from the pharmacy, and provide additional information such as conditions that interfere in the treatment program like the absence of food and extreme poverty. In addition, symptoms indicative of dangerous side effects can be dealt with straight away by sending an SMS to the clinic and arranging an appointment as quickly as possible.[13]

While the internet and communication technologies described above are being widely used in our daily activism, some of the most interesting new ICTs are technologies that directly challenge the foundations that our virtual spaces are built upon. As access is still a significant issue throughout the world (especially for women), free and open software (FOSS) and the Creative Commons are two examples of movements that directly challenge issues of access and regulation for profit, presenting opportunities to close the 'digital divide'.[14]

FOSS is a movement that directly challenges issues of copyright and access. In September 2004, Women'sNet, a South African organization, with the help of the Association for Progressive Communications, organized one of the first workshops on FOSS 'by women for women', introducing Southern African women's organizations to the potential of this software.[15] They stated the potential benefits of this software as follows:

• Open source software is royalty- and license-free, which means that the cost of acquiring the software is lower than that of proprietary software.

• Because the source code is accessible, open source software can be modified to meet the needs of users in particular contexts and languages.

• Users are not trapped into ongoing dependency on a particular vendor for upgrades and support.

• The collaborative open source model of software development offers greater opportunities for local skills and economic development.

• Some free software is recognized as more stable and more secure than its proprietary counterparts.

• Open source software is often less damaging on hardware resources than proprietary software, and can help break the cycle of constantly needing to upgrade hardware to accommodate 'software bloat'.[16]

The Creative Commons is part of the movement to challenge copyrights and intellectual property rights in relation to ICTs.

> It promotes a flexible copyright framework that protects creative works while also promoting access to knowledge. It provides a system of 'some rights reserved' on websites, software, music, films and literary works. An author can for example prevent commercial use of his work, but allow free exchange for non-profit purposes.[17]

This project allows for licensing to be held by the Creative Commons project. Material can be released and disseminated this way, for instance, 'allowing people to download parts of it, but preventing commercial use'.[18]

This has significant implications for access to technology, and works around licensing and regulations in a 'creative' way. Communities, organizations and individuals who otherwise could not have afforded this type of technology thus begin to have access. 'In all, 261 communities are already involved in the project, and 250 more will be included next month.'[19]

The possibilities are endless – but for whom?

Gender disparity in technology is a reality. In order to ensure that women are able to access technology once it is physically in their vicinity, it is paramount that they have the capacity. There are still significant concerns about literacy worldwide – those who cannot read and write have no use for the internet.[20] Girls' illiteracy is still in disproportion to men's globally and this affects the number of women who can utilize ICTs in an effective manner.[21] To close the literacy gap, girls everywhere must be encouraged to stay in school; they must then be encouraged to pursue higher education in information technologies. Ultimately, women should not be merely recipients of technology, but also the creators, visionaries and inventors of new, appropriate technologies. This will ensure that we have available to us the technology that we need to ensure the most effective strategizing and organizing possible.

It is also important to consider the effectiveness of technology, and the supporting infrastructure, being utilized in differing contexts. Using the internet in Canada is very different from using the internet in the Democratic Republic of Congo, for example. I've often heard people commenting: 'I sent them the document three hours ago, why haven't they responded?' – obviously not realizing that internet connections, and technology in general, work differently in different contexts because of the existing infrastructure, as well as access to supporting technology. For some people it takes 30 seconds to download ten emails, for others it takes 30 minutes. Although FOSS, the Creative Commons, blogging and RSS begin to address issues in relation to access, infrastructure, copyright and intellectual property issues, there is still a significant way to go before the digital divide is overcome.

The internet as an *effective* tool for feminists

So while there are new possibilities that ICTs present, there are also new frustrations and challenges. For instance, I spend a lot of time in front of my laptop, using a variety of ICTs. For me, it is essential to evaluate and question the new technologies we are utilizing and creating. I often wonder if they are just the newest 'fad' and if any of these new methods will actually contribute to meaningful change. For my generation, and the upcoming generation of young feminists, ICTs have drastically changed the way in which we communicate with each other, the ways in which we strategize and the issues that we pay attention to, as our inboxes are flooded with cries for help or messages filled with pornographic propaganda. Therefore, we must be selective in choosing the documents we are willing to 'read' and pay attention to. Otherwise our already busy lives would be bombarded with every virus known to the cyber world, and every issue/campaign known to social justice organizing. So the question remains: how do we weed through these mountains of email messages, campaign pleas, newly released reports and 'task force' findings, in order to maximize our time and efforts in organizing for broader social transformation and gender equality? How do we use blogging, SMSing and open source communication to create actual change and not just overwhelm people with new technologies unnecessarily?

I think that we are all in agreement that the internet is useful: very useful and very frustrating. It aids us in the never-ending search for information and statistics, and allows us to communicate with colleagues, friends and family across the world relatively efficiently. As with other forms of communication, the internet can result in misunderstandings, as well as ineffective organizing and messaging. Unless the recipient of your email message or text message or your intended website/blog site/chat room reader is willing to take the time to a) open your message/webpage, b) read it in its entirety, and c) interpret what you are saying in the way that you have intended it, you then have a resulting breakdown in your intended communication. The age of reliance on internet technologies has sped this phenomenon up to a frantic pace. Misunderstandings and miscommunications are rife. Because of our resulting dependence on the internet, other (perhaps more appropriate) communication strategies, such as face-to-face meetings or telephone conversations, for dealing with conflicts, clarifications and new job tasks, are often undervalued and under-utilized.

Therefore we have to be selective in terms of the types of messages and issues that we communicate over the internet for social justice organizing. Internet technologies are tools that must work for us. Therefore, we cannot utilize the same tools for *every* message we want to communicate and *every* issue that we want to address. We must be selective and strategic about the communication technologies we use, and ensure effective use of a wide variety of options.

I see internet communication technologies as key in information dissemination: sending messages, announcements, press releases, and so on, out to a targeted audience. I think that this is where people often go wrong. Messages are often sent with the hope of reaching 'as many people as possible'. While it is logical to think that this is an effective communication strategy, it is often inefficient. Having your message reach people who are interested in your information is perhaps the most essential strategy in messaging and communication. Introducing the topic to newcomers to the field should be approached in an entirely different manner from that used for people already in the field, who are your potential supporters. The internet is an excellent tool for both tasks, but they need different messaging and communication strategies.

Finding the endless amount of data and information that we need for our daily work is also an integral part of the internet's usage as a research tool. However, this can be misused as well. While you can find anything from the number of plant species in South Africa (20,000) to the amount that Bill Gates is worth ($46.6 billion), the information is often unreliable and misrepresented.[22, 23] The internet has become the fastest and often sloppiest way of researching. It can also be an incredibly frustrating experience if you are not familiar with ways to sift through the 35,000,000 sites that Google finds for your research topic. Use the internet for research, but use it wisely. Ensure that your sources can be backed up and that they are from reliable institutions or authors.

The internet is often used for mobilizing people on specific (or sometimes general) issues. This is where internet use gets tricky. It is seemingly logical that the internet is the best way to get the greatest number of people to rally behind your cause/issue. You must ask yourself, however, if this is really what you want and whether this is really what is going to happen. Do you want your issue being filtered to every organization working on development issues or do you need specific people, with specific skills, to rally behind you? You must also ask yourself: whom exactly am I advocating for, and on what issue? Have you consulted with groups who are working 'on the ground' as to whether or not this kind of strategy and support will aid them? If not, it may just exacerbate the plight of the people/issue you are trying to aid, as well as set 'on the ground' work years back.[24] An example where mobilizing people via internet technologies has been successful was in the anti-war rallies to protest about the invasion of Iraq, as well as in organizing around the WTO protests in Seattle and Cancun. Many people obtained information, strategies and press releases via email messages, webpages, blog sites and RSS feeds, as well as by mobile technology in order to coordinate actions, meeting places, rallies, and so on. Another example of ICTs being effectively used in mobilizing people is in countries around election times – both to organize demonstrations and to rally more people to vote. South Korea and the Philippines used a variety of technologies to mobilize constituencies. In South Korea, for example:

more than a million e-mails were sent to mobile phones and online accounts urging supporters to go out and vote. This online rallying cry sent young voters to polling stations nationwide and delivered a narrow 2.3% election victory to the self-proclaimed political outsider Roh [Moo-hyun], who had been summarily rejected by South Korea's conservative media.[25]

In the Philippines, 'text messaging was used by protesters in the 2001 revolution in the Philippines to rapidly coordinate demonstrations that helped topple President Estrada'.[26]

Internet technologies are also useful for specific communication. Email messages, chat rooms, blog sites and online discussions (which can be distributed through list serves or occur in chat rooms), have all become very popular ways of discussing work, sending documents as well as interrogating critical issues.[27] The creation of this very book is an excellent example of how specific internet communication can result in virtual collaboration with people from all over the globe. The book was conceptualized over the past three years by AWID's Young Women and Leadership programme manager, Shamillah Wilson, and her colleague Anasuya Sengupta, who initially established their own relationship via internet communication. Their experiences of collaborating with young women predominantly over the internet, as well as drawing on many discussions regarding critical issues over the last three years, allowed them to conceptualize the book. Once the logistical tasks of arranging publication with Zed Books was solidified (again, mainly via communication over the internet), a call was sent out on AWID's list serves, asking for articles from diverse young women about their perspectives on current global issues. Once these were collected, they were evaluated and selected by an editorial committee, who communicated by internet and telephone conversations (often with mobile phones). After the selections were made, the submissions were sent back to the authors, with input from the editors, and from this point there was a back and forth until the final product was established. And *voilà*, you are now reading it!

Working across countries, continents and contexts

As technological development and innovation marches on, we are presented with many new opportunities, strategies and methodologies for our work, at the same time as many new challenges arise. One of the most interesting challenges of this virtual communication is the way in which we work together to bring forth issues of diversity into virtual spaces. As Anasuya Sengupta explains:

I find it fascinating the way relative strangers coalesce around a particular issue and yet have to negotiate issues of race, class, language, regions etc. in a virtual space. How is that language familiar and yet interestingly different? What makes it so? What makes one style offensive while another is challenging? How much more important the written word becomes when we don't know each other and our backgrounds, our loves, our passions, what makes us tick beyond the computer. How do we cope?[28]

As the primary vehicle for virtual communication is the written word, this creates significant challenges around language, expression and interpretation – not to mention literacy. New languages and expressions (which transcend the written word) are also being created by these newly formed virtual communities. Sengupta explains that this is perhaps why emoticons have become such a valuable part of our online vocabulary.[29]

Internet technologies also highlight the disparities in terms of access to resources and opportunities, as well as the issues of gender inequities that still exist throughout the world. Everjoice Win, in an article that appeared in South Africa's national newspaper, the *Mail and Guardian*, emphasizes that in terms of ICTS,

it is a case of one step forward, two steps back: the Internet has brought pornography to personal computers. Naked girls have become cell phone screensavers. It is now easier to buy and sell women on the Net. And millions of poor women have never seen a computer, let alone have access to public phones for use in emergencies.[30]

Although the internet is in many cases an invaluable tool for our work as feminists, it is also, at times, a space that highlights all of the issues that the women's movement has been grappling with for decades, and still has to find constructive ways of dealing with – identity politics, North–South relations between feminists, and distribution of wealth and opportunities.

'I can't work today, the server is down'

The internet, and the ability to use it, are still elitist in a number of ways. It is our responsibility as young feminists to ensure that we do not become out of touch with other ways of organizing and communicating. This is of particular relevance in the North, where systems and structures tend to work much more effectively than in many Southern countries. For example, many of us in the North do not have to contend with daily power outages, servers being down/busy, and so on. We must be versatile and able to cope with all sorts of situations. The phenomenon of technology leapfrogging has been put forth as skipping over technologies that are considered 'old' or 'archaic' to 'new' and more 'efficient' technology – for example, land line telephones versus cell phones.[31] However, when the supporting infrastructure for the new and fancy technologies comes crashing down, we must be able to carry on working and getting the job done. Rather than being dependent on technology to do our work, we must use it wisely and ensure that we can still sit across a dinner table from someone and be able to have a face-to-face interaction, explaining our histories, our dreams, our identities and how these inform our positions on feminist work and advocacy. We must not be afraid to pick up the telephone and have a conversation with someone because they haven't responded to our email in three weeks. We must be able to lobby ministers of trade at the WTO with a virtual and a real presence, convincing them of the importance of more effective and gender-sensitive policies – persuasively and articulately.

Communication and technology – by feminists, for feminists

Recognizing the challenges, as well as learning effective ways to use the numerous new ICTs, is one thing. Transforming the challenges and benefits of ICTs to push our agendas is another. Besides learning all of the ICTS, ensuring equitable access to them and using them strategically, it is essential that women start taking ownership of this technology. Although the majority of ICTs have been created and developed by men, it is time that women became experts in these realms in order to understand and expand on the existing possibilities. But further than this, it is up to us, and particularly the upcoming generation of feminists, to start inventing new ICTs that work for our own advocacy and activist agendas. Only we have the power to create and utilize tools that work for our causes in the ways that we want them to. It is time we became the creators and innovators, instead of being in the reactionary position of trying to play catch-up and learn someone else's games. Let's play our own games and define our own rules and tools for winning. But let's be sure that everyone can join our games, our spaces, and bring to them their own contexts, cultures, languages and ways of working.

Notes

1 E. J. Win (4–10 March 2005), 'Plus ça change', *Mail and Guardian*, p. 23.

2 Examples of free email providers include Hotmail, <www.hotmail.com>; Yahoo, <www.yahoo.com; or look at examples from Free Email Providers Guide (2005), 'Free email providers', see <http://<www.fepg.net/providers.html>.

3 You can find chat rooms on a wide variety of subjects on the internet. Simply use one of the internet search engines such as Google: <www.google.com> or Altavista: <www.altavista.com>, and key in the subject that you are

trying to find a chat room for. For instance, 'feminist chat rooms', which comes up with over forty thousand links on Google.

4 Organizations such as AWID, <www.awid.org>; DAWN, <www.dawn.org.fj>; APC, <www.apc.org>; Women'sNet, <www.womensnet.org.za>.

5 For more information on the Association for Women's Rights in Development please see their website: <www.awid.org>.

6 J. Emerson (2005), 'On blogs', see <http://backspace.com/action/on_blogs.php>.

7 China View (2005), '"Blog" the word of the year', see <http://news.xinhuanet.com/english/2004-12/05/content_2296755.htm>.

8 Please look at the Blogger website for instructions on how to easily create your own blog site. See <http://<www.blogger.com/start>.

9 APC (2005), 'Tell me more about RSS', see <http://<www.apc.org/english/new/index.shtml?x=28978>.

10 See <http://<www.apc.org/english/new/index.shtml?x=28978> for detailed instructions of how to use this system.

11 BBC (2005), 'Mobile growth "fastest in Africa"', see <http://news.bbc.co.uk/2/hi/business/4331863.stm>.

12 R. Jones (2005), 'HIV/AIDS and mobile technology: SMS saving lives in Africa', see <http://<www.awid.org/go.php?list=analysis&prefix=analysis&item=00235>.

13 Ibid.

14 Please note that 'free' software and 'open software' are distinct from each other. See comparison of 'free' vs. 'open' software at: <http://en.wikipedia.org/wiki/Free_software>.

15 See Women'sNet website at: <www.womensnet.org.za. See APC's website at: <www.apc.org>.

16 APC (2005), 'The first "free software" workshop run for women by women in the world? Southern African women do it!', see <http://<www.apc.org/english/new/index.shtml?x=26360>.

17 S. Milan (2005), 'World social forum: open systems for open politics', see <http://<www.ipsnews.net/interna.asp?idnews=27175>.

18 Ibid.

19 Ibid.

20 J. Emerson (2005), 'An introduction to activism on the internet', see <http://backspace.com/action/introduction.php>.

21 UNICEF (2005), 'The situation of women and girls: facts and figures', see <http://<www.unicef.org/gender/index_factsandfigures.html>.

22 Wikipedia (2005) 'South Africa: flora and fauna', see <http://en.wikipedia.org/wiki/South_Africa#Flora_and_fauna>.

23 Forbes.com (2005) 'William Gates III', see <http://<www.forbes.com/finance/lists/10/2004/LIR.jhtml?passListId=10&passYear=2004&passListType=Person&uniqueId=BH69&datatype=Person>.

24 See the example of the campaign for Amina Lawal in K. Evans (2003),

Cyber girls

'AWID's ways and means: an advocacy guide for feminists', see <http://<www. awid.org/publications/primers/waysmeans1.pdf>, p. 4.

25 J. Borton for Asia Times Online (2005), 'OhmyNews and wired "red devils"', see <http://<www.atimes.com.by-parakeet.gibeo.net/atimes/Korea/ FK25Dg01.html>.

26 E. Ellis for TIME Asia (2005) 'How text messaging toppled Joseph Estrada', see <http://<www.time.com/time/asia/asiabuzz/2001/01/23/>.

27 An example of online discussions can be found on the AWID Young Women and Leadership website. See <http://<www.awid.org/ywl/index. php?do=list>.

28 Personal communication with Anasuya Sengupta, 28 February 2005.

29 Emoticons are the expressions that people use to communicate how they are feeling. For example, :) for happy, or :(for sad.

30 Win (4–10 March 2005), 'Plus ça change.'

31 The term was first introduced to me by Ann Elisabeth Samson, AWID's senior researcher for the Gender Equality and New Technology Programme.

13 | Feminine whispers: notes on hysteria and loving commitment[1]

GABRIELA MALAGUERA GONZÁLEZ

To (with) Giovanna and Gioconda,
for the journey before this arrival.

Scheherazade

Scheherazade's decision to accept to live through what she did was an act of great courage; the daughter of King Shahryar's wazir could have chosen to escape the misogynistic revenge of the king, who, still not satisfied with having beheaded his wife after witnessing her infidelity, decided to marry a different woman each night and murder her the next day.

Scheherazade resolved not to heed her father, who had begged her not to expose herself to the dangerous king possessed by such lethal passion.

'I wish thou wouldst give me in marriage to this King Shahryar. Either I shall live or I shall be a ransom for the virgin daughters of Muslims and the cause of their deliverance from his hands and thine,'[2] Scheherazade implored the wazir.

Resignedly, her father finally gave in and took her before the king. Intelligent and eloquent, Scheherazade resorted to a female tactic: ensuring another woman's complicity in order to achieve her goals.

Scheherazade instructed her younger sister, Dunyazade, to go to the palace and request that she recount a marvellous tale in front of king Shahryar. And so it happened. That first night, the new queen, Scheherazade, began to tell stories and at dawn would discreetly stop talking while her sister kept playing the game, asking about her silence and praising her narrative. Scheherazade responded to her sister using more or less the same words, from that moment on and for one thousand and one more dawns. She said: 'These tales are nothing compared to what I could tell you tomorrow night, if I'm still alive and the king wishes to keep me.'

Marvelling at his wife's stories, Shahryar spared Scheherazade's life night after night in order to continue enjoying each tale. Thanks to Scheherazade's ability to 'weave'[3] words, *but also to know when to keep quiet at strategic moments*, the king finally put an end to the fatal sentence to which he had condemned Allah's daughters.

Dora

Dora's decision to rebel against what she was going through was an act of great courage; the daughter of one of the wealthiest families of Freud's Vienna, she could have quietly accepted what the culture, of her time and of ours, imposed as the 'Ideal Woman'. To concentrate, as Freud said,

all her interests in the administration of the household, offering a complete image of what we could consider 'housewife's psychosis' [and spend the day] cleaning the rooms, the furniture and utensils with such an obsession that it was almost impossible to make use of them.[4]

The 18-year-old woman's relatives were alarmed after noting that she was depressed and sickened with her life: feelings she wrote down in a letter that caused her father consternation. This episode and a subsequent loss of consciousness marked the beginning of her treatment. Dora was reluctant to go into therapy, but finally heeded her family's worries, particularly her father's, whom she loved deeply, and decided to be analysed by Freud.

The clinical sessions between Freud and Dora took place for only three months. During this time, Dora recounted her story: some events in her life that allowed for a slight comprehension of the reasons why her body was full of symptoms. Freud wrote that Dora showed

all the characteristics of a *petite hystérie* with the most vulgar somatic and psychic symptoms: dyspnoea, nervous cough, aphonia, migraines, mood depression, hysterical excitability and *taedium vitae* [boredom with life].[5]

Dora's body protested against the feminine fate imposed on her; a heavy and practically unavoidable fate.

Dora told Freud about the relationship her family, and especially her father, had with the K. family. She spoke of the deep friendship she herself had with Mrs K., for whom she felt a profound admiration and affection. But she also expressed great complaints against Mr K. On some occasions, he had approached the young woman in a fashion she regarded as inappropriate. Once, when Dora was 14 years old, Mr K.

held her in his arms and kissed her on the lips. This situation was thus appropriate to provoke in a virgin girl ... a clear sensation of sexual arousal. But at that moment Dora felt a violent revulsion, untangled herself from K.'s arms and ran into the street ... .[6]

This story prompted Freud to diagnose Dora as hysterical. But the Freudian definition of hysteria is one that, by implication, conceives people, both men and women, as beings who must normally be at the disposal of *somebody else's* desire; if they are not, then they are sick. Says Freud,

I should without question consider a person hysterical in whom an occasion for sexual excitement elicited feelings that were preponderantly or exclusively unpleasurable; and I should do so whether or not the person were capable of producing somatic symptoms.[7]

In Dora's case, one of the representations of the 'Other's desire' is Mr K.'s desire. He was a tired man and too old for her; she was young enough to be his daughter and was just beginning to understand what it meant to be a woman. There was a close relationship between this desire and Dora's father's desire for Mrs K. Dora objected to both, and her objection was revealed to Freud as analysis progressed.

All of this caused Dora such great discomfort that her bitterness increased whenever the thought crossed her mind that she might have been handed over to Mr K. as the price of his tolerance of the relations between her father and Mrs K. 'In fact, each man carefully avoided assuming, from each other's behaviour, those conclusions that could impede the satisfaction of their own desires,'[8] in a sort of male pact whose objective was the exchange of women.

As the case progresses, we realize that Dora was expressing outrage about two situations that were unacceptable to her. First, she could not understand why Mr K. despised his wife the way he did. For the young woman, Mrs K. was the 'Ideal Woman' that she was so willing to accept as a role model, trying to separate herself from the traditional 'Ideal Woman', the one offered by her mother.

Mrs K. personified another ideal – she was desired and appreciated by her [Dora's] father, her double life tolerated by her husband; she was a mother and a nurse devoted to her beloved man, and she possessed a 'sexual knowledge' which she shared with Dora, who was her confidante and friend. In this act Mrs K. introduced Dora to the world of adults, of women as such. If there was anything Dora desired, it was this education that she could not receive from her mother. What do women feel, what do women live regarding men?[9]

Second, there was a great narcissistic wound in Dora, who, as far as Mr K. and the rest of the men were concerned, was being left without any guarantee that in the future she would not be considered just a nobody.[10] Dora also felt the possibility that she would be a victim of male contempt. A sad fate for any woman – and for any person.

This feeling of Dora's that we now expose is a possibility that finds solid ground in some valuable feminist theories of the end of the twentieth century. As Lacan points out:

181

Of what she is, Dora can say nothing. Dora does not know where to stand, nor where she stands, or what love is for. She only knows that love exists, and she finds a historization of love in which she discovers her own place in the form of a question ... . After all, if Dora expresses herself as she does, through her symptoms, it is because she wonders what it is to be a woman.[11]

Dora talked to Freud, but she didn't say it all: at a certain point she kept quiet and went out of his office, where she would return much later to visit the Viennese doctor, but never again to be analysed by Freud himself. What came after 31 December 1900, when the clinical sessions between Freud and Dora ended, are interpretations of what she really wanted. Her story, and her silence, have awakened in many of us great admiration and the need to know about her desire, which was to become a *desiring woman*, instead of remaining at the mercy of others' desires.

The desiring woman

It was a great act of courage for women of our times to vindicate and adopt the hysterical form as a means to protest against patriarchal culture. Not necessarily because the structure of our personality is hysterical, but because we have learned, from Dora and her symptoms as indicators of female discontent, that our socialization as girls, teenagers and women is fraught with messages that turn us into a gender that is valued differently from the way in which male gender is valued. With women's hysteria, we vindicate ourselves as human beings, instead of being considered merely as people who are valuable because of our bodies. As Emilce Dio Bleichmar points out:

A girl enters into the Oedipus devalued for her gender, and step by step, through the maternal and paternal phantoms, she will receive the conflicting mandates concerning her sexuality and her possible fates as a woman. She must be formed and delivered as an object of desire and must, for her achievement, develop with greater or less sophistication the arts of grace and seduction. The body, the beauty, the perfection of what is offered to the eye cannot be avoided and will thus be incorporated into the present forms which awaken admiration and desire from a man.[12]

The object of men's desire: this is the fate that marks our lives even before we become aware of the world. It was this fate that Dora fought against, following feminist interpretation. Other 'hysterical' women also fought against being considered just a 'body-to-have-sex-with', and they are still fighting. The struggle makes even more sense in light of the great cultural contradictions that exist. We are encouraged to feel complete if we succeed in satisfying male desire. We exercise our sexuality, but at the same time we are penalized for it. Dishonour befalls a woman who *decides* to have sexual relations, even when she assumes the role of the object.[13]

Feminist vindications are greatly nourished by this hysterical feature of protest, of rebellion against what is imposed on women as the only way of being: to assume only the role of being desired, but never that of desiring. We have already pointed out that this is what Dora complained about. And those of us heterosexual women, who also complain about this 'Ideal Woman', run the risk of losing the object of our love whenever we openly express our disagreement with certain cultural norms.

There is a very specific point of honour in all of this: it seems that women's love-related and cultural aloneness will increase or decrease depending on how we deal with this key aspect of our lives. This point is precisely the form of protest that is expressed in being capable of assuming ourselves 'as [subjects] of desire and placing in [our] phantom a man as the object which causes it'.[14] More simply, it is the situation in which women go against what is expected of us and dare tell to men, before they say first: 'I want you, I want you now and for myself.'

If there is anything that feminism has tried to vindicate for a good part of its existence, it is the fact that we women should be able to live our own sexuality, taking the initiative about what we wish. In this sense, some feel that it is absolutely natural to go after what our desire demands from us – love, sex, company – anything we may be missing from men at different moments of our lives. This is an important consequence of feminism; a trace we do not always perceive in its full dimension but which is there: in our daily experiences, in our love relationships, in the most intimate corners of our sexuality. Today, some women regard themselves as capable of being *desiring*, but fear of loneliness plays tricks on us. We question how many men are actually willing to let themselves be desired: to be the object of women's desire?

This situation leads to a problematic aspect within affectionate, loving and/or sexual relationships between the sexes. What can we do so that the desiring women of today can build loving bridges to men who run away from the idea of becoming objects? How do we make it possible for loving relationships to exist between women who may be different, and men who may possibly remain the same as they have always been?

The overwhelmed man

I would like to close this attempt with my own act of courage. I need to be courageous in order to feel that I am not betraying myself. It is very difficult to have to examine that which has been a source of pride for us, the rebellious, and particularly for the younger generations. What needs to cool down at this moment is the spontaneous and open expression of desire, the desiring word. The desiring word must be quietened down. Not disappeared or buried but just, perhaps, said in whispers. And, with this whispered word, we need to invite our men to raise their voices and say what they think about us, what they feel with us, now that we are different.

I am speaking of the subjective sphere, the intimate realm of relationships. It is not about neglecting our political struggles; that is not what I am suggesting. Rather, I think that protest, in this sense, is more necessary than ever. It is about betting, in the field of love, on 'asking for the voice of the other and listening to it carefully [so that] this voice [will reach] everybody'.[15]

In this regard, it is necessary to start listening to those male voices that we can hear around us, particularly now with the emerging studies on the construction of masculinity. We know that the divorce between the masculine and the affectionate is a gap difficult to close, so much so that men generally leave to women the task of elaborating explanations of what takes place in their emotional daily lives. And from the daily sphere this has gone to the theoretical: feminism has assumed the task of explaining, in different versions, what men feel, and by recounting those male experiences it has turned men into a real enigma, just as women were to Freud.[16] This enigma was reinforced more than ever at the beginning of the twentieth century, judging by the examples of Scheherazade and Dora. It seems that women know more than men about *their* experiences.[17] Women do not know exactly what it is that men feel, but we talk and talk about them. We assume that they want, or would like, to hear that we desire them or that it is easy for them to become our object of desire. But are they possibly afraid of this? Probably, as Victor Seidler explains,

> it is fear that the dominant mother may be about to overwhelm her son and take away his potency. Although this is not part of feminist intention, it has often been the involuntary consequence of a feminist questioning that has left many men with a feeling of 'not knowing who they are' or 'feeling inadequate with who they are as men' or, in the context of their relationships, feeling that their partners 'know more'. This tends to make men become defensive, rigid and stiff, instead of providing them a means for some sort of significant change. ... They usually feel threatened, withdrawing into shy silence or act with violence.[18]

Just as one day women felt fed up with subordination and decided to be courageous, make ourselves hysterical and protest, men of today seem to be fed up as well. Dora protested with symptoms; hysterical men protest, as Dio Bleichmar points out, by becoming 'Don Juan'. 'I refuse to belong to just one woman, I will not commit to any of them',[19] they say when they feel overwhelmed. This is one of the consequences of feminism, whether we like it or not, just as the desiring woman is.

This is why I suggest we lower our voices a little: just a little, only for a while. We must listen to men, even if they find it hard to speak about what they feel, even if it is only now that they are articulating an emotional language in order to be accountable for themselves, for their masculinities. I would like to declare a truce, because I am still betting on a loving commitment, which is becoming all the more difficult. Although undoubtedly, and as Rubén Darío would say, 'life is bearable, so painful and short, solely for that; touch, bite or kiss in this divine bread for which our blood is our wine'.[20]

Dora developed symptoms, and by so doing she also protested, as a symptom is, as Lacan points out, a signifying element, 'because underneath runs a meaning in perpetual movement'.[21] Again, Dora didn't say it all; and at the same time she said a great deal. She desired. Even in silence, she desired. Let our whisper become that which lets the bet for the loving encounter between men and women run underneath. Let us play with being subjects and objects of desire at the same time. Let us keep a bit quiet and, like Scheherazade, let us awaken the king's desire and rescue Allah's rebellious daughters – not from death, but from loneliness.[22]

Notes

1 This chapter was presented at the 'III Jornadas Ucevistas de Investigación de Género' and the 'II Jornadas Universitarias sobre Diversidad Sexual', Central University of Venezuela, 2004. It was originally written in Spanish and was translated into English by Laura E. Asturias.

2 All quotes from the story 'Las mil y una noches' ('Thousand and One Nights') taken from the website: <http://www.bibliotecasvirtuales.com/ biblioteca/LiteraturaAsiatica/lasmilyunanoches/comienzo.asp>.

3 I refer to Freud's epigraph, which Emilce Dio Bleichmar cites at the beginning of her essay, 'Deshilando el enigma' ('Unweaving the Enigma') in M. Lamas and Frida Saal (1991), La bella (in)diferencia [The Beautiful (In)difference]. Mexico: Siglo XXI: 'It seems that women have made few contributions to the discoveries and inventions in the history of civilization; there is, however, one technique which they may have invented – that of plaiting and weaving.'

4 S. Freud (1905), 'Fragment of an analysis of a case of hysteria ("Dora")', Obras Completas [Complete Works], Vol. III (1900–1905) (Biblioteca Nueva), p. 941.

5 Ibid., p. 944.

6 Ibid., p. 946.

7 Ibid., p. 947.

8 Ibid., p. 950.

9 E. Dio Bleichmar (1985), *El feminismo espontáneo de la histeria. Estudio de los trastornos narcisistas de la feminidad* [The Spontaneous Feminism of Hysteria. A Study of the Narcissistic Disorders of Femininity] (Mexico: Fontamara), p. 204.

10 Ibid.

11 J. Lacan (1957), 'Seminar IV: The object relation. Class 8: Dora and the young homosexual woman', CD-ROM.

12 E. Dio Bleichmar (1991), 'Deshilando el enigma' ['Unweaving the Enigma'] in M. Lamas and F. Saal (eds), *La bella (in)diferencia* (The Beautiful (In)difference] (Mexico: Siglo XXI), p. 109.

13 Ibid., p. 110.

14 Ibid.

15 B. Matamoro (1991), in Lamas and Saal (eds), *La bella*, p. 88.

16 M. Burin (2000), 'Construcción de la subjetividad masculina' ['Construction of Male Subjectivity'], in M. Burin and I. Meler (eds), *Varones: Género y subjetividad masculina* [Men: Gender and Male Subjectivity] (Buenos Aires: Paidós).

17 V. Seidler (2000), *La sinrazón masculina: Masculinidad y teoría social* [Unreasonable Men: Masculinity and Social Theory] (Mexico: Paidós).

18 Ibid., p. 174.

19 E. Dio Bleichmar (1985), 'El feminismo espontáneo de la histeria. Estudio de los trastornos narcisistas de la feminidad' [The spontaneous feminism of hysteria. A study of the narcissistic disorders of femininity] (Mexico: Fontamara), p. 79.

20 Rubén Darío, in M. Hernández (1997) 'Una mirada al amor desde la psicología social' [A look at love from social psychology] *Revista Avepso*, XX(2): 47–58.

21 Lacan (1957), 'Seminar IV'.

22 Thanks to Anaína Rivero and Miguel Ángel Tamburini for revising the English version of this chapter.

14 | We exist! Voices of male feminism

DEAN PEACOCK

Across the world, men are working creatively to end violence, prevent HIV/ AIDS and foster gender equality. In Nicaragua, the Men's Group of Managua launched a national campaign making the connection between the devastation caused by Hurricane Mitch and male violence against women. To make clear that violence against women is not a natural disaster but very much man-made, they used the tagline: 'Violence against women: A disaster that men CAN do something about'. The Male Initiative of the Society for Women on AIDS in Kenya works in remote rural communities to encourage men to support their partner's full participation in prevention of mother-to-child transmission programmes. In Brazil, Instituto Promundo works with young men in the urban slums or *favelas* surrounding Rio de Janeiro and São Paulo to promote gender equitable values and practices. Similarly, in South Africa, EngenderHealth has worked together with a wide range of organizations and institutions to implement the Men as Partners Programme (MAP), which uses an explicitly human rights framework to promote gender equality and greater male activism through a combination of community education, grass-roots organizing and advocacy for effective implementation of policies and legislation. Reflecting this groundswell of work with men across the world, one of the two themes for the 2004 United Nations Commission on the Status of Women was 'The Role of Men and Boys in Achieving Gender Equality'.

Many of the initiatives mentioned above draw upon three interconnected principles, each related to an understanding of the many negative ways in which the unequal balance of power between men and women plays itself out. Contemporary gender roles are seen as conferring on men the ability to influence and/or determine the reproductive health choices made by women – whether these choices are about utilization of health care services, family planning, condom usage or sexual abstinence. Second, contemporary gender roles are viewed as also compromising men's health by encouraging men to equate a range of risky behaviours – the use of violence, alcohol and substance use, the pursuit of multiple sexual partners, the domination of women – with being 'manly', while simultaneously encouraging men to view health-seeking behaviours as a sign of weakness. Such gender roles leave men especially vulnerable to HIV infection, decrease the likelihood that they will seek HIV testing, and increase the likelihood of contributing to actions and situations that could spread the virus. Third, men are seen as having a personal investment in challenging the current gender order both because it is in their health interests to do so, and because they often care deeply about women placed at risk of violence and ill health by these gender roles.

The words of three young men currently involved in the MAP Network in South Africa make clear the ways in which these three principles inform their commitment to promoting gender justice. They also reflect the honesty and rigour with which they have examined their own roles and perceptions; they can well be an inspiration for feminist engagements by men, across gender, generations and geography. These words are deeply personal and may resonate with other men, across the world, who are making attempts to challenge themselves and the worlds around them, in similar ways.

Lee Buthelezi, a 25-year-old from the Johannesburg township of Thokoza, says:

I was socially brought up knowing that if you want to have sex with a girl and she doesn't want, you just *klap* [hit] her two or three times and she will give you what you want. I grew up doing those things, you know, beating women and forcing myself [on them] and all that. After being in contact with MAP a couple of years ago I realized that the way that I grew up was actually wrong; it wasn't supposed to be like that. If you want to have sex it should be a mutual feeling, both from your partner and you, and you agree on doing that. But when I was growing up I wouldn't wait for [an] agreement or consent of some sort. I'd just do exactly the way I wanted, you know ... We were brought up in a manner that women should be beaten in order to get what you want from them. But we're trying to change that stereotype ... and show [other men] that you should talk, discuss and reach a consensus together with your partner.

Lillo Phalandwa, a gender activist with the MAP programme for nearly two years, shares his experience:

Five of my family members are HIV positive, and my father was abusive to my mom. Before I went to the workshop, I thought it was normal because when I was three my father started abusing my mom. I was verbally abusive towards women. Now I treat them as equal to me.

Thami Nkosi, who is 22 years old, also describes his commitment to working with men on gender-related issues, in very personal terms:

188

My dad passed away from HIV last March and my uncle two months before, so the reason I'm here is to address issues surrounding HIV. After taking the workshop, I saw that the relationship between gender and HIV has a lot to do with promiscuity and violence. I didn't grow up with violence in my family, but it was all around me. A girl near where I live was raped at gunpoint just recently. They bribed her not to press charges. So that's the type of issues I'm faced with everyday. We've still got a lot of work that needs to be done; so for me, this is just a life-long fight.[1]

A significant body of literature exists that documents the work of various organizations doing work with men across Southern Africa. By and large, these chronicle accomplishments and describe lessons learned, and have been written by research- and evaluation-focused organizations. To date, the voices of those actually *doing* this work have not been captured to a great extent. The interview that is included in this chapter attempts to remedy this void. It was conducted in early February 2005 during a planning meeting held by the South African MAP Network in Johannesburg. Participants in the discussion were Boitshepo Lesetedi, the MAP Programme manager for the Planned Parenthood Association of South Africa; Dean Peacock, EngenderHealth's South Africa programme manager; Dumisani Rebombo and Rodney Fortuin, MAP Programme Officers for EngenderHealth, Mbuyiselo Botha, secretary-general of the South African Men's Forum and Regis Mtutu from Padare-Enkudleni Men's Forum in Zimbabwe.

During a conversation that went late into the night, we shared our own process of becoming involved in these issues, and reflected on what had kept us involved in work that has at times led to ostracism and isolation. We also shared how much we have gained as men and as individuals through establishing, in some instances, far more rewarding relationships with our partners and children and, in other cases, with male friends and colleagues. Finally, we grappled with our understanding of our role as men in the broader struggle for women's rights and gender equality, and explore what we see as important challenges and 'next steps' for the still embryonic work to engage men in promoting gender equality.

Interview with Dean Peacock, Rodney Fortuin, Boitshepo Lesetedi, Dumisani Rebombo, Mbuyiselo Botha and Regis Mtutu[2]

Dean Peacock: What brought you to this work and what sustains you, particularly in relation to how we've promoted dialogue between men and women in ways that advance the agenda of gender equality?

Mbuyiselo Botha: I'm from the South African Men's Forum, an organization focusing on what men can do as a collective to change both the mind-set

189

and the behavioural tendencies of men. What brought me into this work was seeing the link between the oppression of black people in this country, and the same oppression that women are faced with. It is actually our duty as men, in particular black men, to say that we cannot allow a situation where our own sisters are dragged into a situation similar to the past, before 1994. You can't separate one freedom and say it is actually more important and urgent than the other. In the oppression of men lies the oppression of women. And in the liberation of women lies the liberation of men.

Regis Mtutu: I'm Regis Mtutu from Padare-Enkudleni Men's Forum on Gender in Harare, Zimbabwe. For me, it was the view that it is possible for men to actively work towards gender equality and not see the responsibility only on women to work in issues of gender. For us, what was more critical was being part of a movement that is initiating the possibility of men actually being part of, as Mbuyiselo says, the liberation of not only men but also to complement the good work of women's movements, especially in Zimbabwe.

Dean Peacock: I am with EngenderHealth and the MAP Network. I came to the work as an anarchist activist. I had been involved in anti-apartheid struggles here in South Africa before I left in 1986, but in the US I had been part of a group of people involved in putting together an anarchist newspaper collective and very involved in anti-Gulf War activism leading up to the first Gulf War. As a white South African living in the US, I was really grappling with the question of what is appropriate social justice work for me to do. I remember my girlfriend at the time was working at a battered women's shelter. During her orientation there, she came back one day and said, 'You know I was at this training at the shelter provided by a man from Men Overcoming Violence.' I was quite taken aback that there was an organization dealing with issues related to domestic violence. It had never occurred to me previously that men actually do this. A light went off in my head, and I began to think about becoming involved in this kind of work. Once I began to volunteer at Men Overcoming Violence, I was invited to observe a men's group for men who had battered and there was something very different about that. It gave me an opportunity to engage in reflection around my own socialization. I think that's what kept me involved.

Rodney Fortuin: I was introduced to this work in 2002. I was quite curious with regard to the impact that gender had on the spread of HIV/AIDS in South Africa. At the first MAP Workshop, I started asking myself, 'What am I doing here?' You know the issues that are being raised here are issues that I've never ever thought about, as a young coloured man growing up on the notorious Cape Flats in Cape Town.[3] As we went along through the workshop, I started to realize that I can make a difference.

I was married for quite a number of years back then and I started to realize, 'Hang on, if I make these changes to my own personal life then that will be an immediate improvement with regard to my relationship with my wife, my relationship with my children, and also my relationship with other men and women.' I had never even thought about the issues surrounding gender-based violence. Growing up on the Cape Flats, I experienced a lot of violence with friends and families – seeing my friends running away from their homes, from their dads being violent or drunk.

Boitshepo Lesetedi: For me, this is more personal than political. I got involved in 1994 when I was still working for Young Christian Students as a general secretary. At that time, I never thought I would get married simply because I never liked how my dad treated my mom. We had a session on gender-based violence as part of our studies with Mmatshilo Motsei, who is a founder member of ADAPT, and from there I never looked back.[4] I joined the board of ADAPT; and in 1997 I joined them as part of their staff. For me it has become my life's work. I've just realized now that I haven't always recognized the impact that my life and my work has actually had on a lot of people. Last week, I was invited to a show on Khaya FM (a local South African radio station). It was a show on my life – on being a good man, on where and how I started [my activism]. I think I came to acknowledge the fact that, even if I'm trying to be modest, things are making a difference. People, who I never thought would, called [in to the show] from Kagiso (where I'm from).

Dumisani Rebombo: I got into this work about six years ago. I was working for an NGO called Hope Worldwide. Our mandate was to work at an informal settlement with mainly unemployed single moms because the government thought that they might be a high-risk group in terms of HIV infection. For three years we did HIV prevention, educating women on condom use and negotiation skills. Because they were unemployed, we also started income-generating projects. When we checked the impact of our work, the findings were alarming. Although the women knew more about how to use a condom, and although they might now have some money, some reported that the men took the money, and others reported that their partners wouldn't utilize the condoms. So, while the women were becoming enlightened about HIV prevention, there weren't any tangible results, despite the three years we had been doing the work. It then became clear

191

that for the project to work we needed to engage the men. That's when as an organization we approached EngenderHealth and were trained in the MAP methodology.

Immediately after this, I realized that you can't do this work for others without starting with yourself. I needed to do my own introspection and look into how I personally was socialized and brought up as an African man in a small town. I carried my own attitudes around masculinities and I had to change a lot of things personally. The way I was brought up, when it came to sexual matters, my wife had to just comply with my sexual advances because, 'Hey, I mean as a man, this is what I do.' She was also socialized that whatever your husband wants from you, you go with it. As a man, you go to church, and whenever these issues were brought up, I was given the opportunity to say, 'It's not that bad – after all I'm the head of the family and she needs to be submissive to me.' So I had to change all of this before I could engage other men on these issues.

I've seen a lot of changes in my personal life. My relationship with my kids prior to this was more of, 'I provide and give you money – that's it! What more do you want?' Today, all of my kids are my friends. I respect my wife's decisions. At the same time there are other men that I can talk to. Sometimes I find myself doing those things that perhaps I shouldn't have been doing. But that support mechanism is there so that I can open up about what I am doing and other men can suggest: 'You could have done it this way.' Together there is more hope and a clear vision on where we're going. That keeps me going!

Mbuyiselo: I am interested in what Dumisani was saying. What we tend to do is to be more outward, and in so doing we forget to have sufficient focus on introspection. Not knowing my father has been a critical thing in my life. When I had my kids, I then decided that I would not become an 'ATM father' and only provide money. But I would want an experiential, emotional bond with my kids.

Regis: I agree with Dumisani. I have two daughters and I tend to see them as my friends. It's also sending a message that it's possible for them to actually have a much more fulfilled relationship with a man that is not based on hierarchies of power.

What strikes me is that when I was growing up, I had this relationship with my friends where we really supported each other, but in very negative ways – to act out negative stereotypes of being men. I feel like this work that I'm doing has given me the opportunity to be able to have relationships with my friends where they can say: 'No, in this matter I think you are going astray,' and we discuss that in a very positive and supporting atmosphere without feeling defensive.

Dean Peacock: And it brings us back to the question we were engaging with, of what this work on men and gender equality is all about. What we are hearing here is a sense that certainly it includes this process of enriching our own lives. But I want to discuss what is difficult about that, because one of the questions that is often posed is: 'Aren't you being naive?' or 'Are men going to quickly give up their power, give up the patriarchal dividend?' I want us to explore how we engage with/share or negotiate power in a relationship. When it gets difficult, how do we grapple with that?

Mbuyiselo: I think on two levels it is extremely difficult and lonely. You are often expected to be manly – in your outlook, your perception and your perspectives. Now doing the work that we do, you are often challenged on your manhood: what does it mean in real terms? And you even doubt: 'Am I still masculine?' 'Am I still a real man?' It can be dangerous if one does not have a support system. The MAP Network, as a collective, begins to provide a support system in the positive sense, as opposed to previously where one would walk alone and be encouraged to do things that were demeaning, degrading and/or dehumanizing to women.

Rodney: I don't think it's easy to bring about personal change. I realized I have been in a position of power with my wife where I have made all the decisions, and that I have certain expectations of her as a woman. What makes it difficult is when I don't communicate with her why I am doing what I'm doing and asking how she feels about it.

One example of this is that my wife and I spend time together (go out or do things as a couple) every Monday night. Previously, I always decided for us, based on what I liked and what made me feel happy, but forgetting that she has needs and might want to do other things. As a man, I thought I needed to make all those decisions and that she just had to tag along with it, even if she was not happy about it. Eventually I was able to engage with her on this topic and tell her, 'This is what we've been doing, this is what I've been doing, let's do things that you would like to do.' For example, I love movies but she's not a movie fan; she only went because I wanted to go. She loves to go for coffee and talk. I do like that, but as a man you want to sort of protect and set certain boundaries that you only expose yourself so far.

Regis: For me it can be difficult not only in my personal life but also in

193

public. How do you relate to female colleagues? For example, if you were to go to a meeting and there is a discussion going on; immediately men want to jump in and start engaging, without necessarily giving space to the women in the meeting. Actually realizing this has been really useful; creating spaces even for junior male staff so that there isn't a hierarchy of masculinities and power in the organization.

Dean: It is interesting, this whole question of power and democratizing our relationships – whether it is with our intimate partner or our colleagues. I worked for a long time in collectively orientated workplaces. Tonight, for instance, we were debriefing the workshop and were really struggling around one or two activities for tomorrow. There was a moment where I thought I could draw on the power I have as the manager of the programme and have it go my way – and sometimes it feels that that's almost what people want. But my political analysis leaves me with a deep distrust of power of any sort. One of the things that is so difficult about more hierarchical models of power within an organization is that it leaves me feeling very lonely in my workplace. The expectation is that I have the final say, that I can't talk to my colleagues about some of the more difficult staff issues, and so there is a sense of loneliness. I imagine it is the same for a father who inhabits the space as the patriarch: he makes the final decisions and the difficult disciplinary actions. It must leave a father in a position of some isolation within the family.

As a man doing this work, while I experience some of the isolation that you have described, Mbuyiselo, I think there is another interesting dynamic. I think I get more attention from women as a pro-feminist man than I would if I wasn't doing this kind of work. I feel that I really have to watch what I do with that. So when I run a workshop, I can see who's checking me out sometimes ... I think it is because there is this notion that 'This is one of the good men, he is not going to exploit, he is not going to be like my ex.'

Regis: For me the major difficulty is when women actually make very clear that they want to have a sexual relationship, and they see that as part of their independence; it's their choice, you know. When we are doing work, especially along sexual lines, it is again like, this power that men also have over sexuality – it is like us either initiating or, if a woman initiates, you even feel more powerful. How do you deal with this power?

Dean: This intersection of masculinities, sex and sexuality is an interesting phenomenon. When I have engaged in risky sex, I think it has often been tied to my own notions of masculinity. For example, if I am not completely turned on, and I fear that if I stop to put on a condom, I might lose my erection. I think the notion I carry somewhere inside my own head is that, as a man, I can't acknowledge to my partner: 'No, I don't want to put on a condom, because I'm afraid I might lose my erection.' There is something that gets cross-wired between sexuality and masculinity.

Boitshepo: Doing this work, I sometimes get called names – 'sissy', 'soft', and so on. There has been a tendency for me to want to prove my manhood: that I'm straight, that there is nothing 'wrong' with me and I'm not all these negative terms. I find myself doing this by engaging in promiscuous behaviour that proves that I am straight and that I can actually charm any person and therefore 'be' with any girl.

Mbuyiselo: There is a lot of stress that is placed on men – about the 'triple Ps': providing, protecting and procreating. If men work together with women, and understand that there are instances where men can't pro-create, men can't provide, men can't protect, this reduces the pressure.

Dean: One of the main things we have to do in our analysis and discussions with other men is highlight the costs to men of contemporary male socialization. I have also been grappling with the question about how useful our personal stories/narratives are as a very deliberate strategy, because it seems to me there is a tremendous silence about men's privileges and about the costs to men of male socialization. There is also tremendous denial about men's behaviour in society. Maybe what's much more powerful, in fact, is personal reflection.

Boitshepo: I think that it is very powerful. In my initial comments, I acknowledged having seen my father being abusive to my mother. Ultimately I have also been abusive to a few partners that I have had. The acknowledgement of this has actually led to being demonized to a point where I doubted whether I could make a change. And the detriment of this is, sometimes you draw negative attention to yourself if you acknowledge some of your past. If it is an acknowledgement of one's personal experiences in a safe place, I think it is easier. However, I think in bigger platforms, one does not necessarily know how much sharing could still put one into trouble.

Regis: I like the notion of appealing to positive notions of masculinity. Typical masculinity defines men as 'risk-takers'. So in a sense, Boitshepo, going to Khaya FM is taking a risk, but taking the risk in a very calculated positive manner that benefits us all. We need to advance this agenda and perhaps, strategically, this is the risk that we are taking to advance the agenda we need to see moving forward.

Dean: And it's also about reframing these issues, right? As men, there is something about masculinity that is associated with risk-taking, so we reframe this.

Dumisani: At the same time for me, it's about asking myself how honest I am. To me, gender inequality is an epidemic that has been around for years, even before HIV. It should be treated just like a state of emergency. Therefore, I think whatever is needed to redress this I'm willing to risk it – not because it is masculine, but because this is part of the remedying process.

Dean: We have talked about framing this work as being in our interest and having a stake in it. We haven't talked much about our relationship to women and women's organizations.

Mbuyiselo: The temptation often is to impose what *we* may think that women want. For me, that re-creates negative masculinities. 'Let us avoid the temptation to set the agenda.' This is a struggle that we are not going to lead; this is a struggle that we are going to be led in. And being led is also part of healing ourselves and listening to what the cries are all about.

Dean: I think this question of leadership is one where there is contention, and it isn't often articulated. Are women leading work that happens with men, or are men and women leading this together?

Boitshepo: I was groomed and capacitated around these issues in the women's movement. Sometimes not all women are willing and ready to accept men into this kind of work.

Dumisani: As men, we are not [often] victims of gender-based violence. I think women who lead many of the women's organizations have been victims of gender-based violence of some sort hence they are extreme in terms of their [articulation of] feminism. So the approach doesn't tend to be: 'Let's work with men.' I want to listen, and together then devise the strategies that can involve both men and women. I think that would work better than women rejecting men, or men continuing with negative masculinities consisting of wanting to lead and take charge.

Dean: It is true that sometimes when one engages with women's advocacy organizations, or with women who are feminists and activists, there is a certain kind of scepticism, a certain kind of defensiveness and anger that we are sometimes met with as men doing this kind of work. I don't think we should be surprised by it. As a white South African, I anticipate when I interact with black people, whether here or in the US, that I will be met with a certain level of distrust and a certain amount of anger. I feel like that is part and parcel of coming to terms with the legacy of oppression; if you are part of the group that has been responsible for oppression, you better believe people are going to be angry with you, especially when they have experienced oppression at a very violent level. That doesn't mean it's easy and that it is not tempting to sometimes say, 'Hang on, I'm not one of those people.' But as a white person, I am one of those people at some level, and as a man, I certainly am. I continue to exercise privilege in both of those identities. I think it's important to help the men we work with anticipate that they are going to be dealing with a certain level of scepticism and that it comes with the territory.

We have talked mostly about gender and gender-based violence. We have talked a bit about HIV and AIDS. Are there any other issues, or strategies that perhaps you think we need to consider in terms of gender equality?

Mbuyiselo: Religious groups are one terrain where women continue to face constraints. In South Africa, there is only one woman who is a bishop in the whole country. I also think the message that the religious community is sending to the girl-child, as they grow, is that it is okay to be subservient. As we move forward, it is important for us to have a particular focus on how we begin to work with faith-based organizations.

Regis: I think the women's movement has done tremendous work in focusing on the girl-child. But I always ask myself, what are the implications of this? Is the resocialization of the girl-child producing a clear-minded young girl, a young woman who is aware of her rights? And who do these young women have to deal with? They are dealing with young boys – young men who are still 'doing time', who are still in the prison of masculinity and patriarchy. We need to be able to redefine gender roles from an early age, so that when these two meet, when they start either falling in love, engaging, they are doing so on an equal level, because right now for me, this is what leads to gender violence. When that empowered young girl engages with this young man, he cannot engage, and all he can do is to resort to violence, sexism and so forth. Let's really look at how we resocialize the young boy from that early age onwards.

Rodney: I think we should develop strategies to reach men and women in the workplace.

Dean: I think, in our work, we need to recognize that most workplaces are gendered institutions, not simply because of who sits in the positions of power, but because of the gendered arrangements that make it difficult for women to compete with men: when they are not allowed to take maternity leave, when women's roles as mothers become impediments to gaining access to positions of power in organizations.

Dumisani: To add to that, we need to create an enabling environment. Let me give a scenario: if I am abusive at home to my little girl and she goes out on to the streets, and the boys who are out of school abuse her on her way to school, and when she gets to the classroom, the teachers do the same, even if she has some knowledge about her rights, the environment is not such that she can exercise those rights. So if we target everyone and mobilize the community around these issues, the environment that this work is being taken forward in, is conducive to us reaching the desired goal.

Dean: We've talked a lot about men and masculinities and gender. We haven't talked about homosexualities; we haven't talked about how we work to address the needs of men who have sex with men and gay men. We haven't talked about homophobia and its relationship to the work that we do.

Boitshepo: We have a heterosexual bias in terms of gender-based violence. We still think men are the ones perpetuating violence against women. This is true, but we are not thinking about men who are violent to other men. It is an area where, unintentionally, we might still feel uncomfortable. There is very little knowledge and very little literature that we have access to about this topic. But we could empower ourselves by partnering with organizations who work around issues of sexualities to bring those issues into our work.

Mbuyiselo: We cannot separate the struggles. The struggle [against homophobia and heterosexism] is the same as the struggle about how we relate to the disabled. You raise the issue of homosexuality as a minority issue, but the disabled in this country are also a minority. The difficulty is the so-called 'normal' people – their frame of reference is systemized on their normality and is predicated on the notion that all others are not important;

this is where you find abuse. This is where people believe or you tend to think in a very parochial, in a very small-minded manner. I am returning to what I said earlier, that the struggle for equality affects and impacts all of us!

Regis: In our culture as black African men or women, it is a very difficult subject to look into. Sometimes I feel that when you talk about 'leaving no one behind', is that not somehow trying to cover up, not to confront the issue of gay relationships directly? When, Boitshepo, you say we don't have enough knowledge, have we not created the knowledge that informs our work? The whole question of gay relationships, to me, also goes to the core of patriarchy, of redefining manhood. In our work, among ourselves, we are very quick to hug ourselves. I think we have to make a very conscious decision to address this issue. You see, if we had to raise the question of disability, there's nothing controversial about that. But as you raise the question of gay relationships, people think, 'Ah, Mbuyiselo, but I thought you were a real man.'

Dumisani: I also think that it is not because people are afraid of what people 'out there' would say about them or about us, but I think we, ourselves, carry a certain bias that we don't want to confront immediately. For instance, I accept gay people, but I think that when I analyse that acceptance it is in a particular way. I accept them, I'm fine with it, but in a particular way.

Mbuyiselo: Are you not then being condescending, patronizing? Like under apartheid, whites would say, 'Among my best friends are black people', and you immediately knew that what they meant was, 'Actually, I'm okay with black people so long as they are not in my back yard.' I'm just wondering when you say 'in a particular way', what this means?

Dumisani: What it means is that I could interact, but I won't always make the initiative. I wouldn't take the first step to initiate something: friendship, for instance. That's particular, whereas if it's Mbuyiselo, I can initiate that first step.

Dean: I think what you did, Dumisani, is what I'm hoping we can all do: acknowledge the struggles and the limitations of where we've gone, and where we still need to go. And part of where we still need to go is home. It's late.

Notes

1 Quotes from unpublished MAP Mural case study written by Kristy Siegfried.

2 The interview was conducted by Dean Peacock on 7 February 2005 in Johannesburg, South Africa.

3 The Cape Flats is located on the outskirts of Cape Town and is where non-white people were relocated to during the apartheid era, under the terms of the infamous Group Areas Act.

4 ADAPT is a South Africa-based NGO that works towards preventing domestic violence.

15 | Separation anxiety: the schisms and schemas of media advocacy, or 'Where are you tonight, Langston Hughes?'

PAROMITA VOHRA

'Theme for English B'
The instructor said:
Go home and write
a page tonight.
And let that page come out of you –
Then, it will be true.
I wonder if it's that simple?
...
It's not easy to know what is true for you or me
at twenty-two, my age. But I guess I'm what
I feel and see and hear, Harlem, I hear you:
hear you, hear me – we two – you, me, talk on this page.
(I hear New York too.) Me – who?
Well, I like to eat, sleep, drink, and be in love.
I like to work, read, learn, and understand life.
I like a pipe for a Christmas present,
or records – Bessie, bop, or Bach.
I guess being coloured doesn't make me NOT like
the same things other folks like who are other races.
So will my page be coloured that I write?
Being me, it will not be white.
But it will be
a part of you, instructor.
...
Sometimes perhaps you don't want to be a part of me.
Nor do I often want to be a part of you.
But we are, that's true!

(Langston Hughes)[1]

When did they start to call political art media advocacy? I'm not sure, but possibly around the same time that the feminist movement began to be called the women's movement.

At some point we ceased to see art and media projects as expressions of our political ideas and came to regard them as receptacles – some sort of fast, cheap and convenient carriers of 'content': disseminating tools.

Media for social change is a decades-old institution in India.[2] It is tied to the conception of nationhood, either to build or critique its practices, right from the paternal governmental vision of Doordarshan and All India Radio,[3] through to the left and liberal film-makers of the 1970s and 1980s, the media collectives of the 1990s until today, where there is a growing diversity of alternative media initiatives. Media advocacy follows roughly three routes: the making of alternative media, for example documentary films, the critique of mainstream media and the handing over of media tools to untrained groups in order to demystify the process and give them the power to tell their own stories.

With respect to the feminist movement in India, media advocacy has been of particular relevance. In part, this is because the media seemed like a very good way to combat the cultural attitudes that underpin patriarchy and prevent the success of organizational or developmental projects. In part, it is because video records of women's initiatives and experience overlapped so easily with the idea of oral history, as well as 'the making public of the personal', hence rendering it political.

There have been important moments in this engagement, like the oft-noted Video Sewa experiment or the formation of Mediastorm, a women's documentary film collective in Delhi. But over the years, barring a few exceptions, much of this media work has remained at a sort of early stage.[4] While in more recent times the Indian documentary film movement has seen a proliferation of *styles* in feminist films, it has seen fewer new feminist approaches or narratives; there is a stronger tendency to clarify a position than to speak from it. In a sense there is an industrial strength replication of pre-established narratives with only the tiniest of modifications, a preference for sticking close to familiar modes. From being a philosophical political narrative, informed by the ideas of feminist thought and activism, a lot of women's media advocacy (and a lot of other social-issue advocacy as well) is example-oriented, a reiteration of known ideas, not a deepening or widening of the feminist discourse. Having established the importance of a woman's room, it is as if it stays there safely rather than challenging and disturbing the calm surface of political correctness. How did it all get to be so thoroughly domesticated?

'Women's issues' rather than feminism

There is something to be learned from this trajectory of women's media advocacy, and it is crucially tied to the growth of feminism as a dynamic, meaningful philosophy. Much advocacy work has tended to circle around the idea of 'women's issues' rather than feminist approaches to the world. This is in large part because there is, in fact, an industry around this – of funding and promotion – which considers women being on film sufficient, women picking up a camera empowering, women making movies an amazing achievement, and asks not much else of it. Funding for media advocacy often proceeds along these concretized lines. It is relatively easily available for a list of appropriate issues – say, women and housing, or adolescence, or violence. These have a programmatic nature and are illustrative rather than exploratory projects. The issue is seen as being quite clear, and it asks that the project have a result that is equally visible and unambiguous: something we can touch and see in our lifetimes. In government terms, it's what we call 'implementation'. As the industry expands, the work grows further away from the central ideology that it once radiated from, becoming a free-floating process of routine and, eventually, a dead metaphor. Those who become absorbed into it, do so by professional routes, carrying out the job rather than seeking to subvert these processes.

In effect, this approach also stems from a fixed, rather than evolving, delineation of what is political, and what are the problems of being an Indian woman. The tendency then is to speak of women primarily as examples of their socio-economic location, and only in terms of the problems they either experience or triumph over. At some primitivist level, it is as though women do not negotiate complex compromises or produce theory, or, heaven forbid, art. It is a pseudo-socialist aesthetic: where determined sameness is a metaphor for equality and the world of imagination is an exiled counter-revolutionary.

The new rhetoric of accessible technology makes this process even more pedestrian. Technology is seen as sufficient to counter the intensely ideological weight of cultural life, as if material access were the sole separator of the marginalized from the privileged. To suggest that there may be need to understand a medium aesthetically or semiotically, to explore the implications of form, is at best to be told, 'Well, this is not an arty film, it's an issue-based video', or its variation, 'We are not artists, we are activists.' At worst, it is to be accused of being 'brahminical' and 'anti-people's media'. It is a matter of unending wonder that the very people who underline the inequities born of language politics – the fact that education in English confers privilege – dismiss the language of media and art, deny that it has its own nuances and political weight, and effectively separate entire communities of artists and audiences from the alternative discussion of political life.

In a fundamental sense then, media advocacy has abandoned the very rich theoretical and political underpinnings of feminist thought, and domesticated itself into an industry. It has fallen into a cautious, conformist mode, using the most hackneyed conventions in self-justification – seeking not the poetry of felt observation, the creation of an alternative culture, but a mechanistic and essentially conservative approach.

It is certainly true that this concept of media advocacy has paralleled the rise of the NGO sector. But these same floating mechanics can be found outside the purview of the NGO film as well. For instance, another form popular with women has been the personal film. Born from the feminist idea that 'the personal is political', it is now a shadow of that idea. It has become a diary form, akin to the slip-dress, where it is more a case of what is inside is outside, where it is enough just to speak of one's personal life or centralize the narratives of inspiring female relatives, and imagine that it will translate into political meaning. But, sister, we are a long way from letting it all hang out and calling it a revolution. The magic of the phrase 'the personal is political' was that it made sense backwards as well – 'the political is personal' – and it is a suggestion that we render the personal political through something we do in expressing it.

Further, this malaise is deeply tied to a similar crisis within party or union politics. Within political movements, the prescriptive approach to media, or (let's face it) propaganda, has existed for a very long time. In terms of form and intent, it is not that different from the state's own didactic mechanisms, and it is often tied to moral lessons rather than ethical issues. More disturbingly, what leads from this is the inherent, implicit, but overwhelming hierarchy of issues. In this roster, feminist issues are just not considered that important, no matter what lip-service is paid to them.

Obviously there has been a long journey from early denouncements of feminism as an elite, Western conspiracy to divide the people's movement, and the refusal to accept that patriarchy was a category by which power could be understood. At a quick glance, it seems that in a pervasively patriarchal understanding of the world, many – though by no means all – activists have (roughly) this order of important issues: communal conflict, defence policy and peace movements, land rights, indigenous people's movements, labour or allied economic issues, women's issues – preferably to be discussed around 8 March – and then, child rights. If there were a catalogue, it would read: 'Category: communalism,[5] Subcategory: women'. In this automated perception, the issue connotes urgency, rather than the moment that the issue finds itself within.

When surrounded by this powerful but unarticulated environment, it becomes difficult to assert a more complex voice with confidence. For many women, it translates into a highly ambivalent relationship with being called 'woman artist' or 'feminist media practitioner', because it is seen as an apologist stream, a limited identity. The limitations exist equally in both domains that have now become so separate from each other – activism and art. While the romanticized figure of the radical male artist evinces a perspective that his work pertains to all, the woman artist is stereotypically seen as being grim or kooky, her concerns being herself and her fluids.

Isms, schisms and schemas

This is a mind-set of schisms and schemas. Faced with this separation of feminism from the world, by its being recast as women's issues, media advocacy done by women flutters anxiously between addressing women's issues and experiences, and making tense, circuitous disclaimers about how their work is not just, well, 'women's work'.

It is all the more confusing because the double-speak of caring about the 'women's question' is the very thing that facilitates and gives space to so much of the work. But its boundaries are firmly drawn with invisible ink. Why is it so difficult to see that one needs more intuitive forms to counter this intuitively felt prejudice?

The schisms are binary. The separation is not only between women and the rest of the world, or feminism and women's issues, but just as strongly, and more fundamentally, between what is perceived as cultural/artistic, what is seen as theoretical and what is considered political. This approach sees art and culture in a fragmented way – as mere adjuncts to the real work of a society, as an illustration of social and historical moments. All media can be clearly identified via a schema, in which art or media work is commercial if it entertains, personal if it is expressive, and political if it is didactic and unambiguous. Everything that seems betwixt and between is problematic.

This suspicion of art is the same as the suspicion of feminism. Both approaches – of art and of feminism – undermine what has been the dominant tendency of academic and organizational thought: a strongly objectivist tendency, uncomfortable with the modes of intuitive observation and ambiguous responses. Both subvert the very structure of thought, not just a point or two in it, and so the anxiety of keeping them separate from the mainstream of *the alternative* is stubborn.

The identikit and the moment of ambivalence

Several years ago, I was involved in a project called *A Woman's Place*, which was a cross-cultural exploration of how women strategically redefine power, around the world. It was a collaborative effort between film-makers from India, South Africa and the US, meant for broadcast; an attempt to work in a mainstream format but with a greater focus on process, rather than just product. Predictably, funding for this was not easy to obtain, and I got quite used to wearing Indian dress to meetings with funders, as proof of my authenticity. Along the way we met with an established women's media network. We were told by its president that the only people entitled to tell the stories of women of a specific context were those women themselves, as indeed this group had facilitated in some places. For us to aspire to do so was to usurp their voices.

Almost a decade later I made a film, *UnLimited Girls*, in English, about feminism and varied people's responses to it; it was quite rooted in content and form within various urban contexts. At several screenings I was lectured about how I ought to be making films about rural and underprivileged women, and told that by speaking of my own and allied contexts, I was effectively silencing the women of rural India (I've met a few of these rural women and I can't remember speaking much in that encounter, but that's another story for another time). One person even sent me a four-page academic article about how my film was elitist, as was my persona. Therefore, by implication, the film could not be a valuable political document because after all the 'real' India is in the villages and the rest is, I guess, *maya*, illusion.

Identity politics has its roots in a very important tenet of equal but different, not same; it resists the power structures of caste, class and gender within progressive politics. In fact, it often seems to have become a peculiar form of wielding power: as if, now that your box has been recognized, you dare not leave it. A sense that we must forever work along the lines of what has been codified and ordained; blurring these lines is not permitted. It creates an effective medium of conservative caution – the focus is on what should be said, and who should speak for whom. This process has a militaristic aesthetic, and it effectively disallows the most fundamental questions of form, essential both to feminism and art – now that we know what we want to speak of, *how* shall we speak of it? How do we join what is individual and human in us with the universal, the socio-economic common identity we each embody?

As importantly, if I am not permitted to speak of others' stories, does it mean by implication that I need never listen to them? Or that I tell them with a comfortable disclaimer, acquitting myself of responsibility? Optionally, if speaking of my own experiences is a political indulgence and so to be eschewed, then what am I? Someone set apart from the need for change and accountability? These questions and uncertainties are a natural corollary of change. But it seems to be enough to plug these anxieties rather than to use them as a means of developing a deeper conversation.

It is almost as though a checklist has been created on which you can tick off a set of identity representations, rather than plunge into the messy questions: how do we speak of heterosexuality without undermining same-sex relationships? How do we speak of Hindu identity without ignoring Muslim women's issues? When does anxiety about not speaking *for* others translate into not speaking *of* them? How do we find a way for the many identities within us to form a fluid whole; that there is a little of me in you and you in me, loved, hated, othered, that we imbue in each other?

How, in other words, do we find a new complex language rich with ideas and questions, as opposed to clarifying a prescribed understanding? If this is the room that media advocacy lives in, then we have to wonder: what exactly is it advocating? Like some great continental drift, as art separates from politics, theory from activism, intellect from emotion, how do we find a way to integrate these vital aspects of understanding, communication, ideas and ways of knowing and doing?

Perhaps we need to return to an early lesson of feminism: that the thing we know intuitively has meaning. That, by articulating the intuitive, what we thought was a random personal inclination begins to form a map of larger political meaning: that it is not enough to articulate the intuitive, but necessary to join it with the experience of others, in order to find other ways of being.

When I was making a film on feminism for Sakshi, a Delhi-based NGO, I went through all the fears and anxieties I have outlined above. I was scared of not representing everyone, of not covering all the bases. Underneath it were all the things that had bothered me for years: that while the ideas of feminism had been very powerful for my life, the encounters with many feminists whose work I admired had left me with suppressed questions. Where was I to go to find a feminist history if I wasn't already 'in the know'? Why in the discourse of empowerment did no one tell me that some of my choices would be so hard, and render me alone and confused? And now that I have found myself in that state how do I speak of it and find a new meaning for it? How can I purify my choices?

But my task was to make a film that would invite young women to rejoin the politics of feminism. If I were to speak of these confusions, would it not put these women off? Was it therefore not more strategic to tell a tale of achievements, and advertise all the advantages? Perhaps it may have been. We'll never know, because in the end I made a film untidy with both doubt and certitude, moody with questions and answers, in no particular progression. I had a great desire to speak to my audience; to do so, I had to let go of the anxiety about what they would go away with, after watching the film. I had to open myself up to the uncertainties of a conversation, choosing this form over the comfortable elevation of media advocacy. Conversation presumes knowledge and it takes certain things for granted. It is an exploratory exercise of clarification in which we take the time to listen to each other. It has wit, and, it is to be hoped, honesty, rather than posturing. But it also has elements of performance that charm the listener, a persuasive statement of one's views – in other words, a deep concern with form. At its heart is the desire to be understood and to understand, and then to seek, together, some answers.

In this, I believe I was true to what I think is the place of art. It is not the work of the artist to place strategy above ideas, truisms above honesty. Most of all, art is a place of honesty, where the nature of art – which is affective as much as explicit or intellectual, something that allows us to feel or sense as much as see or understand – allows for a certain arrangement of contradictions and dilemmas. The honesty and form can then, perhaps, lead to a slow resolving or acceptance of these contradictions. The creative endeavour is a constant reconsideration and refining of politics. It is a spontaneous form of politics but also vulnerable because of its openness. We cannot claim with art: 'Don't shoot me, I'm only the messenger.' We cannot claim an unassailability that the category of media advocacy purports to provide, with its procedures and methodologies and/or politically indignant films. Nor does art ensure recognizable and unmistakable responses in a range of registers – outrage, opposition, sympathy, empathy, gratitude at being informed, and the desire to act. These are time-honoured emotions and have their importance in the world, but ... perhaps there are other ways? To take on more conversational or form-al and creative approaches may mean accepting less definite responses, it may mean that we have to abandon the anxiety that our message needs to be crystal clear, that our stand should be perceived as unequivocal.

I found few of these cast-iron responses to *UnLimited Girls*. Yet, to date, I feel this has been one of my most useful films, leading to few certain statements, but perhaps many moments of questions. I have had the odd reassuring, definite response – 'I always thought I am not a feminist although I believe in equal rights, but after seeing the film, I am proud to call myself one.' But more often, there are the long exploratory discussions about the self, the world, feminism, feminists, men, women, parents, love, anger, violence, and change – interesting and involved but inconclusive. For audiences too, this is unfamiliar, not the know-it-all territory of a quiz. Yet every time I see an audience moving on from the straitjacket of that quiz to the liberated wanderings of saying what's in their heads, to a conversation, I think perhaps that honesty and openness are what films and art and the media in that form can spawn: they can build a culture of exchange and the desire to understand. Does that change people? Who can say for sure, but it does change the tone, shift the paradigm.

This is the place of art – to provide that moment of pausing, the moment when our audience does not say what we want to hear (although once in a while that feels good), but tries to listen to what it is telling itself; what the travel writer Robyn Davidson describes as 'ambivalence – the space in which we can make up our own minds'.[6] That moment of interiority is the potential moment of transformation: one we must learn to trust, without anxiously searching for proof that the message has indeed reached the other end.

I wonder if it's that simple ...

As any parent will tell us, it's all very well figuring things out for yourself but it's different when you have to make decisions for your children. So, as predictable as a parent, when I began working with a group of teenage girls, I found myself often falling back on traditional workshops about gender, media analysis, creating a personal diary, and so on. But as my colleague and I discovered in our work with the girls' media group, political correctness is a mainstream media all of its own, and girls are as canny at reproducing model versions of themselves as they are at replicating the cool images from MTV within a few days of learning to use a video camera. And despite our best efforts, the truth is that at the end of the first year, they did a little bit of just that.

With due respect to the people who pioneered the placing of technology in the hands of the underprivileged, we have to move on. It is still surprisingly in vogue to hand cameras to women, children and other underprivileged groups as if they were a *tabula rasa*,[7] noble savages whose truth will automatically emerge.

But as Langston Hughes asked in the poem that I quoted at the beginning of this chapter: is it really that simple? Are people's truths so simple that a digital machine in their hands is enough to unravel them? There is no denying the first surge of power that comes from being able to write, draw, take a picture or record a voice. Can we declare, though, that the beginning is the end, that the means are the ends, and then say that we've killed two birds with one stone? Can our process of change really be suspended for ever in that poster moment? There seems to be a strange smell of charity to that act. Clearly the point of media advocacy is not to turn people into media practitioners. I would imagine that it is about mutually finding a new language for us to express the complexities within – the mutuality that is called conversation.

In the second year of working with the girls' media group, we abandoned

Separation anxiety

much of our anxiety about how pedagogical we were being, and whether we were addressing all the right feminist points, even though we did so in an innovative way. We replaced most of the workshops with creative ones: open-ended, conversational, expressive. At the end of the year, it was quite clear that the work that emerged had a tremendous honesty in it, but, more importantly, a certain integrity and intelligence. Yet I cannot imagine going to a funder and describing the project as it played out in the second year, and coming away with anything resembling a cheque.

One of the advantages of writing this chapter in the twenty-first century is that hindsight liberates us; we can simultaneously be loyal to a political idea or movement as well as sharply critical of parts of it. The feminist movement both theoretically and politically opened up a rich space of subjective knowledge and ambiguous experience – declaring all these to be equally important ways of knowing. In a sense it provided a means to incorporate, seriously, the creative process as a fundamental part of the processes of political examination and growth. Along the way, it has allowed itself to be swept up by the anxieties that this is not enough, and scrambled to shore itself up with more conventional methods of academic proof or empirical administrative targets.

So perhaps from within it and without, it is time to start advocacy for media as an affirmation of this creative way of being political, and to put our energies behind the idea that art, like the intuitive, experiential documentation of history, is not an inferior, less political record of life and thought.

When we produce media in an industrial fashion, along respectable, predictable, formulaic lines, we function as an establishment and we remove these artefacts from context, anxious to create a value-free, problem-free cultural product. But it is not the place of the alternative to become the mainstream, just as it is not feminism for women to become just like men or the other way round. We need to abandon the safety of justifying mechanistic, commercial, value-for-money approaches as mass media or media advocacy, and push for the unverifiable veracities of creativity. Art becomes a meaningful political space only if it is emotionally viable to people – and it is so only if it is a place where they can make meanings of their own, instead of merely consuming those that they are given. Moreover, it is a place where we allow nascent ideas to exist and slowly grow; a place of constant renewal and change, which should not be harnessed in an instrumentalist manner, working against its very grain. As feminists, as political people and activists, we have to accept the responsibilities of art along with its delicacies, and its particular ways of understanding reality. We need to allow it to fill us with a sense of possibility, the easier to imagine a 'different world' and fantasize the details of how this world will be.

Notes

1 L. Hughes (1951), *The Collected Poems of Langston Hughes*, © 1994 Estate of Langston Hughes (New York: Knopf and Vintage).

2 I address issues of art and advocacy from within the context of my life and work in India. However, there may well be resonances and reverberations of the schemas and schisms I describe in other parts of the world.

3 State-owned television and radio channels in India, respectively.

4 SEWA (the Self Employed Women's Association) is a trade union of over 250,000 poor women working in the non-formal sector in Gujarat, India. In 1984, 20 women in SEWA received training in videography techniques; today the Video Sewa project is a formal cooperative, providing information and communication services (<http://www.c4c.org/india.html>).

5 In other parts of the world, 'communalism' or 'communal conflict' would be called 'fundamentalism'.

6 R. Davidson (2000), 'Against travel writing', *Granta*, 72 (Overreachers), p. 249.

7 In the philosophy of John Locke, the seventeenth-century English philosopher, a young unformed mind, not yet affected by experience.

16 | Moving the personal to the political: personal struggles as a basis for social justice advocacy

SALMA MAOULIDI

This chapter is deeply personal and represents a personal trajectory, a discovery, of sorts, of what influences and accordingly grounds my advocacy in social justice. Inevitably, the exploration is neither smooth nor straightforward, as I allow the process to evolve, building on insights in order to draw meaning. In the end, the process and content are as informative to the subject, as they are the subject.

I delve into the personal because I want to recast the incidence of heroism, since we, as activists and advocates, are by default concerned with saving others. While we spend our energies fighting the demons of humanity – discrimination, injustice, intolerance, human rights abuses – we forget that the demons are not just out 'there'; they may inhibit within. Likewise, our advocacy platform is shrouded in abstract terms so fickle that it can be a weapon of attack in one instance and equally come under attack in another.

In our engagement with the boundaries of human rights advocacy, we increasingly operate from shifting sites of apposition and opposition, our ideology being the only constant. Many aspects of our life remain surreal since, other than the issues we subscribe to, we do not, as activists, maintain deep attachments. We are in constant motion: dashing from one forum to another, travelling from one city to another, taking on new issues and joining new alliances. Sometimes we are with familiar faces but often we are with new ones. We are everywhere and really nowhere.

Our lifestyle runs the risk of making our advocacy impersonal – almost clinical. As we become absorbed in the activist culture, we can easily lose sight of what gave our activism life. We accumulate histories from our various journeys and in the process carry away a lot of baggage, which has the potential to be cruelly unloaded on to others.[1] Or worse, we may become paralysed by the burden. To evade this fate, I recognize that I am a woman with my own history, my own struggles, which shape my worldview and inform my activist agenda. I find it challenging to find a balance between ideal and practice, present and past, in order to forge a desired future.

In our advocacy, we take on issues or causes 'out there', where the particular is generalized and divorced from the individual experience. Because we define our advocacy as an intervention that reaches out to 'the other', distance is created between the action and the actor, raising questions as to where we, as activists, position ourselves within our own advocacy efforts.

My reflection, however, seeks to recognize the personal struggles we face as activists, sometimes in intimate aspects of our lives, and how this impacts on our ability to live and realize our values. After all, this is the basis of why we engage in 'principled advocacy' and how we ground ourselves in this. In this chapter it is my intention to explore my personal struggles around faith, family and relationships to discern how they inform my association with larger advocacy agendas. Certainly, it is through our ability to make personal associations between cherished and propounded values – the praxis that we apply to ourselves – that we cultivate and live our advocacy in a conscious manner.

Situating myself

I am an activist. Activism, for me, is a calling: a way of doing something, a particular consciousness in an ideology aimed at transforming thoughts and processes within and without. My activism is done not in a vacuum but in a context. For example, the organization I am affiliated to is concerned with developing the leadership and organizational capacities of women, young and old, to enable them to exercise active citizenship.[2] This process is neither linear nor singular. I intervene in the process of 'others' as much as I engage with my own practice and values. Indeed, a conscious development practice demands scrutinizing the bearing that my own biases and values have on my practice such that I do not transfer my 'baggage' on to others. This consciousness forces me to have a certain level of humility to recognize and respect an ongoing process, as well as the people partaking in it, irrespective of academic qualifications or social status.

To *do* advocacy one must have fire in one's belly. Many believe that activism involves emotion and passion but it can also be impersonal. Activism is increasingly defined and outlined in purely technical terms where the paramount objective is efficiency, i.e. the output, which in turn leads to a saturation of passion. Likewise, the time-defined nature of an advocacy agenda allows us flexibility in so far as how deeply we want to engage with the issue and process. Hence, while we may oppose land reforms, it is not necessary to have an attachment to key subjects of the reforms, say pastoralists. And while our activism may recognize some of their realities, it does not fully represent those realities. It is an impersonal intervention. Our expertise in a particular discipline, not our commitment, gives us legitimacy and authority in a particular instance. Equally, there are instances in which we become very attached to a process or a situation, where it becomes 'ours'. It may be because a key principle we believe in, and which informs our work, is involved, such as gender justice.

For me, the distinction between advocacy as a calling and advocacy as a job became clear when working on child rights issues. About a decade after the National Summit for Children to popularize the Convention on the Rights of the Child, I participated in a national effort to put children's rights back on the agenda. This was done via a Children's *Baraza*,[3] convened to coincide with the annual Day of the African Child. To attract maximum publicity, we convened the *Baraza* at the legislative capital of Tanzania, Dodoma; even the prime minister agreed to grace the event.[4] Participating organizations, mostly child rights organizations, facilitated the presence of about 300 children from all over Tanzania. Guidelines for the *Baraza* were indicated, including making the issues of security and hygiene a priority.[5] Alas, by the time the children were scheduled to arrive for the *Baraza*, nothing was done about security and hygiene. Instead, valuable time was spent squabbling over money. Unwilling to expose the children to health and other hazards, I opted to book the children into alternative accommodation where they could wash and rest until the matter was resolved.

The organizing committee opposed my decision. They threatened me with executive sanction. How dare I tamper with 'Tanzanian children' against the wishes of local agencies? My arrogance and defiance were attributed to the fact that I worked for an international organization. In reality, the attack was grounded in the fact that I had not acceded to their demands for more funds. Additionally, I was a young, independent-minded woman, who was well placed in the organization. What I was not prepared for was the use of the lives of innocent children to make their point.

My decision to act in the best interests of the children became the cause of my public humiliation. Ironically, my accusers were a group of people who claimed to be 'child rights activists'; some headed child rights agencies, while others were long-serving civil servants working on children's issues.[6] Their behaviour was not only shocking but also disappointing. Most saw no problem in appropriating donations meant for the children, such as bottled water, while the children went without. When some of them learnt that each child sponsored by my organization had a change of t-shirt, they protested about receiving only one. This was supposed to be a 'children's event' but the 'child rights activists' showed minimal interest in the children or their needs. Their concern was with using this rare opportunity to maximize personal benefits. Yet they felt justified in rebuking me for upholding a value I believed in. I stood my ground and questioned my colleagues: 'If these were your children, would you leave them at a place with no running water and an overflowing cesspit, or are hygiene and security dispensable because the subjects are poor rural children?'

In our pursuit of justice we often assume that we share the same ideals with others 'like us'. This incident left me disillusioned about associating myself with a collective whose practised values differed from mine. The experience made me realize that, in actual fact, each individual has a singular and personal interpretation of particular human rights principles, and similarly decide the extent to which they will apply these principles to their own life.

Perhaps a more fundamental lesson from this experience was recognizing the value of anger in fighting for causes. It is not enough to be concerned about an issue. Rather, one must feel outraged and affronted to embark on social protest. Many times, political and economic considerations, in my context, silence the impulse to confront injustice. No one wants to be singled out and punished for an unpopular position. Similarly, the bonds of kinship or comradeship censor one's activism. Our engagement, therefore, remains at the efficiency level: it is something we do and get paid for, rarely something we would die for.[7] In many ways, this has stunted the impact of social justice advocacy in the region where I work, being perceived as foreign and Western, not a local agenda worthy of pursuit. Indeed, principled advocacy is a lonely, hardly lucrative enterprise.

To complicate the situation further, in my context, the risk of challenging the status quo, in a radical way, is intricately associated with people's histories, the relationships they have formed and the cultures they have cultivated. This amplifies the divide between those who 'fit in' and embrace the dominant values of social justice advocacy from those who are categorized as problematic and ostracized.[8] Younger, hungrier voices wanting to push the limits of 'what we know', and thereby giving greater legitimacy to the causes pursued, are quickly suppressed. Social justice advocacy is reduced to a routine, a profession.

Yet, at its dawn, advocacy was not complicated. Passion and time were the only 'qualifications' required to become an advocate. Now one requires academic and political standing to engage in advocacy. Consequently, rather than seeing younger advocates as a resource to local movements, pioneers in the field see them as a threat to their position and purse. Years of sacrifice that have gone unacknowledged have hardened attitudes: some have become apathetic, while others have become bitter. Those who have dared to remain engaged and defiant may provide young activists with inspiration, but not necessarily acceptance, since they too are often outcasts and have never been part of the mainstream. It is phenomenal that while we become advocates to fight social exclusion, in our practice, we exhibit politics of exclusion mainly to legitimize or delegitimize issues and personalities. It is, therefore, not surprising that rather than focusing on political agendas, activists become consumed with personal vendettas, disillusioning potential converts.

Working with inherent tensions

My induction into human rights theory, and work subsequently, focused on the public and private spheres and how these dictate women's lives. Rights-based advocacy poses great tensions in human rights theory and discourse. The human rights frameworks view human rights as inherent entitlements, which come to every person as a consequence of being human.[9] Therefore, one cannot justify opting out of using this framework on account of 'difference' while such difference, similarly, should not be the basis of discrimination. Effectively, human rights advocacy is about demystifying what is particular about identities on account of the personal – religion, culture and ethnicity, traits normally kept beyond the reach of the public – by subjecting these to universal standards.

A further challenge to human rights advocacy pertains to its domestication, i.e. bringing human rights from the international arena and incorporating the ideals into domestic law. While many countries willingly sign human rights treaties, translating the ideals into their specific contexts continues to prove challenging. Sovereignty is often invoked to resist the adoption of universal standards.

I have come to the conclusion that the tension inherent in rights-based advocacy, and particularly between the public and the private, is not only legal or political, but essentially human, and therefore more encompassing. Traditionally, advocacy efforts for compliance to human rights norms focused largely on state responsibility, rarely challenging established practice. Moreover, a history of cultural, gender and economic domination clouds the case for the universalization of values.

Certainly we, as individuals, have the potential of leading multiple, and at times parallel, existence(s): that facet easily recognized in professional circles becomes alien in the personal and vice versa. What we show and what we keep hidden is *de facto* political. In some instances, it is well orchestrated and designed to meet some motive, some objective. In other instances, it is more spontaneous, almost subconscious, perhaps an indication of who we really are. Similarly, what we are can become so inextricably mixed with what we do that it becomes difficult to distinguish the person from the vocation. While our concern is with 'others', our own practices, as advocates, barely come under scrutiny. Do we indeed lead by example such that we move beyond the commitment to human rights, not only on the basis of conviction, but also in action? If the boundaries are thus blurred, where do we then find legitimacy in our strict association with human rights and social justice work?

The origins of an identity

Where is the soul of my advocacy? In answering this question, I find resonance with remarks made by Mahnaz Afkhami, an Iranian human rights activist. She observes:

> Women's struggle to define an identity has been in part a struggle to become visible to themselves and to others. As we become increasingly involved in the economic, social, cultural, and political fields, our interest, that is, the foci of our rights, spread over the entire range of human concerns.[10]

My activism finds its origins not only with my upbringing but also from my encounter with politics of exclusion: from within and without. I am an activist because my personal trajectory involves fighting bias on account of my race, my disposition, my size, my sex and my politics or lack thereof. I am a black, African, Muslim, petite woman. But I also harbour other complexities that add to my identity and, in a sense, give me my multiple identities.

A question that increasingly becomes relevant, for people similarly situated, is from what basis should an identity be constructed? Should it be on the basis of affinity, ethnicity or nationality? Or should an identity be imposed, claimed or assumed? I see myself as a world citizen, identifying myself with the general but in doing so, continuing to be very aware of the particular. Perhaps it is the fact that I come from a small island nation, yet my affinity to it is as intense as my attachment to the mainland and rural Tanzania where I live.[11] Some define me as *Mzanzibara* (a Zanzibari of the mainland). My parents are from two different communities, which they know about from word of mouth and not through their own experience. Thus their being 'this' or 'that' is more on account of lineage than attachment. It is, however, easier for them to identify themselves as Zanzibari, while my siblings and I see ourselves as Tanzanians. Our itinerant lifestyle has allowed us to create our own culture: one that represents our experiences growing up in different parts of the world amidst different cultures and subcultures. This polarization of location and experience has also meant that the sense of attachment my parents have with their siblings, and the extended family, is something my siblings and I do not share; we cannot be as close-knit. Much as we do try to keep the family bonds warm, the reality is that there is too big of a gap for traditional propinquity.

This is the reality of an ever-globalizing world that churns out satellite citizens like me; people who may share more with people thousands of miles away than with someone just a few miles away, even if this person is a relation. Therefore, the fact that I live in Tanzania does not make me a representative sample of an ordinary Tanzanian, nor does the fact I am an African who lives on the African continent make me a generic African. Rather, I think I represent the inherent diversity in my country and in my continent; a reality that activists, politicians and the media have largely chosen to ignore.

Defining the particular

There is an overwhelming assumption that all Africans either live in rural areas or emanate from rural areas. Such views became official in my country with the propagation of 'peasant politics', which rendered those groups with no, or weak, peasant ties invisible. I, for one, come from a cosmopolitan society; the Swahili are largely urban folk. For the better part of my young life, my relationship with the 'rural' was a three-acre *shamba* my father had three kilometres outside Stone Town.[12] It was a place we looked forward to going to every evening and most weekends. *Shamba* for us was fun – allowing us to appreciate another side of nature but also allowing us to spend time with our father, who travelled a lot when we were children. My development work, however, exposes me to another reality of rural life and people's attachment to their land. I have come to appreciate the connectedness of rural life to land in rural realities. Urban folks only realize something is wrong when it is unavailable in the market or on the store shelf.

However, social and political pressures deny us the ability to disassociate ourselves from dominant stereotypes because by doing so you are perceived as being a 'wannabe', and denying your origins, which are unfortunately predetermined for everyone. By default we have no voice or choice to assert who we are, since the voice of the dominant is deemed representative. Perhaps because of my heritage, I consciously resist the over-generalization of people's realities. In particular, I take issue with the generalization of women's realities as I find this disempowering, particularly when realities do not fit neatly into empirical approaches and modern notions of rights and progress. It has, for example, been common to say that African women do not own property; as activists, we lobby for law reforms to enable women to own property. The problem is we have never questioned the validity of such claims and, when challenged, we react in patronizing ways. We assume that what we know and do is the norm.

Yet lived history can challenge our frames of reference. My grandmothers, for example, all had property: movable and immovable. To maintain their autonomy, the men moved into their homes and understood that they remained there at my grandmothers' good will. This, however, has changed during my mother's, as well as my, time. Increasingly, educated women are becoming more dependent on their men, drawing their identities from them and referring not to 'my property' but to 'our property', or worse, 'his property'. Incongruously these women now go around convincing their 'less enlightened' sisters that they are deprived!

Celina Romany made a similar observation when recounting the experiences of women from the Global South at the Vienna Conference on Human Rights. She hinted at how Northern women objectified women from the South yet claimed solidarity, a situation reminiscent of the class and racial struggles of the white or elite left. She observed that 'most women were left to feel [like] powerless clients represented to the world by the enlightened advocates of the north. Women were once again cast as sinners for the redemption script of missionaries.'[13] In the process, we develop a level of arrogance, often unconscious, when we recognize that our education, race or social status puts us on a pedestal from where we claim legitimacy for our agendas. Ultimately, we perpetuate the same vices we vow to condemn, albeit subtly. We assume that because we have an education and have mastered modern terminologies and technologies, we somehow are above the 'masses'. It is therefore incumbent upon us to bring these masses into compliance through 'sensitization and awareness-raising sessions' with agreed human rights and social justice norms. It is not that the upholding of human rights and social justice principles are not noble. Rather, what is problematic is the desire, often unacknowledged, to influence a dominant conception or particular category without allowing it to evolve organically and thereby acquiring its own legitimacy.

Surviving the betrayal of ideals

Home was my first school in social justice. This is where I was taught core values of tolerance, equality, justice and compassion. This is where I learnt to 'walk the talk'. Thus when my parents' marriage of over thirty years crumbled, I felt betrayed in many ways. But mine was not a selfish motive, wishing that they remained together to suit some social expectation. As far as I was concerned, they had done their part in bringing us up. If they were now happier apart, so be it. What was disconcerting was the way in which it occurred. My father unilaterally decided that he would end the relationship. When there was an attempt at reconciliation, he wanted his way or no way. My mother's work-related travels became the focus of his discontent, which suggested a façade mainly because she has always worked; the only time she did not work was when she went back to school. So this could not have been a valid reason. I suspect that my father was depressed, suffering from the retirement syndrome, and that the insecurities that came with it were heightened by my mother's work-related mobility. Unable to articulate, or rather admit and share, his fears, he chose an escape from his frustration in the form of a divorce.

The most difficult thing to cope with was perhaps what ensued, or rather did not happen, after his unilateral decision to leave. There was no property settlement or discussion on the implication of the separation. Instead what was validated was his capacity to make such a decision. This was a blow to my activism. Where is the justice when, by a unilateral act, one person can wipe away the years spent building a life together? I spent the better part of my early activist work in a legal aid clinic assisting women realize their rights in the family. I did not contemplate that one day I would be faced with a situation where one of my biggest supporters, my father, would stand guilty of denying my mother recognition for her contributions, direct and indirect, made during their marriage. To say the least, I was outraged. Yet, society questioned how I could be outraged with my own father![14]

My mother chose not to pursue the matter. Like many Swahili women, she was too proud to entangle herself in a property dispute. Doing so would lower her status. This may well be so, for a woman with means and some form of support, but what happens to countless homemakers, mostly women, who sacrifice their youth bringing up families, if this support counts for nothing? Will their pride feed them and see them through old age? Moreover, what gives a husband the prerogative to end the relationship at will, with no due consideration of the other? And why is there the assumption that it is up to the man to be merciful, and that he solely has the discretion of giving or not giving his wife a parting gift upon divorce? More importantly, why should this be a gift and not a right by virtue of one's contributions in acquiring the property?

I do not know if I can ever come to terms with the fact that my father, the man who taught us our values, our belief in humanity, who ingrained in us a sense of justice and fairness, would first think that what he is, and what he has acquired, is solely by his own account. Nor could I have imagined that he would be ungracious and deny my mother some share of the property they acquired together, even if symbolically. If, after years of intimacy, he could dispense with her well-being, could he, or anyone for that matter, truly be passionate and committed to those less familiar to him? Certainly, charity begins at home. If we cannot be compassionate to those closest to us, it is unlikely we will be to others. And, if we cannot require those closest to us to exemplify social justice virtues, what mandates us to demand it of others? I have no qualms that equality and justice are standards I will not compromise on, but I realize that demanding it from others also requires that I share personal challenges in upholding the values I espouse. Doing so allows us to move from the abstract to the personal, thereby situating ourselves squarely between the tensions of social justice advocacy.

Moving the personal to the public

Our realities as citizens of the world expose us to external forces, which compound our internal struggles. My Islamic identity is increasingly a burden that I, and many others, have to endure as a result of a global assault that on the one hand defines you as an aggressor and a terrorist, while on the other it paints you as a victim and backward. Consequently, being Muslim gives others a licence to judge you based on assumptions they may have. For instance, many expect the same level of groove in my social life as they see in my advocacy. But because I am profoundly spiritual and very subdued in lifestyle and character, I am labelled 'conservative'. On the other hand, the conservative group thinks I am too liberal, too opinionated, and too Western; they approach me with much suspicion. My life and choices are thus under constant scrutiny. Likewise my authenticity is constantly in question. The conservative camp asks, 'If you are a Muslim, why aren't you married? Why don't you wear an *abaya*?'[15] Feminists ask, 'How do you reconcile being Muslim and progressive?'

It strikes me that if one is Muslim then the concern with balancing religion and activism is heightened. Activists I have come across who happen to be religious or spiritual from other faiths hardly attract the same scrutiny in the movement, nor do they get the same exclamations and questions about the fact that they are Hindu or Christian.[16] Their faith is hardly extraordinary, nor is their religious heritage assumed to influence their outlook the way Islam is assumed to cloud mine. Clearly being 'Muslim' invokes, for many, images of cloaked women, sexual repression and high levels of ignorance. Yet I approach my faith as something personal. I do not use it to attract acceptance or to allow me to fit in. I recognize that even my understating of doctrine and practice may differ with others who identify themselves as Muslim. My philosophy is therefore to live and let live.[17] I do not fit the profile of 'the ideal' Muslim, nor do I seek to. The same applies to my activism. I believe that who we are is partly genes, partly a product of our environment. It also results from the choices we make as human beings. I may be Muslim, but I have a choice in what I do and what I don't do. I choose not to drink, I choose not to sleep around and I choose not to tolerate injustice, in any form. Choosing not to do these things is a lifestyle choice of being sober, sane and content.

While the politics of exclusion are rife in our lives, and they may indeed compel one to claim an affiliation, I choose neither to remain on the fringes nor to be fully absorbed. Rather, I want to chart out my own destiny, create my own space, which I can share with diverse others while still undergoing an experience that is deeply personal. To do this, I have to defy stereotypes. Defiance, though painful, remains for me an empowering option mainly because when defying, you not only go against the dominant, but also challenge yourself to reason, and to accept the consequences of thought and action. Nevertheless, one must defy on principle and not just for the sake of being exceptional. Social justice advocacy, therefore, should give expression and recognition to personal marks of resistance in challenging deep-seated prejudices that permeate human reason and action. Otherwise, it loses significance and passion. Certainly, the challenge in advocacy rests with the personal. Core values we espouse can no longer concern just 'those people' out there but must concern 'us' right here. Nor can they be externalized or dealt with in a technical, mechanical or surgical fashion. I have to search my soul not only to make peace with my conscience but also to accept the consequences of my conviction.

Notes

1 I use 'baggage' to refer to the unresolved issues, questions or fears we need to work with in our development but fear to do so. Consequently we push them into our subconscious but because the issues are unresolved they keep on resurfacing in different ways, including extreme cases of denial, which is more a manifestation of our sense of insecurity when faced with the inevitable than it is about the issue or person prompting the feeling. But because it is easier evading addressing our fears we often load them on to others and justify to ourselves and to others that they are the problem.

2 Sahiba ★Sisters Foundation, a Muslim women's development network.

3 Children's Council.

4 Commemorated every 16 June in memory of schoolchildren killed by the South African racist police in Soweto in 1976 while protesting against apartheid, which denied them many rights, particularly the right to education.

5 The *Baraza* site was a government secondary school. Lavatories were blocked, there was no running water or lighting on pathways and dormitories had no mosquito nets.

6 Unlike the rest of the organizations, we made an undertaking with the parents of the children before signing them up for the trip. We knew most of these children as they came from our programme areas.

7 This and the ensuing comments are based on my experiences working in the East Africa region.

8 I think this has denied us of critical minds allowing us to move our advocacy from a basic to a more strategic level.

9 UN (n.d.), *Human Rights: A Basic Handbook for UN Staff*, p. 3.

10 Mahnaz Afkhami (1995), 'Identity and culture: women as subject and agents of cultural change', in Margaret A. Schuler (ed.), *From Basic Needs to Basic Rights: Women's Claim to Human Rights* (Washington, DC: Women, Law and Development International), p. 220.

11 I was born in Zanzibar but have lived most of my life on the mainland.

12 This was a result of revolutionary government policy in redistributing a maximum of three acres of farm land to all Zanzibaris.

13 Celina Romany (1995), 'On surrendering privilege: diversity in a feminist redefinition of human rights law', in Schuler, *From Basic Needs to Basic Rights*, p. 548.

14 By implication the suggestion is that it is only justifiable to be outraged by the acts of others, not your own.

15 A long black outer garment that serves as a cloak for women.

16 Just to demonstrate, a noted lady judge in a lawyers' association I belong to attends morning mass every day, attracting praise from the members, whereas the fact that I pray brands me a jihadist or extremist. Because there is an assumption, and this is a lay person's assumption which the educated may also harbour, that other faiths are somehow more progressive or tolerant, the fact they these women identify themselves as activists or feminists is perceived more as a bonus and not as a drawback. Emerging work on women's experiences with fundamentalism across faith, however, reveals a trend for faith establishment and communities to censure them.

17 Nevertheless, being part of the human family, I subscribe to some minimums in etiquette to facilitate co-existence, recognizing that this cannot be left to chance.

17 | Feminist leadership for feminist futures ...

SHAMILLAH WILSON

It is not the strongest of the species that survive, nor the most intelligent, but the most responsive to change.[1]

In the past few decades, women's and feminist movements have made great strides in advancing the rights of women. The engagement of women in international development processes following the UN Decade of Women (1975–85) signalled a transition for women's movements; they began developing holistic analyses of the issues impacting on women's lives, and made connections between political, economic, social and cultural realities as well as the local, national and global spaces for organizing and advocating. The resulting engagement of women's movements with institutions also signalled a transition from loosely formed social and feminist movements to the rise of institutionalized NGOs.[2] According to Charkiewicz, funding guidelines and UN access rules disciplined social movements to make the transformation to organizational structures that included staff, management and a board. This reorganization has had important implications; some good, in terms of organizational accountability and effectiveness, while others are more challenging. In a reflective process, evaluating this transition, Ruth Ochieng asked why violence against women is still rife despite the way movements have been able to restructure and the supposed levels of sophistication in our organizing.[3] Her enquiry pushes us to reflect on whether, in our haste to adhere or conform to new forms of organizing and engaging, we have been able to integrate the 'old' discourses and lessons learned, with new effective and relevant strategies. In that same conversation, Ruth Ochieng questions whether we should return to the older methods of working, i.e. 'Should we not go back to mobilizing grass-roots women?'

It would be easy to say 'Yes, a return to the old is all that is needed,' but I think that one of the lessons we have learnt is that connecting our issues and working at multiple levels is a challenge we cannot afford to abandon. At this very moment, given that it is ten years since the adoption of the Beijing Platform of Action, women from all over the world are collectively reflecting on whether we *actually* have been able to advance women's rights since 1995.

This evaluation is critical as we examine the role of women's movements in their engagement with the state and institutions of authority. Currently, we are operating in a context where (many of) our governments have ratified important international treaties, conventions and charters, which bind them into the responsibility of being providers or at least guardians of social well-being within their countries. In practice, however, governments are more apt to follow the social and economic policies recommended by multilateral entities such as the World Bank, the IMF and the World Trade Organization. Reflection on our own effectiveness needs to take into account what our current engagements with governments and institutions look like. Who defines this engagement? How do we strategize and allow ourselves to reimagine our relationship and engagements with states, vis-à-vis the feminist agenda?

As feminist movements, we have to contend not only with shifting contexts and factors, but also with a range of issues within our movements. The very nature of feminist movements is diverse, with common as well as differing goals. Our history of organizing includes the challenge of engaging with this diversity within and among movements: identities defined by race, ethnicities, class differences, geographic location and, of course, age. As feminist movements, we must role-model internal democracy, consensus finding and the recognition of diversity as practice, and not only theory.

According to Leslie Calman, the success of movements can be gauged by analysing three potential arenas of action: (i) a movement can target society, particularly with regard to social consciousness and ideology; (ii) it acts to influence the state; and (iii) it can act on participants within the movement itself.[4] All of these are intricately connected with overlapping ways of measuring outcomes.

In this chapter, I attempt to address the effectiveness of feminist movements. Through an exploration of the notions of leadership within, I explore the 'feminist futures of feminist movements'. What I am proposing here is not any different from what has been proposed before; I am simply urging us to revisit and recommit to the manifesto of the feminist project with vigour and enthusiasm. As young women, we do not propose to change the vision for social justice; our goal is to propose a revolutionary (new ways of looking at the same issues) approach to tackling challenges. Our moment in time is different, and we recognize that it will require a combination of experience, wisdom and new ways of risk-taking. One example of this was the DAWN Training Institute of 2003, where there was a transfer and sharing of experience, wisdom and strategy from the DAWN team, but at the same time, as the young feminist attendees, we were able to share our issues and concerns, and our ways (sometimes quirkily creative) of dealing with them.[5] The goal remains that we do not lose sight of the integrity of the issue we are trying to take on, yet we should not remain clutching at an ideology without assessing why that ideology (or the strategies leading from it) does not have the impact we want it to have.

Contemplating the task ahead

As we envisage the tasks before us, we can become overwhelmed by the magnitude of what needs to be done.[6] This sentiment is echoed by Peggy Antrobus, who notes that social justice work is full of risks, but a commitment to personal change will allow us to find sources of power among us that cannot be taken away by external forces.[7] Therefore, the 'self' as the individual is a starting point. However, the self as a movement is another important aspect of this reflexivity. Throughout this anthology, young feminists from all over the world have made varied proposals for dialogue in many different realms and at many different levels (local, regional and global), as well as possible actions to accompany the dialogue and changing discourses. Therefore, as we contemplate the way forward, it is important for us to be clear that what we need is thoughtful *action*. But to change the rules, the very core of the social order, I firmly believe we need feminist leadership. According to Peggy Antrobus, what makes feminist leadership different from other forms of leadership is that it is transformational: 'with a passion for justice, a commitment to change things, beginning with oneself'.[8]

Starting with ourselves: the feminist movement's internal challenges

Feminist movements today face a range of challenges that can be framed in two critical areas: soul and strategy. While we have placed much emphasis on making the personal political, we have not spent nearly enough time on making that very same politics personal. How do we internalize the politics we advocate for in the world out there as feminists and as movements? If the basic tenet of feminism is to deconstruct power, and to propose alternative paradigms for power sharing, feminism has been concerned with redefining democratic communities on more participatory grounds. In all honesty, though, how have we fared in this regard? How have we dealt with issues of power? According to Edwards and Sen, if we are to transform society and cause a fundamental shift in values, one that is sustainable and freely chosen, we can do so only if we have undergone personal and inner change ourselves.[9]

Who are we? There are different kinds of feminisms – different interpretations and applications. In addition, my interaction with other young women over the last few years (electronically and face to face) has exposed me to the diverse relationships of young women to feminism and feminist movements. I will limit myself to only a few of those. Some young women avoid overt identification with the movement and to the label 'feminist'. They may be engaged in addressing different forms of oppressions – human rights abuses, racism, heterosexism or poverty, with social justice at the centre of their analysis – yet many of them feel isolated and excluded from the feminist movement. They feel that the movement has not adequately challenged power and multiple oppressions. According to one such colleague:

> I feel that at this moment in time, feminism does not apply to my experience and often due to class, race and gender gaps with consistent visions/versions of feminism, it forces me to leave out parts of my community.
> It too often asks me to prioritise the needs of women and girls, without challenging me/us to be leaders and advocates for the entirety of our communities.[10]

Some young women have mixed feelings and misconceptions about the meanings of feminism and the movement, while others feel that openly identifying with the movement makes them vulnerable, in their local contexts, to 'anti-feminist backlash'. In an email discussion in 2003, young women noted that 'in an era of increased militarization and fundamentalisms, where women are often relegated to traditionally oppressed roles, it is of the utmost importance to have an awareness of the consequences for young women of identifying as feminists'.[11] In broader discussions with other young women, living in contexts where it is 'easier' to come out as feminists, these young women are often criticized as not being willing to go the extra mile to really live their activism.

The 'professional' feminist is a phenomenon that has surfaced over the last few years. This identity often comes about from those young women who enter and network with the feminist movement through women's and gender studies programmes at their universities. Through their research, they start engaging with issues of social justice and then eventually find employment in the field. However, a colleague from Peru last year pointed out that although it is important for young women to have a historical, analytical and theoretical framework, it is as important for these young women to find local spaces for their activism that does not involve (paid) 'work'.

The last group of young women that fall into the 'feminist' category is what I would like to call the 'new generation feminists'. This group feels that feminism and the movement is the key to achieving social justice.

Many of them are engaged in local struggles but also engaged in critical analyses on the issues affecting women, and young women in particular. These young women actively seek and create spaces to learn from 'previous generation' feminists to engage across generations and critically reflect on strategies and on their own feminism. They are keen to bring new analyses and ways of looking at power relations, different strategies and ways of organizing into the movement. Although this group may be critical and reflective about the movement, its dynamics and relations within, they do so without disengaging. Many of these young women are working in contexts where organizing is very complex, engaging with a range of power relations, and they therefore understand the need to push through the tensions in order to achieve desired outcomes.

I have highlighted only *some* of the feminist identities of young women that I have come across and 'labelled'. While we recognize the importance of choosing the feminist identity for political reasons, it is as important for us to scrutinize how we build alliances and support those who may not openly identify as feminists, but who are part of other movements for social justice.

Diversity As a movement, at the global, regional and even national levels, issues of diversity create a complexity that continues to challenge and perplex us. The fact remains that there are feminists identifying as black, rural, indigenous, lesbian, transgender, HIV positive, disabled, as well as young. In terms of representation, we seem to have our bases covered, but our weakness is in discerning how to ensure *meaningful* participation, while also acknowledging that this diversity will sometimes entail moments of conflict, disputes and contradictions.

When trying to address these issues, we always resort to the reference of 'embracing' complexity and diversity. However, working with diversity is tough, messy, and can get difficult because it is intensely personal. It is important for us to recognize this tension but also to commit ourselves, our energies and our humour, in order to handle diversity with grace and honesty.

Fragmentation is, however, not only a result of different identities. We also have ideological differences among us, some of which are due to our diverse backgrounds, some due to the changing global contexts around us. The reason for these ideological differences can be narrowed down to three general causes: interpretation, application and politics. There are different ways of interpreting and applying feminist ideologies. Politics (or lack thereof) is an issue that has emerged particularly in the last decade. For instance, it is felt that gender mainstreaming has coopted the language of gender, but without the discourse on power and patriarchy. In addition, we have grown specialized in our areas of attention (human rights, peace, environment ...), but find it difficult to incorporate this into our global strategies.

The fragmentation of issues has also had a specific impact on how 'sub-movements' see the feminist movement and its efforts to engage or support them. For example, women who are disabled might see themselves as part of the feminist movement, but might form a 'sub-movement' for disabled women in order to give identity and focus to the specific challenges facing them. Similarly, HIV-positive women have long felt that the feminist movement has not taken up issues of HIV-positive women with the urgency and attention they deserve. According to Gracia Violeta Ross, an HIV-positive young woman from Bolivia, women who form part of the HIV/AIDS movement are all fighting for the same goal as feminists: a better life for women. However, she feels that the feminist movement needs to take cognizance of the victories of the HIV/AIDS movement, while also finding ways to support the activism of HIV-positive women within the broader HIV/AIDS movement, and through the feminist agenda.[12] At the AWID Forum in 2002, Sisonke Msimang, a gender and AIDS activist, endorsed this by saying:

> Our sisters in the North need to develop a consciousness about the fight against AIDS as a feminist fight. One that, if we lose, could have profound effects on the lives of girls and women into the next century. A feminist analysis of the impact of the HIV/AIDS epidemic on women's lives is necessary. But it is not enough. We need global solidarity, an admission that the processes of structural adjustment that devalued currencies and scaled back on social services have made it that much more difficult for Africa to cope with the epidemic. We need to hold those who now glowingly talk about the need to address poverty and gender equality, accountable. But first we need solidarity between and amongst women of the North and South.[13]

Language, and how we use it, is another issue that needs critical reflection. Are we cognizant enough of the connections between language and power? For example, the language of technology has given us access to many more ways of communicating and organizing ourselves, with greater possibilities for regional and global alliances. However, we also know that there are still many more women who do not have access to technology. At a global level, it is important for us to stay connected and informed of what is happening in other countries. At local levels, where the work at a societal and community level is happening, how does technology impact on our ability to include or exclude women who identify with the feminist agenda? How is it changing our ways of working with each other and with other movements?

Antrobus also touches on issues of language by noting how English has taken on hegemonic power, excluding the majority of women in the world.[14] Language is critical and powerful as the means to convey our politics, but also in its ability to include or exclude, based on privilege, ideology and culture. In our strategizing, with the resources at our disposal, we have to find innovative ways of acknowledging and then addressing these issues.

Passing on power – what about the power in sharing?

At the Dawn 20th Anniversary Celebrations in October 2004, younger feminists organized an inter-generational dialogue where it was acknowledged: 'We need to understand that young feminists are today's leaders and recognize our own accountability in power relinquishing and power sharing within feminist movements.'[15] There have been difficulties within the feminist movement, where there is a 'generation gap within the women's movement, and a marked absence of younger women in leadership positions', in dealing with power issues and leadership.[16]

Many feminists before have argued that the feminist movement needs to become truly multi-generational. Lydia Alpizar and Shamillah Wilson argue the importance of the movement(s) in encouraging young women's participation in order to: (i) allow the movements to reinvent themselves; (ii) maintain consistency with the principles and values of feminism – and, as we are challenging power and privilege, it is important that we also do so amongst ourselves; (iii) build strength and sustainability.[17] A committed engagement with these issues will provide the foundation for developing inter-generational solidarity and power. Given that so many people have talked about this, are talking about this, I think the time has come start acting and take on this challenge. Now.

I suppose the starting point is that, as younger feminists, our challenge is finding ways to create a bridge between our own lives and past feminist action. According to Rosas and Wilson:

> Young women today are born into a reality where the gains made by the earlier generation are a reality, if no one talks to us about the struggle and history of achieving those rights, we take them for granted and assume that they were always there. As young women, we acknowledge the wisdom and experience of our predecessors. At the same time, we want to find ways of creating interactions of exchange and learning where we can gain this knowledge, but also where we can share our 'knowledge' as well.[18]

Building on this argument, so many of the problems and so much of the angst in the movement are related to issues of giving and taking power. We are extremely self-conscious about wisdom. As young women, we need to acknowledge the history and wisdom of previous generations much more than we currently do. At the same time, we need to recognize that in acknowledging wisdom and experience, we can still challenge each other. In renegotiating our relations of power with each other, we need to recognize that at different moments, we will either give or receive inspiration/wisdom/ideas and momentum from other members of the movement (and this is not based on any age-defined principles). We need to create accountability mechanisms to take on this challenge with honesty and respect.

Spirituality

In conversations with young women who attended the 2003 DAWN Training Institute in Bangalore, many of the young feminists felt that feminist movements do not support their practice of spirituality; or at least the feminist movement proposes a very particular practice or engagement with spirituality that is secular in nature. The reality is that many women do find themselves as part of 'organized religion' and feel that the disengagement of the feminist movement means that they are unsupported in their practice and in their challenge of dominant paradigms of religion, from within. For example, questions such as, 'Is it possible to be a Muslim and a feminist at the same time?' tend to fuel the fires of women who already have to defend such identities in their own communities. Assumptions and reductionist thinking about faith and spirituality are powerful divisive forces in the global context. Within the feminist movement too, we need to ask ourselves the tough questions: does being spiritual mean that we cannot be political as well? Can the two qualities co-exist individually and in the collective? We have to find ways to analyse and act in solidarity, and disengage, as do cultural relativists, because we feel we are not 'conversant' with the issues. Finally, if we are to be holistic in how we function, we need actively to make space for women to share their faith and spirituality with us.

Sustainability

The last aspect of how feminist movements function is the issues related to sustainability. Very often we hear that 'We do not have the capacity,' or 'We cannot be everywhere, advocating on all issues.' This thinking results in the reactive rather than the proactive pursuit of our agendas. We have so far explored issues of sustainability in terms of personal relations and tensions. However, the issue of well-being is critical to sustainability of the movement itself – at the individual as well as the collective levels. According to Rosas and Wilson:

> Many of us experience illness, depression, poverty, anger and conflict. Many of us are struggling with addictions, not just to substances but also to obsessive work regimes which do not allow us time to reflect, or breathing space. Being a feminist means we have many fascinating, complex experiences, trying to create a new culture, and re-create our own lives. But the destructive aspect of it, the guilt and sacrifice, at work and in our lives more generally, is a tremendous challenge.[19]

Being an activist means that we make passionate engagements, with constant personal sacrifice. There have been many discussions around these issues, between young women.[20] Although we personally value the need to be devoted and committed to and passionate about the cause, it is crucial to recognize that a longer and sustained fight is likely to have more impact than one that is interrupted because of a withdrawal of activists, through ill health and exhaustion.

In an email discussion hosted by the Association for Women's Rights in Development's Young Women and Leadership Programme in 2004, one of the young women asked:

> Does activism have to make one feel burnt-out? Maybe it does, but I have a sense from the discussion thus far that the type of burn-out people are expressing is not necessary to work for social justice. So I would put the question this way ... after the revolution, once we have won the battles for justice, what do we want the world to look like? Now how can we start living that way today?[21]

As a movement, our challenge is to find ways to prevent such a culture of burn-out from proliferating, as well as finding ways to start addressing it if it does exist in our organizations and networks. At the Young Women and Leadership Institute in 2003, Pregs Govender advised participants:

> What you [need to] look at – because as young women you are at the start of what is a lifelong journey – is how to sustain yourself. You can learn all about economic policies but you will get depressed, burnt-out, you will despair, you will want to give it up. Because it is too overwhelming. So through the work you do you have to actually say, how will I make sure that I sustain myself? That the joy you experience is there in how you live your life and how you work. If we work without that, if we allow the system that we are fighting against to destroy our joy, we don't stand a chance. We cannot let the horror of what we are fighting against destroy our soul.[22]

We need to find different ways of retreating into spaces of our own, for rest and rejuvenation. We need to do this without feeling guilt or feeling 'selfish', and we need to support each other while doing so.

Relation to other movements – allies or adversaries?

The feminist movement is one of the predominant social movements engaged in the fight for equality and justice worldwide. According to Sunila Abeysekera, social movements are generally described as conscious, collective activities to promote social change, representing a protest against the established power structure and dominant norms and values.[23] However, contemporary social movements are no longer guided by the sense that they are completing a universal plan. Their agenda is not always shaped by long-term fixed goals (for example, anti-privatization movements), and the mobilization they undertake is rooted in specific times and places.

> Activism implies acting upon, acting against, acting for causes and issues of social concern, not only personal concern. There is an implied sense that it is for the social good, working towards social change, and a move towards something better. By its very nature, activism creates a polarised tension, a dichotomy, of two opposing camps, us and them.[24]

These camps that are referred to are like two groups of protagonists: those who are 'on the right track' and those who are not. In the current global context, we are faced with the possibility of forming alliances or adversarial relationships with a range of role-players. We find ourselves opposed to right-wing fundamentalists, and at the same time, in different spaces, we might form very specific alliances with more progressive religious groups. There is also the possibility of working with corporations with a commitment to social responsibility while taking an adversarial position, in general, towards the hegemonic powers and practices of corporations. For this chapter, however, I will focus only on our alliances with other social justice movements and our relationships with the state.

Whenever the issue of how we relate to other movements is raised, I sense that there is the assumption that there is no history of feminist engagement with other social movements. Yet many feminists were part of resistance/national liberation movements within their own countries and contexts (for example, the ANC Women's League played a very active role within the South African resistance movement). While engaging with these struggles, women were also fighting patriarchy, although often not explicitly. This is one of the reasons the feminist movement was born: women's rights were not getting appropriate attention in other movements and struggles. For example, in the South African liberation struggle, women

233

were told, 'After liberation we can deal with your issues.' In an online discussion by ISIS, it was noted that:

> We have always expressed solidarity with the issues raised by a host of other social movements, and two, that we have more often found ourselves supporting the agendas of other movements, without actually being able to transform these movements from within. To a vast extent, these movements have remained patriarchal in nature.[25]

However, it is also true that feminists have continued to work with other social movements, and that we are at a moment in time where we have come full circle. We realize that in order to survive and have strength, we need to find ways to influence these other movements to incorporate our agendas.

Our task now is to build strategic alliances. According to Antrobus, we cannot build a movement for social transformation without making strategic alliances with men. She encourages the feminist movement to distinguish between men who are open to partnership with feminist leadership and those who are not, and to make strategic alliances with those who do understand that there is no justice for men without justice for women.[26] Working with young men, in particular, is an opportunity to ensure that a new generation of leaders sees the necessity of addressing systemic gender inequality in order to achieve social justice. In addition, we also need to support women who are working within other social movements, through analysis, through dialogue, and also to support them in advancing the feminist agenda within those movements.

The world is volatile, and in order to be effective and to survive as a movement and a species, we need to assess moments and opportunities accurately, prioritizing when various actors need to work together. There are also moments when we will have an adversarial relationship with other movements, but this is all part of the context we engage in. We need to accept the challenges of apparent paradoxes in our ideologies and our actions, in order to achieve our visions.

The state and institutions of authority

The institutionalization of NGOs has changed the terrain of engagement of women's and feminist movements, requiring an explicit focus on states and their allies. Women's NGOs, in particular, find themselves in the predicament of having to choose carefully the way in which they interact with the state. While there are opportunities and a necessity to work with the state around concrete issues affecting women, such as education and health, they also run a risk of being coopted by the state. This has implications for the potential to challenge the state. Alternatively, they can adopt an oppositional stance towards the state, which in particular contexts might influence their access to resources, or have implications of repression in some instances.

In order to be effective, women's rights groups find themselves in the position where they have to engage at the global, regional and national levels. This has had serious implications for women's groups in developing countries, where many are left behind because of limited available resources. Those who are able to organize themselves at the different levels find themselves speaking for 'everyone', and issues of legitimacy have come in question.

According to Patricia McFadden, there are those who define our politics in relation to the neo-colonial state, to decide what intellectual tools we use in understanding inequality and injustice: she feels that we are even allowing them to redefine the language we have struggled so hard and long to find, which speaks most deeply to the social and bodily violations that confront us.[27] Charkiewicz is also very critical of engagement at the institutional level, and the fact that feminist groups have allowed themselves to be moulded into what the institution can handle. 'The pursuit of the strategy to speak the language of the system is based on the assumption that it will change global governance from within – the problem is that these strategies subtly change the movement.'[28]

This brings up the age-old debate of whether, as feminist movements, our engagement should be one of resistance or reform. At the end of the day, there are benefits and disadvantages to both prospects. The threat of cooption is real. As autonomous women's movements, we need to ask how can we ensure that the organization and issues are not coopted by a modernist yet repressive state (or institutions)? How do we engage with the state on our own terms? Is it possible to work on feminist policies within the state? According to Pregs Govender, we should not aspire to fit into and function within institutions of power. Our goal should rather be that we should set our agenda, understand our values, and try to transform those institutions.[29]

As we strategize, it is important to see many possibilities, often simultaneous, for our engagements. First, it is important that we do work with the state, but without losing our autonomy to challenge. Instead of adopting a simply adversarial role, we need to recognize that we can achieve more by engaging and getting our voices heard in the institutions that govern. However, engaging with *only* the state is also problematic. It is important for us to work across spaces in order to address our issues in authentic ways. In addition, our engagement with the state will push us to engage with much more vigour with the internal challenges (within our organization and movements) that we need to address; for in our challenges to the state (or other institutions) for their lack of democracy and accountability, we should not be guilty of the same charges. I am not trying to be simplistic about the complexity of engaging with institutions of authority; however, we need to consider honestly how effective we are in our intended outcomes, and the various possibilities that may need to be explored, in our quest for social justice.

Moving forward

There is a need to evaluate our feminist engagement at all levels and in all issue areas that we work in. Personal issues that women identify with and their links (or lack thereof) with institutional politics provide challenges for how we engage. Our aim is not only to engage with the state or within the movement itself. Our aim is to transform patriarchal structures, so we need to be clear how we are going to do it. Are we focusing a skewed amount of our attentions on the state and institutional levels? What is happening at the community or national levels? As I said earlier, if we are to effect real change, we need to employ a combination of strategies, at multiple levels, involving a range of different players.

According to Srilatha Batliwala, 'feminist leadership requires incredible agility and resilience because each step forward creates new and some-times graver challenges/backlash. This makes feminist leaders stronger and smarter strategists and negotiators.'[30] We have paid considerable attention to the soul of the feminist movement. Throughout this book, we have des-cribed some of the external and internal challenges that we face. As young women, we want to push the boundaries around the debate of leadership. As a movement, we need to assess how we are able to adapt to changes in our own environments on a continuous basis. How does this get integrated into long-term strategy and also, ultimately, effectiveness?

Here are some of the challenges I feel we need to tackle if we are to take on the leadership in advancing the social justice agenda:

1 We are always responding to challenges and we are not always as able to be proactive around them. We need to find ways to generate new knowledge and variations around the issues we are engaging around so that we can stay ahead – for example, the recent tsunami disaster. Have we, as feminists, really integrated natural disaster responses into our core strategies or agendas? Now that the tsunami has happened, how are we supporting grass-roots groups who are involved in helping people pick up the pieces? Also, how do we take on and push for issues

that are not necessarily within public memory, that are not 'sexy'? How do we renew strategies and interests for the 'old' issues that are still plaguing us?

2 We find it difficult to mobilize around new issues. For example, the fragmentation around specialization of issues such as new technologies and genetic engineering have meant very little joint responses to these new engagements.

3 We need to build the capacity to know why we succeed/fail, to understand why change does, or doesn't, happen. This should inform how we strategize and implement new strategies for effecting social justice. We also need to put in place systems and measures of accountability, and for evaluating change.

4 Our survival and strength depend on our best use of available and limited resources. In our current context of organizing, we are constantly made aware of the competition for limited resources. We need to make intelligent, informed, and, ideally, collective choices about how we use these limited resources.

5 How do we engage with the mainstream and challenge it at the same time? How do we define our agenda and ensure that we constantly revisit our engagements with the state and with institutions?

6 How do we connect to global movements and build even stronger connections to our local and regional movements?

If we want to be effective, if we want to be strategic, we need to realize that in order to be different, cutting-edge and innovative it might mean that we run at loggerheads to the customary notions of an activist movement. We need to capitalize on our strengths, home in on our weaknesses, and be responsive and able to adapt to an environment that poses some unique challenges, with high levels of uncertainty and complexity. The biggest hurdles we face are how we deal with issues of power, accountability, leadership and bureaucratization, both within the institutions we challenge and within our own movements. We must move out of the boxes we seem to have trapped ourselves in – to act with courage and to 'revolutionize' the ways in which we engage within and without. Speed, choice and innovation are critical if we want a world where there is freedom from fear and freedom from want, and where obstacles to human security are a thing of the past.

Notes

1 C. Darwin (n.d.), see <http://<www.writersmugs.com/quote/Charles_Darwin/32.html>.

2 E. Charkiewicz (2004), 'Women in action: beyond good and evil: notes on

global feminist advocacy', see <isiswomen.organisation/pub/wia/wia2-04/ewa.htm>, p. 2.

3 Ruth Ochieng in N. Montes-Rocas and M. Ibanez (2004), 'At the crossroads: rethinking the critical advocacies of the women's movements', see <http://isiswomen.organisation/pub/wia/wia2-04/malen.htm>.

4 L. Calman (1992), *Toward Empowerment: Women and Movement Politics in India* (Boulder, CO: Westview Press), p. 5.

5 In September 2003, the Third World feminist network DAWN (Development Alternatives with Women for a New Era) held its first Feminist Advocacy Institute with young feminists from the global South.

6 P. Govender (2003), 'Transcript of Association for Women's Rights in Development Young Women and Leadership Institute' (Cape Town, South Africa: AWID).

7 P. Antrobus (2004), *The Global Women's Movement: Origins, Issues and Strategies* (London and New York: Zed Books), p. 166.

8 Ibid.

9 M. Edwards and G. Sen (August 2000), 'NGOs, social change and the transformation of human relationships: a 21st century civic agenda', *Third World Quarterly*.

10 Y. Chlala, N. Ngugi, A. Sengupta and S. Wilson (2004), 'Transformative leadership: the "now" and "future" of the movement', *Agenda* 60, see <http://<www.agenda.organisation.za>.

11 K. Evans and S. Wilson (August 2004), 'Views from her(e): young women's perspectives on gender, human rights and development', see <http://<www.awid.org/publications/primers/yw_fact_sheets_en.pdf>.

12 G. V. Ross Quiroga (2004), 'A bridge needs two sides: partnership and collaboration between women's movements and the movements of HIV positive women', paper presented at the Global Roundtable, Countdown 2015, Sexual and Reproductive Health and Rights for All in London.

13 S. Msimang (2002), 'Human rights for all: understanding and applying "intersectionality" to confront globalization', plenary presentation at AWID's 9th International Forum, see <http://<www.awid.org/forum2002/plenaries/AIDS_and_Feminism.html>.

14 Antrobus, *The Global Women's Movement*, p. 146.

15 S. Abeysekera (2004), 'Women in action: social movements, feminist movements and the state: a regional perspective', see <isiswomen.organisation/pub/wia/wia2-04/sunila.htm>, p. 18.

16 Ibid.

17 L. Alpizar and S. Wilson (forthcoming), 'AWID Spotlight, 2005: making waves: how young women can (and are) transforming organizations and movements'.

18 A. Rosas and S. Wilson (2003), 'The women's movement in the era of globalization: does it face extinction?', *Gender and Development: Women Reinventing Globalization*, see <http://<www.awid.org/publications/gen_dev/rosas-wilson.pdf>, p. 138.

19 Ibid., p. 140.

20 Unpublished online discussion summary by AWID's Young Women and Leadership Programme, 'How do young women sustain themselves?'

21 Ibid.

22 AWID's Young Women and Leadership Programme (2003), 'YWLI: Africa Regional Young Women and Leadership Institute – transcript', see <http://<www.awid.org/ywl/ywli/transcript2003.pdf>, p. 6.

23 Ibid., p. 1.

24 N. Nair (2004), 'On 'being' and 'becoming' ... the many faces of an activist', *Agenda 60*, pp. 28–32.

25 E. Charkiewicz (2004), 'Women in action'.

26 Ibid., p. 148.

27 P. McFadden (April 2004), 'Why feminist autonomy right now?', *Fringe Feminist Forum Online Journal*, see <www.fito.co.za/april_2004/articles/mcfadden_why_feminist.htm>

28 Ibid., p. 3

29 AWID's Young Women and Leadership Programme (2003), 'YWLI: Africa Regional Young Women and Leadership Institute – Transcript', p. 6.

30 S. Batliwala (2003), 'Women's leadership, what's the difference: insights from an international study of 20 innovative feminist women leaders', unpublished.

Feminist leadership for feminist futures

You wonder why I say I'm feminist

GABRIELLE JAMELA HOSEIN, 2005

You wonder why I say I'm feminist
Don't I know that's out of style?
Don't I see when people don't challenge me
Just shake their heads and smile?
Don't I know people feel sorry for you
If they think you are addicted to a cause
But can't decide if it's the 'death penalty'
Or 'pro-abortion' laws?
How do I carry this label?
Don't I realize people (still) ask if I hate men?
You try to place me because I seem unafraid
And yet even have a boyfriend!
You find it's hard if men don't accept you,
But at least having a man in your life
Makes it okay to speak out for women
Because you feel easier than lesbians to like.
How could I think women are still 'oppressed'?
Don't I look around and see?
We have all we want, though we know
Not to shout out our new equality.
Yes, it's true we would not have these rights
If women didn't struggle, question and write
But now who has that time?
And can't those other people look after their own fight?
You haul over all these stereotypes.
Wonder who would burn the push-up bra
Or think women need to work with men
So we don't take everything too far.
You wonder why I say I am feminist
And what it really means.
Don't I get fed up all the time
Of having to defend my dreams?

Editors and contributors

Editors

Shamillah Wilson (age 32) is the Young Women and Leadership Pro-gramme Manager for the Association for Women's Rights in Development (AWID). She has a BA from the University of Cape Town and part of her research included a focus on Muslim Women's Social Reality. She is in the process of finishing her M.Phil. in Futures Studies at the University of Stellenbosch in South Africa. She is a founding board member of the Youth Against AIDS Network, a regional network of youth leaders in Africa, and acts as a member of the Advisory Council for the Africa Region for the Global Fund for Women. She is also the coordinator for the HIV/AIDS Learners' Network of the Western Cape, a group that builds young people's leadership from a gendered perspective to enable them to fight HIV/AIDS. Shamillah has set up and facilitated various networks in the region and internationally aimed at linking up different role-players in order to share information and to strategize around key issues related to young people, HIV/AIDS, sexual and reproductive rights and women's rights.

Anasuya Sengupta (age 30) has an economics (honours) degree from Delhi University. She worked as a Programme Officer for 'Samuha', a rural de-velopment organization in north Karnataka (India) and went on to do an M.Phil. in development studies, as a Rhodes Scholar at the University of Oxford. For the past three years, she has been coordinator of a UNICEF project with the Karnataka police, working on violence against women and children. She is also a researcher and facilitator for Gender at Work, an international knowledge network on gender and institutional change. She is an adviser to different organizations on issues of gender and governance, and is actively involved with regional and national networks against funda-mentalisms. She is a former member of the Young Women and Leadership International Advisory Committee for the Association of Women's Rights in Development (AWID), a trustee of JournalServer.Org (for online journals), member-secretary to the Institutional Ethics Committee of Samraksha (an NGO working on HIV/AIDS), and a board member of Krishuka Pradhana Abhivruddhi Samstha (an organization for farmers' support services and community development). She is old-fashioned enough to believe in the power of the collective and new-fangled enough to believe in future pos-sibilities for generating that energy.

Kristy Evans (age 26) has worked with the Association for Women's Rights in Development (AWID) in varying capacities for the past three and a half years. She holds a BSc in Biology and a minor in Peace Studies from McMaster University. She is currently working towards her master's degree in public health at the University of Cape Town. Kristy has worked in various capacities for local, regional and international NGOs and institutions. Over the past year she has worked on projects for UNAIDS, Actionaid, the Atlantic Centre of Excellence for Women's Health in Canada and the Interagency Coalition for AIDS and Development. Her interests include fostering leadership skills in young people, and she works in her spare time as a coordinator for the HIV/AIDS Learners' Network of the Western Cape. Strategizing, writing and the promotion of global justice and gender equality preoccupy her thinking. She is currently focusing on building strong young women's analysis through research, participation and dialogue.

Contributors

Zakia Afrin (age 27) has an LL.B. from Dhaka University in Bangladesh and LL.M. in public international law from Golden Gate University, California. She is working towards her doctoral dissertation on transitional authorities under international law. Zakia is a research analyst for Kreddha International, working on conflict resolution and existing autonomous arrangements in the Asia-Pacific region. A feminist by nature, Zakia has published a book on existing laws aimed at violence against women in Bangladesh and numerous articles in newspapers and magazines. She has worked as a journalist specializing in women's issues and as a campaign coordinator for Amnesty International's 'Stop Violence Against Women' campaign in California.

Aziza Ahmed (age 26) has a BA in Women's Studies (Emory University) and an MSc in population and international health (Harvard School of Public Health) and is currently a law student at the University of California, Berkeley. Aziza worked with DAWN Caribbean on issues of sexual and reproductive health rights in the Caribbean, and also worked in Johannesburg, with the Planned Parenthood Federation of South Africa. Her work has focused on gender, health and human rights. She has also explored the interaction of these topics with religion and migration. Aziza Ahmed is a second-generation South Asian Muslim American woman.

Sushma Joshi (age 31) is an independent anthropologist and writer, and consultant for UN and ICIMOD. After graduating from Brown University in 1996, Sushma returned to Nepal to coordinate the Global Reproductive Health Forum in South Asia. Through this, she started *re/productions*, an

243

online journal, and also Bol!, a mailing list with 600 subscribers and lively discussions on gender. She also directed *PANI*, a documentary on how women and lower-caste communities are cut out from decision making on water, which was featured in *Q and A* with Riz Khan on CNN International. For the last year, she has worked as staff writer of the *Nation Weekly* magazine, Kathmandu. She believes in versatile activism that mixes politics with vision, and creativity with compassion.

Gabriela Malaguera González (age 27) is a Venezuelan psychologist and graduated from the Universidad Central de Venezuela, UCV (Caracas, DC). She has 12 years of experience in the field of sexual and reproductive health and rights. Gabriela has advocated for gender equality and sexual and reproductive health within the World Bank's policies, through the Consultative Group of Young People Venezuela's New Voices. She graduated in gender and development studies from the Universidad de Chile, and for two years has been a professor of communication psychology at UCV's Social Communication School. Gabriela is committed to achieving the highest degree of equality in these areas, for the people of her country.

Salma Maoulidi (age mid-30s) is the executive director, Sahiba Sisters Foundation in Tanzania. She is trained in Law (LLM from Georgetown) with a focus on human rights and women's law. Since 1997 she has been working as a development practitioner and consultant mainly with grass-roots organizations in East Africa on institutional strengthening, leadership development and social justice advocacy with a keen interest in culture, religion and human rights.

Dean Peacock (age mid-30s) is the South Africa Programme manager, EngenderHealth. He has been working with men to promote equitable and healthy relationships for the last twelve years and has a BA in development studies and an MSc in social work. Dean feels enormously privileged to do the work that he does and is fundamentally optimistic about engaging men in efforts to promote gender equality.

Jennifer Plyler (age 24) has a BA in international development studies from the University of Toronto, Canada, and is currently working on an MSc in social work at the University of Toronto. She is currently interning at the Davenport-Perth neighbourhood centre in Toronto. She also coordinates the International Solidarity Movement in Toronto. Jennifer Plyler is a student and community organizer committed to radical social change that challenges poverty, racism, ableism, heterosexism and imperialism in ways that are dynamic and sustainable.

Suzan Pritchett (age 26) has worked with international human rights organizations in Belgium, London and the USA and has spent time studying and researching in South India. She holds a BA in religion and gender from Grinnell College and a masters in gender and development from the Institute of Development Studies, University of Sussex. She is currently working towards a law degree at the University of Iowa, where (not surprisingly!), her particular research interest lies around the intersection of gender, religion and rule of law reform in developing country contexts.

Ann Elisabeth Samson (age 30) is the senior researcher of the Gender Equality and New Technologies programme at AWID. She has a BA (*cum laude*) from Harvard University in history and science and an (M.Phil.) from the University of Cambridge (UK) in the history and philosophy of science. Her academic work has focused on women's health, contraception, the public understanding of science, genetics, genomics, molecular biology and biochemistry. She has also worked on various freelance writing and research projects about science, technology and health. She has been a feminist from an early age, and has always been interested in how women understand their bodies and the world through scientific knowledge and technology use.

María Alejandra Scampini (age 30) is an adviser on education, gender and citizen matters and coordinator of the Programme on Education for Policy Influence and Advocacy for Red De Educacion Popular Entre Mujeres (REPEM). She has a master's in education from the Catholic University of Uruguay. She works closely with REPEM/DAWN coordination, specifically in Latin America, and has published articles for various e-bulletins and other publications. Alejandra is a teacher and a feminist who strives to grow continuously. She is in constant equilibrium between these two passions and is passionate about everything she does.

Amy Schwartz (age 25) is the young women and leadership intern for AWID. She has an honours BA in international relations and economics from the University of Toronto. Her research interests include the intersection of a rights-based agenda for women's movements, the political economy of development and international governance. Between studying and working she has divided her time volunteering with a HIV/AIDS youth-peer education network in South Africa, for a rural land-rights movement in India, for BRAC in Bangladesh, instructing youth-leadership training programmes for schools such as Outward Bound Costa Rica, working with immigrant support programmes for youth in her hometown of Halifax, Canada, and finding new ways to experience the world.

Contributors

Haidee Swanby (age 33) has been working in the field of sustainable agriculture for the past ten years as a trainer and networker. Her experience includes coordinating the South African desk of the PELUM (Participatory Ecological Land Use Management) Association and acting as media and training officer for Biowatch South Africa. A love of diversity is at the core of many of Haidee's interests. She lives an eclectic lifestyle, always with many pots on the boil.

Alison Symington (age 31) is the research manager at AWID. Her work focuses on issues of globalization, trade policy, human rights accountability, international institutions and women's economic and social rights protection. She holds a law degree from the University of Toronto and a master's in law in international legal studies from New York University. She has held several research positions based in the University of Toronto, looking at issues of international women's rights, the use of international and comparative law in domestic jurisdictions, the politics of trade negotiations and the citizenship and nationality rights of women and children.

Paromita Vohra (age mid-30s) is an independent film-maker and writer. She has directed several films, including *Work in Progress: At the WSF* (2004); *Cosmopolis: Two Tales of a City* (2004); *UnLimited Girls* (2002); *A Short Film About Time* (2000); *A Woman's Place* (1999) and *Annapurna* (1995). Her films as writer are *Khamosh Pani* (Golden Leopard, Locarno Film Festival, 2003, Best Screenplay, Kara Film Festival, 2003), *If You Pause: In a Museum of Craft* (2004), *A Few Things I Know About Her* (Silver Conch, Mumbai International Film Festival 2002) and *Skin Deep* (dir. Reena Mohan). She is the India coordinator of A Woman's Place, a collective of women using media for social change and teaches scriptwriting as visiting faculty at Sophia Polytechnic.

Indigo Williams Willing (age 32) was born in Vietnam and was adopted in 1972 by an Australian family. As an activist and academic, her work primarily addresses the rights of orphaned children who are adopted abroad, and has recently expanded to examining how gender issues shape their migration. She is currently a PhD candidate investigating transnational adoption at the School of Social Science, University of Queensland. She graduated in 2004 with an MA by thesis from the University of Technology, Sydney, and was a 2003 Rockefeller Fellow at the William Joiner Center for the Study of War and Its Social Consequences. Indigo is also the founder of Adopted Vietnamese International and support member of the Intercountry Adoptee Support Network, Australia. Indigo believes that even the smallest steps can lead to greatest of changes – this is how she makes sense of her life.

Index

environment, feminist engagement with, 73–4
environmental degradation, 44, 137
ethnicity, 104, 105
eugenics, 51
exclusion: social, 117, 216; politics of, 222
extension services, appropriate, 69

family planning, 13
famine, 65
Farrah, activist, 140–2, 145–6, 147
fatherhood, 192
female-headed households, 121
females, assumed to be unwanted in traditional society, 98
femininity, concept of, contested, 101
feminism, 111, 128, 183, 184, 202–5, 206, 207, 227, 241; anti-feminist backlash, 227; avoidance of identification with, 227; definition of, 146; diversity of, 226; engagement with environment, 73–4; engagement with science and technology, 57–8; perspectives on poverty, 119–22; scepticism about, 145 *see also* diversity, of feminist movement *and* male feminism
feminist futures of feminist movements, 225
feminist multiperspectivalism, 15
Fernández, M.C., 127
food, as a weapon, 53 *see also* women, as producers of food
Food and Agriculture Organization (FAO), 68, 69
food insecurity, 43; and genetic engineering, 65–78
Former Yugoslavia, 152
Fortuin, Rodney, 189–200
fragmentation of issues, 228–9, 237; overcoming of, 16–17
Francisco, Gigi, 126–7
Frankenberg, R., 101
free and open source software (FOSS), 167, 170
Freud, Sigmund, 180–2

fundamentalism, 17; divisiveness of, 12–14; effect on women's freedoms, 13
funding: for media advocacy, 203; guidelines for, 224; of projects, 210

gender roles, traditional, 12; as coping mechanism, 14
Gene Revolution, 67–8
General Agreement on Tariffs and Trade (GATT), 36
genetic engineering, 49, 51–2, 58, 237; and food insecurity, 65–78; costs of, 68–70; of crops, 53; of foods, 55; of germline, 57
genetic technology, gender aspects of, 55–7
genetically modified organisms (GMOs), 66–7; as living pollution, 71; testing of, 70
genocide, 163
girls: education of, 35, 84, 171; experience of armed conflict, 160; media group of, 209; resocialization of, 197
globalization, 79–94 *passim*, 125; challenge of, 14–15; struggles against, 74
GM crops, resistance to, 73
Govender, Pregs, 232, 235
government, engagement with, 225
Grand Theft Auto, 26
Green Revolution, 67
guerrilla war, women in, 91

Haddad, Sergio, 126
Hague Convention on the Protection of Children, 99
Harris, Mike, 142
Hawthorne, Susan, 11
health of women, 57
heterosexuality, 12, 21, 24, 28, 198
Hindu society, 79, 84
HIV-positive women, 229
HIV/AIDS, 20–33 *passim*, 39, 43, 52, 69, 97, 187, 188, 191, 197; and mobile phone technology, 169;

Index